AF291584

The History
of Navigation

The History of Navigation

Dag Pike

Pen & Sword
MARITIME

First published in Great Britain in 2018 by
PEN & SWORD MARITIME
An imprint of
Pen & Sword Books Ltd
47 Church Street
Barnsley
South Yorkshire
S70 2AS

ISBN 978-1-52673-169-2

A CIP catalogue record for this book is available from the British Library.

Typeset by Concept, Huddersfield HD4 5JL.
Printed and bound in England by TJ International Ltd, Padstow, Cornwall.

Pen & Sword Books Limited incorporates the imprints of Atlas, Archaeology, Aviation, Discovery, Family History, Fiction, History, Maritime, Military, Military Classics, Politics, Select, Transport, True Crime, Air World, Frontline Publishing, Leo Cooper, Remember When, Seaforth Publishing, The Praetorian Press, Wharncliffe Local History, Wharncliffe Transport, Wharncliffe True Crime and White Owl.

For a complete list of Pen & Sword titles please contact
PEN & SWORD BOOKS LIMITED
47 Church Street, Barnsley, South Yorkshire, S70 2AS, England
E-mail: enquiries@pen-and-sword.co.uk
Website: www.pen-and-sword.co.uk

Contents

Introduction

Navigation is part of nearly all human activities. When you walk or drive from your house to the shops you are navigating. When you catch a bus or train you are navigating. These are probably very familiar routes that you follow instinctively but stop and think for a minute: how do you know the way? You recognize it by the various landmarks that you pass: traffic lights, distinctive houses or trees, perhaps a roundabout that you have to negotiate along the way or by consulting timetables. You navigate almost by instinct in so many ways and you follow routes almost without thinking, but it is landmarks that guide you and you should quickly become aware if you have taken the wrong turning.

Landmarks have been the key to navigation for thousands of years. Ancient man probably used landmarks such as trees or stream and river-beds to help him find the way on land and, more importantly, to find his way back. Today on land we have signposts that help with navigating the intricate network of roads and footpaths, and these roads and footpaths are a form of landmark in themselves because they help to delineate where you can and cannot travel. One of the reasons it is so easy to get lost in a forest is because of the absence of any landmarks and the trees all tend to look the same. There are either no or at best very few distinguishing features in a forest that can give you a guide to the way back.

It is the same at sea, and out on the open sea there may not be any obvious landmarks to guide the sailors. Close to land there is the shoreline to provide navigators with landmarks as the basis for their navigation. The early navigators at sea had little else on which to base their navigation; this is why they tended to keep close to the shoreline where they could see landmarks (headlands) that would help to guide them in the right direction or could at least give the navigator some idea of his location. Out on the open sea where there were no landmarks, the navigator had to find much more subtle clues for navigation such as birds, fish, the wind and the sun, or even smells to give clues about the direction of land. However, the navigator going to sea needed something more than just knowing where he was. He needed direction so that he had some idea of where he was going. This is where both the wind and the sun would be a help. Just like navigating on land, you need some clues to help

The Polynesians are thought to have been the first ocean navigators.

you get to your destination and at sea the clues can be quite hard to find and even harder to understand, which is why a good navigator was highly respected.

A direction clue can come from the sun because its direction does not change very much in the course of half an hour so this could be a short-term guide to give a consistent direction by which to steer. It is much the same with the wind and it will blow largely from the same direction at least in the short term and give a useful guide to continue heading in the desired direction. However, the wind was a lot more important to those early navigators because it was often the motive power for the vessel and those early sailboats could only head downwind. This meant that the navigator's choices about his direction might be limited by the direction in which the boat could travel. The weather was an important factor in those early days of navigation and this is still the case today where weather routing and the avoidance of storms are essential factors in assessing which route to follow. No navigator is likely to go to sea without having first obtained a weather forecast.

This was all pretty basic stuff in terms of navigating, using clues from the natural world, and in a different guise it is still in use today by many leisure sailors who head out along a coastline. The yachts of today are considerably more agile in terms of the direction in which they can head but you can still judge your route by recognizing the coastline along which you are sailing.

It sounds so simple just sailing along a coastline, but of course navigating is never that simple in real life if you want to arrive safely. Sailing close inshore is something that experience will soon tell you to avoid. Sailing along a coastline is a balance between keeping in touch with the shore so that you can recognize landmarks and knowing where you are and keeping offshore so that you are a reasonable distance away from the dangers of the shoreline. Inshore there can be shoals and rocks, the wind can be fickle and varying in direction and when sea breezes pick up in the afternoon you can find the wind blowing you towards the shore. This is where experience comes in and those early navigators who survived would learn from their experiences and make mental notes about what was good practice and what could get you into trouble. Experience is such a vital part of navigating and that is as true today as it was 5,000 years ago. The experienced navigator knows what will work and what could put you into danger, certainly in terms of coastal navigation.

Of course, man was never satisfied with just heading along a coastline and it is easy to see the temptation to head out over the horizon to see what lay there. Probably the first ventures out of sight of land were not intentional. Most likely the vessels were blown away from the coast and out of sight of land by storms because, remember, in those days there was no such thing as weather-forecasting as we know it today. You might look at the sky for clues but, as in navigation, the clues about changes in the weather could be very subtle. If you are blown out to sea by a storm then you need to find your way back or you might even discover a new land over the horizon as a sort of accidental discovery. Accidental navigation and discovery were probably a significant part of early voyages. Years later man would head out to sea intentionally, not knowing what lay over the horizon; this would be a brave venture but explorers have been going into the unknown for centuries. Direction might still be obtained from the sun and the stars as navigators learned a lot more about them and the clues they can offer, but what courage it must have taken to head out to the horizon day after day in the hope that land would be sighted. Or was this sheer foolhardiness? Some did not even know if the world was round, which might have proved a challenge when there was the prospect of 'falling over the edge' when you came to the end of the known world.

So navigation moved on from being by guesswork and by God into a realm where science and technology started to provide some of the answers. Science was slow in coming to the aid of the navigator because what might work on land to help fix a position or point you in the right direction might prove very challenging to use on the deck of a moving ship. However, navigators had found a reliable way to measure latitude with reasonable accuracy so they

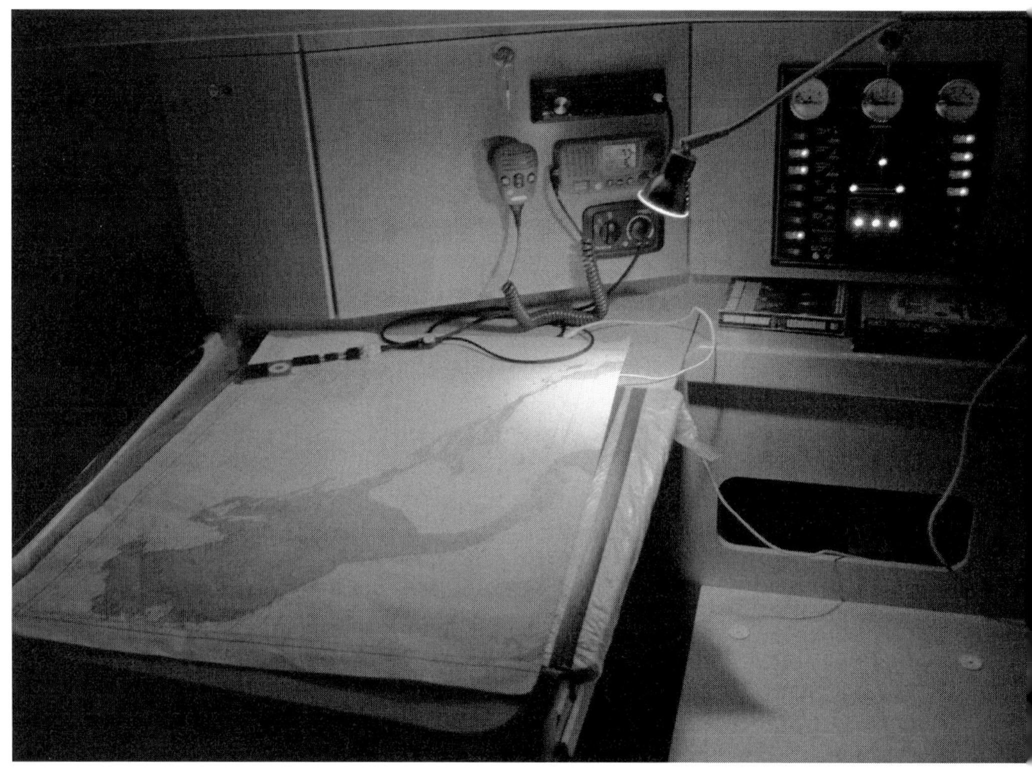

The chart or map has been and still is the basis of all navigation.

would sail a line either east or west and then head north or south once new land had been sighted. The quest was on to find a solution to measure longitude and it was not until Harrison invented his wonderful clock that this problem was solved. Yet it was another 100 years before versions of this clock could be used reliably at sea on a moving ship and a position could be determined with a reasonable degree of accuracy. Finding equipment that would work at sea on small ships where the movement could be violent and where there was damp and spray could add to the challenges of making equipment that would work. It was the same when electronics started to offer alternative solutions to navigating at sea and trying to keep a Decca Navigator receiver, with its seventy-two valves, working in the harsh marine environment was a constant challenge.

Not much changed in navigation for another couple of hundred years and when I went to sea in 1950 we were still using a sextant and a chronometer to work out our position. The electronic revolution that would change navigation forever was just starting to happen but, as always, trying to develop electronic equipment that would work in the challenging marine environment took considerable time. Then there was still the challenge for the navigator in making the transition from the relative safety of open ocean waters to the increased dangers of coastal waters. Close inshore you needed to know your position with a high degree of accuracy, while on the open sea if you were accurate to within 5 miles that was probably good enough.

Fixing the position has always been the key to navigating. If you know where you are then it is possible to work out where you will be going with a degree of confidence. However, a position on its own is just a collection of numbers and letters when shown as a latitude and longitude. It has little meaning until you can plot that position on the chart when the position of the vessel can be seen in relation to the land and to possible dangers. Charts have been in use for centuries and are a vital piece of the navigation jigsaw but like position-fixing itself, the paper chart has succumbed to the lure of electronics so that today not only is the position determined by electronics but the chart on which the position is plotted is generated electronically. Electronics may give us an unprecedented level of navigation information but this in turn raises the question of 'Can it be trusted?' As the saying goes: 'Electricity and water do not mix and if they do then the water always wins.' Having said that, modern marine electronics are remarkably reliable and it is hard to picture navigating these days without them.

The development of satellite navigation systems such as GPS has revolutionized navigation. Instead of the navigator having to use all his resources

A replica of the *Matthew* in which Cabot discovered North America.

just to establish a position for his vessel, GPS now offers a position at the touch of a button and what is more, that position can be incredibly accurate. It is like the Holy Grail of navigation; a highly accurate position on demand. On paper this should mean the end of navigation as we knew it because now with such accurate position-fixing the need for navigation and the navigator should be redundant.

When navigating on land or in the air the dangers to safe navigation should be visually evident, assuming it is daylight and there is no fog or cloud. At sea things are very different because most of the dangers for shipping are hidden below the sea surface and cannot be seen. So soundings were a vital part of navigation at sea as the only means of 'seeing' what was going on below the surface. Now navigators put their trust in accurate charts to show what is below the surface, but to be effective that demands accurate position-fixing.

Satellite navigation has certainly revolutionized navigation but, as with all good things, there is a down side. The very weak signals from the satellite that are necessary to fix the position can be easily jammed and even spoofed and they can present a tempting target for those who want to undermine civilization as we know it. Then there are the charts on which positions have to be plotted for them to have meaning, and trying to keep charts up to date with changes in the sea bed and in navigation marks in order to match the accuracy of GPS positions is another challenge. Just when we had the Holy Grail of navigation within our grasp its reliability is becoming suspect so we have to continue the search for alternative solutions.

Throughout the ages navigation has been a challenge to establish the position and the heading and we are close to reaching the perfect solution but it seems that it is just outside our grasp. This book traces the development of navigation at sea throughout the ages and it is a fascinating tale of endeavour and challenge with a strong flavour of developing technology. From basic visual navigation through to highly-sophisticated electronic systems we are almost there, but can we close the gap to total reliability and accuracy that is the Holy Grail for the navigator?

Chapter One

In the Beginning

For the early humans the sky and the sea must have been a confusing and threatening part of their lives. On a clear night there would be the myriad stars moving in the sky with perhaps the moon joining in, while in daylight the world would be dominated by the sun. On a cloudy day the clouds could present a constantly changing picture, sometimes passive and picturesque, while at other times threatening and dominating. There would be hourly and daily changes as well as the longer-term seasonal changes that would be reflected in the weather conditions and in the visibility. On the water the conditions could be equally changeable. The surface of the sea would reflect the strength and direction of the wind, but the picture could become confusing with local changes in conditions depending on the depth of the water and other factors. In many parts of the world the water level would rise up and down on a regular basis as the tides ebbed and flowed and this would also create currents.

When you think about the picture that was presented to early man it must have taken a long time to make some sense out of this confusion, particularly when there was not the means to record the constant changes. Many of the changes and events that were reflected by the visible changes that could be observed would be noted to take place on a regular basis, while others would appear quite random. Gradually patterns would have emerged such as the regular changes made by the tides and the rotation of the stars in the sky, but even these would have been challenging to identify because there was no easy way in which to measure time. The movement of the sun across the sky in daylight would have provided a guide to time, but even here the picture would have been confused with longer-term changes that occurred with the changes in the seasons. These seasonal changes would have been noted in the way that the weather changed over longer periods. Even today it can be a challenge to understand and be aware of the daily, monthly and annual changes in the weather, in the tides and in the movement of the heavenly bodies so without the deep understanding that we have now it must have taken ages to establish the intricate patterns of the natural world. However, it was the understanding of these patterns that formed the basis of early navigation techniques as man took to the sea for trade and for warfare.

Then early man had to take into consideration the short-term and largely unpredictable natural events. Today we understand all about rainbows but they must have presented a startling event to early man and it would be much the same with thunderstorms and violent squalls. Trying to make sense of all these natural events and to factor them into a means of navigating both on land and on the water must have been challenging and it is easy to see why they enlisted the help of the gods to explain some of these natural events. The gods would not change the weather, but at least they could provide an explanation. In the Mediterranean, which was one of the first places where man ventured out onto the sea, the conditions were more predictable than in many other parts of the world with negligible tides and currents and with winds that were reasonably predictable both on a daily and a seasonal basis. Under the influence of the sun the land heats up during the day, which can generate winds during the afternoons in quite a reliable fashion. The winter months are noticeably the time for bad weather in the Mediterranean and reports about the early navigation of the seas in the Mediterranean suggest that it was mainly carried out only in the more settled conditions of the summer months.

From this it can be seen that early navigation was largely dictated by the weather and particularly by the wind direction as the primitive sailing systems only allowed the craft to sail downwind. What was noticeable about these early navigators was that they were not under any of the time pressures that we see today and the navigation techniques reflected this. Navigation was largely visual, sailing along a coastline when the wind was favourable and then beaching or anchoring the craft at night when the visual navigation information disappeared. In much of the Mediterranean there is relatively deep water close inshore and there are fewer of the off-lying dangers such as rocks and shoals that are found in other parts of the world. This meant that visual navigation was a valid technique and when there might have been doubt about what dangers there were underwater then a sounding pole was used as a guide to the shallow water that might be found in river estuaries or when beaching.

So with these relatively benign conditions it is not surprising that the Mediterranean was one of the cradles of early navigation, but it was possible that this reputation was enhanced because this was one of the regions where writing and recording events was developed so the history of some early voyages has been recorded in words and drawings. Compare this with waters outside the Mediterranean such as northern Europe where very different conditions prevailed. Here you can find tides with the sea level rising and falling, and with those tides there can be tidal currents which in turn can generate offshore shallows and sandbanks. The rise and fall of the tide could have made places accessible when the tide was high and where most of the ports would dry out at low water. The currents generated by the movement of the whole body of water as the tide ebbed and flowed would have been both a benefit and a handicap to the early navigator, helping to carry him to his destination when the current was favourable and slowing him when it was not.

To add to the challenges of navigating in northern European waters was the much more unpredictable weather and areas of offshore rocks and shoals, both of which were hazards for the unwary sailor. Records of early techniques for sailors in northern waters are virtually non-existent and the development of sea-going vessels was considerably slower than in the Mediterranean, although when the Romans sailed their sea-going craft northwards across the Bay of Biscay they did find well-developed sea-going craft being used. What is interesting is that the records of the Roman voyages into northern waters makes little mention of the tides and currents that would have a significant effect on navigation in these waters. While the winds would have helped progress when they were favourable, it does seem likely that the tidal currents would have had a significant impact and you have to wonder if the techniques used on the River Thames for handling barges without motor or sails were used in the open seas. Even seventy years ago the bargees on the Thames would drift downstream using just the current for progress and guiding the barge which had no engine or sails into the desired berth or alongside other barges using a steering oar. When the current flowed upstream the reverse procedure could be used and this was a highly-developed skill that might have been used to good effect in inshore waters, although the craft used are likely to have had sail assistance as well and possibly also had propulsion by oars.

There seems little doubt that navigators in these northern waters needed a higher level of skill to cope with the challenging conditions, which of course would be the reason why the development of sea trade was a slower process. However, the Romans did report that they found local sea-going craft making voyages across the English Channel. The reports by the Romans take us to a point in history a little over 2,000 years ago and what we are missing is where and how navigation developed prior to the Romans coming onto the scene. It is likely that it was line-of-sight navigation similar to that used in the Mediterranean but with the added complication of using the currents to help progress. With the narrowest part of the English Channel at the Dover Straits enabling a visual sighting of the other side, it seems highly likely that the early navigators could roam far and wide using just visual navigation with two-way traffic across the Channel. The cultural and language similarities between the peoples of Brittany, the English West Country and Ireland suggest that early navigators were making voyages between these areas.

There is every reason to believe that the same sort of development took place in the Middle East and the Far East, but the evidence of navigation is

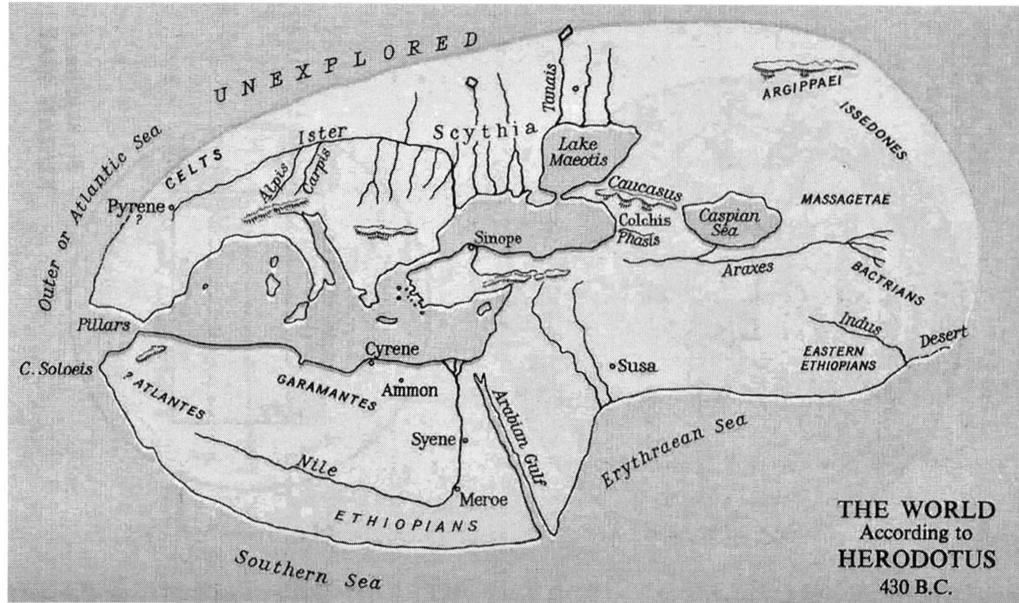

A very early 'map' based around the known areas of the Mediterranean.

well hidden. In the Pacific there is a long tradition of open ocean voyages using basic navigation techniques using natural indicators. These techniques have been in use up until recent times and the navigation technology has been well researched, leading to speculation that the Polynesians were well ahead of the game when it came to navigation. Because the Pacific is a series of islands rather than large land masses, the navigation techniques were specific to that region and you get the impression that in other parts of the world navigation developed using basic line-of-sight techniques that to a certain extent we still use today in familiar waters under what is termed pilotage navigation.

Perhaps we should look at the types of boats that were developed in the various regions to give us a clue about navigation. The types of boat discovered buried and preserved mainly in riverbanks and sometimes used for ceremonial burials are relatively unseaworthy, which would suggest that they were used in the calmer waters inshore and probably first in rivers and then moving out to estuaries before venturing onto the open seas. Using dug-out canoes and similar basic craft, the occupants might have been more concerned with staying afloat than with navigation. With many settlements located along riverbanks, the first ventures on the water are likely to have been to cross the river, which is line-of-sight navigation. As more seaworthy boats were developed so it seems possible that the voyages became more adventurous, but in assuming this it is necessary to find a reason for such voyages. In the Middle East and the Mediterranean we know that voyages were untaken to find cargoes of exotic spices and similar valuable commodities and it is possible that this was the case in other parts of the world. Some metals such as Cornish tin were valuable commodities and their transport could have spurred more adventurous voyages. Fishing was another possibility for venturing out onto open sea waters.

The reasons for developing more capable craft and for venturing further afield may be hard to define without written records, but the navigation techniques used were likely to be visual which tended to mean navigating in daylight. If you head for the next headland you have a visual reference to steer by, which could account for the term 'headland'. You also want to know what is underwater and the very simple sounding pole was used to dip the water over the bow to determine what was underneath. Dipping with a pole like this might not give you too much of a clue but it could at least tell you if the water was getting shallower or deeper. Small craft have been using similar visual techniques to navigate along a coastline up until recent times, backed up by other clues as and when it was possible. Of course these modern navigators had the benefit of a chart that could give them reassurance about the dangers that might be lurking below the surface.

A few years ago we went right back to basics when navigating in fog. Our aim was to round the Lizard Point where there is a line of rocks stretching for a couple of miles offshore. These are dangerous waters with strong tides so we had the idea of closing the rocks close inshore where they were very visible to

Very basic boats in which navigation would be entirely by visual signs.

see if we could find a way through the rocks in our small RIB (Rigid Inflatable Boat) with its shallow draft. In the calm foggy conditions this was a feasible solution and we closed the towering rocks just off the headland and headed for the gaps. The water here was clear and in the calm we could see the bottom so we headed for a gap and with two crew peering into the depths over the bow we found a way through without touching bottom. Purists might argue that this was a dangerous way to navigate but it worked and saved us a long journey offshore in the fog. As a navigator, there is nothing quite like being able to see the dangers so you can find a way around them. This could have been a valid way to navigate for those early navigators in the clear waters of the Mediterranean where sight plus the sounding stick could have provided a sort of solution.

The problem with just relying on seeing the bottom of the sea and sounding with a stick is that it only tells you what is happening directly underneath the craft. If the water is too shallow then the vessel is probably in trouble by the time it is discovered and this type of navigation just gives information in the very short term. A longer-distance solution to navigation might be found by reading the surface of the sea and this can produce some useful answers to help avoid danger. The surface of the sea tends to reflect the sky so

The sounding pole being used by the crew on the right was the earliest navigation 'instrument'.

at any distance from the vessel it is not possible to see through these surface reflections. However, if there is shallow water or perhaps a patch of rocks ahead it may be possible to see their location by the disturbance in the water surface. If there is a swell in the water or waves then this may create an area of breaking waves over the shallow water and if there is a tide or current running then there could also be a local area of disturbance over the shallows.

I used this effect about thirty years ago when we were trying to set a new record across the Atlantic. After leaving New York the large ships keep out to sea to avoid the extensive Nantucket Shoals. With our shallow draft I wanted to keep close inshore which would shorten the distance by about 100 miles. However, this meant heading across these changing areas of shallows and they had not been surveyed for more than thirty years so the depths shown on the chart could not be guaranteed. Should we take the risk of the short cut or should we play it safe by going outside? I decided to take the risk of going over the shallows on the basis that if there was dangerous shallow water then we would see the breaking waves that the swell coming in from the ocean would create. It was a high-risk gamble because our project was very high-profile and the world was watching but we broke the existing record by just two hours which was the time we saved by going across the shoals. We did see some areas of breaking waves and were able to avoid them, and this could have been similar to the techniques that ancient navigators used when voyaging along a coastline.

When the waters are tidal, any dangers that are underwater at high tide can be exposed at low tide. Early navigators may have started their explorations in the rivers where they had their settlements. Even if they were not tidal waters, rivers' levels would rise and fall depending to a large extent on rainfall or perhaps melting snows further inland. This rise and fall of the water level would have helped to expose dangers and perhaps allow the early navigators to plot a visual route. These are the techniques perhaps used on the Nile and the Rhône, large rivers that exit to the Mediterranean which is non-tidal. Outside the Mediterranean where the seas are mainly tidal the rise and fall of the tide would have exposed sandbanks and rocks every few hours so a navigator could perhaps have anchored over low water and seen the dangers and then got under way when the waters rose. The navigators would have also been aware of the flow of the current and could have used that to make progress in a desired direction. The same techniques could have been used along coastlines and we have to remember that, unlike with the navigators of today, there was little or no pressure of time so they could wait for the right conditions to make progress in the desired direction.

In the absence of any instruments for measurement or guidance about direction, those early navigators would have been reliant mainly on the signs from nature, the seas and the skies. The skies would have been an indicator mainly about the weather and a skilled navigator would have been able to interpret the clouds and prevailing conditions to give an indication of what conditions might be like in the short term ahead. The wind direction could determine in which direction progress might be possible and the signs from the sea and the coastline could indicate dangers. We have to rely mainly on speculation about the navigation skills of early navigators and the skills that were required have been largely lost as we now have the luxury of accurate charts, weather forecasts over the radio and position-fixing of unheard-of accuracy. However, these luxuries could lure us into a false sense of security and the signs and skills used by the early navigators can still give useful warnings and indications of danger as a back-up for the modern systems. You ignore the signs of nature at your peril when navigating.

Chapter Two

Over the Horizon

Even in the early days of navigation as detailed in the previous chapter, there were vessels that had to find their way back to shore either because they had been blown away from the land by storms or because they were skippered by more adventurous seamen who had decided to undertake voyages away from the coastal routes. The more you delve into the history of navigation, the more you find that there were navigators who were prepared to undertake voyages where the outcome was far from a foregone conclusion, where they were heading over the horizon without knowing what lay beyond that great divide. Long before Columbus made his epic voyage of discovery across the Atlantic and going back thousands of years, we find that there are records of voyages made over the open ocean. These must have been the ultimate adventure: undertaking a voyage without knowing what the outcome might be. What is fascinating about the voyages is not only the excitement of discovery, but the navigation techniques that were used.

Those early ocean navigators must have been great observers of nature because they record many techniques that would signify the nearness of land. The movement of the sea can change significantly as the oceans grow shallower, there are birds and sea life that are only found close to land and clues such as patches of seaweed would all point to the possibility of land being close over the horizon. Following these clues to the possibility of land that was out of sight but within close sailing distance was one thing, but the big adventure was in setting out with the thought that there must be land somewhere out there if only you sailed far enough over the horizon. Navigators had always found land within a few days of sailing when they sailed about the Mediterranean even when they did not actually know that the land out there actually existed, and it seems possible that this was the philosophy followed by the more adventurous navigators when faced with unknown waters beyond the Mediterranean. There must be land out there so let's set off and sail into the unknown to find it.

The probable pioneers of ocean navigation were the Polynesians who currently inhabit many of the islands in the Pacific. It has been suggested that they set sail from Indonesia and the Philippines several thousands of years ago and headed out into the Pacific, seemingly intent on finding new lands to inhabit. Quite what prompted them to undertake such a voyage or voyages is not clear but they found the islands in the Pacific and proceeded to settle there. These Pacific islanders are now recognized as some of the most competent navigators in history and they were able to navigate from island to island in their canoe-like craft. These slim, sleek craft had a good turn of speed and were balanced by outriggers, and these open boats appear to have been remarkably seaworthy and were used extensively to travel between the groups of islands and even undertake more extensive voyages.

One of the techniques used on their inter-island travel was simple visual navigation. While the islands themselves tend to be low in the water, they become much more visible from a distance because of the characteristic clouds that form above them. This means that instead of being visible from just a few miles away, the high clouds could be seen from up to 50 miles distance so that making a landfall could be achieved from a long way out at sea. This cloud technique has been used by many ancient navigators but the islands in the Pacific were particularly suited to it because the skies were usually clear and the rising air over the islands heated in the sun created these characteristic clouds.

It is easy to suggest that the navigation technique was simply to sail in a fixed direction using the wind direction and the sun as a guide until first the clouds and then the island were sighted and a landfall made, but research suggests that the techniques employed were much more sophisticated. Much of this was developed by constant and detailed observation of the sea and the sky and of the wildlife, mainly in the form of birds. For the latter it has been suggested that they could have followed the routes of migrating birds, reasoning that if a bird was flying off in a fixed direction there must be some land in that direction. It has been suggested that this was how the Polynesians first discovered New Zealand, which would have entailed a voyage of more than 1,000 miles from the Pacific islands. While noting the heading in which the birds were flying, it does demand that the navigators had developed a way of following a chosen route across the oceans and for this it seems that the sun and stars were the main indications of heading, and possibly the aid of the consistent winds that are found in many parts of the Pacific Ocean.

What is amazing about the navigation techniques that were developed by the Polynesians is that they had no access to the written word. Competent navigators were held in high regard in the island communities and it appears that there was a sharing of information among the elite navigators. This information and the techniques used were handed down through the generations without anything being written down so potential navigators had a long apprenticeship of experience. It has been suggested that one way of transmitting this navigation information was by means of songs, and wooden one-dimensional stick models have been discovered that are suggested as representing maps showing ocean currents and winds. Polynesian navigators employed a whole range of techniques including use of the stars, the movement of ocean currents and wave patterns, the air and sea interference patterns caused by islands and atolls, the flight of birds, the winds and the weather.

Polynesian navigation also used some navigational instruments, which certainly predate the more scientific instruments developed in Europe but mainly they relied heavily on close observation of sea signs and their large amount of knowledge gained through oral tradition. There are numerous traditional Polynesian devices used for navigating and/or teaching navigation. These include charts, spatial representations of islands and the conditions around them, and navigational instruments such as those for measuring the elevation of celestial objects. They also include non-physical devices such as songs and stories for memorizing the properties of stars, islands and navigational routes. In many ways the techniques used mirrored those developed by navigators initially in the Mediterranean such as measuring the angle of stars above the horizon with basic instruments, but there was a basic difference. Much of the ocean area in which the Polynesians navigated was close to the Equator so they would not have access to the Pole Star which can give a quick reading of latitude by measuring its altitude. It is much more likely that they would have used the altitude of significant stars as they passed their zenith based on experience and measurements taken in known places; a system also in use in Europe in the early days.

It does appear that the Polynesians were past masters of putting together a number of clues about position and progress in order to arrive at a navigation solution. Before the advent of electronic position-fixing systems, navigation was a bit like detective work. You found a number of clues about your position such as bearings, soundings and observations and from these you could have a pretty good idea of your position. Techniques like this were still used when I went to sea in 1950 and it seems likely that the Polynesians had developed the art of these navigation techniques to a very high degree. Finding islands after a long ocean voyage is much harder than trying to make a landfall along a coastline. To pinpoint an island you need to have both an accurate course and distance travelled; for a coastline only an approximate course is required to find land, something much easier to achieve.

Another technique was to use wave and swell formations to navigate. Many of the habitable areas of the Pacific Ocean are groups of islands (or atolls) in chains hundreds of kilometres long. Island chains have predictable effects on waves and on currents, and navigators who lived within a group of islands would learn the effect made by various islands on the formation of waves and swell that would give another clue about the approach to land. If they were approaching a group of unfamiliar islands it is suggested that they could determine this by their experience of changes in swells and waves. Once they had arrived fairly close to a destination island, they would have been able to pinpoint its location by sightings of land-based birds and certain cloud formations, as well as the reflections made by shallow water on the undersides of clouds. A unique navigation technique was the use of frigate birds; birds that could not land on water as their feathers would become waterlogged. By letting a caged frigate bird fly free, it would return to the craft if there was no land in sight or it would head to nearby land if it was close enough, thus giving the navigator a vital clue about the direction in which to head.

Prior knowledge of islands was an essential part of Pacific island navigation and Captain James Cook had a local navigator who had knowledge of up to 130 islands, most of this knowledge handed down from past generations rather than from actual visits. Of course it could be argued that there were so many islands in the area that you were bound to encounter one if you set off on a voyage. It is thought that the Polynesians travelled as far as New Zealand and there is some evidence that they even made it to the ice fields of Antarctica, but it is hard to imagine people from the tropics wanting to continue heading south into these very cold regions.

Thor Heyerdahl has tried to suggest that the Polynesians migrated from South America on balsa-log boats and he made his voyage in a replica craft to try to suggest it was possible. However, more recent research has suggested that the opposite was true and that the Polynesians travelled from their island homes to South America and back. Such a voyage would require a knowledge and experience of the prevailing currents and winds.

History has given the Polynesians the credit for being some of the best navigators in the world, being capable of undertaking long ocean voyages and finding their way to tiny islands in a vast ocean. Such navigation would have challenged modern navigators before the advent of technology and electronic systems, and several historians have suggested that the Polynesian reputation for ocean navigation has come from the lucky ones who set out on voyages to distant islands and made it. Once having found an island, it tends to be easier to find your way home because you know where it is. What history does not record is the possibly large number of these ocean travellers who set out and did not make it, dying somewhere out on the lonely ocean. As we shall see later in this book, there were large numbers of ships that set out on voyages and were lost without trace and we only know these numbers because their departure was recorded. Without the written word for records, we will never know how many Polynesian vessels set out never to be seen again.

Clouds over the land could give an early visual clue about where the land was.

While the Polynesians are reputed to be the masters of exploration and navigation thousands of years ago, it does appear that the Chinese were close behind them. They were using bamboo rafts similar to those of the Polynesians and it is likely that the two cultures explored side by side. One suggestion is that the Chinese headed in a more southerly direction towards Australia, which in terms of sea journeys only involves quite short voyages across the open sea. People from the north of China headed across the Bering Strait to 'discover' the American continent, again a short sea journey. It is proposed that the Chinese sailed around the coast and through the Malacca Strait towards the Indian Ocean and even crossed the Pacific. In the years going back to 1000BC the Chinese became a significant seafaring nation but even then it tended to be a closed nation, which is why records of the long voyages are hard to authenticate. There has been talk of large fleets of quite large ships undertaking exploratory voyages and it does seem that the navigation skills of the Chinese were quite advanced for their time.

Chinese navigators are credited with developing the first compass which was probably a water compass in which a piece of magnetite (a ferrimagnetic mineral) or lodestone with magnetic properties was floated in water on a piece of cork and it would settle in a fixed direction that could be used as a steering reference. It seems likely that such a 'compass' would not work on a small craft such as the cane rafts or canoes that were used by some of the early explorers and the use of this compass might partly explain why the Chinese started to use larger ships that could provide a more stable platform for such a compass.

Having such a heading reference could have given the Chinese navigators a significant advantage. They also developed a way to measure speed which was by throwing a floating object overboard at the bow and measuring the time it took to float past the stern. The time was measured by a verbal count, which would likely give a relative speed rather than an absolute measurement. A way to measure absolute time was also developed and again it was a simple solution, having an incense candle that was known to burn for a fixed time. However, this might have been more useful for timing the period for the watches for the crew rather than for navigation. As with most of the early navigators, the latitude was measured from the altitude of the Pole Star or the Southern Cross depending on whether they were north or south of the Equator and simple instruments were developed to give a more accurate measurement. Basic charts were also used as well as sailing directions so that the Chinese captains had all the ingredients for navigation in a basic form, except of course that one vital aspect that vexed navigators for many more centuries to come: the measurement of longitude.

The peoples of the Mediterranean were also advanced in the development of basic navigation techniques, but they also wrote things down so that we have a better history of how they navigated when they ventured away from the shores onto open seas. We know that coastal navigation was quite advanced with some significant headlands being identified by marks such as a cross or a temple, but it was not long before longer voyages were being undertaken. These were nothing like the extensive open ocean voyages of the Polynesians and Chinese because the open sea areas in the Mediterranean are limited, but trade demanded longer voyages out of sight of land and techniques were developed to meet this requirement. In many ways the techniques developed were similar to those already described but on just short voyages of two or three days the main concern would have been heading information in order to make landfall at roughly the right place. The sun and stars would have provided this information and been a reliable source for such short voyages and soundings were regularly used when making landfall. Some areas of the Mediterranean also have seasonal winds coming from a steady direction that could have provided a heading reference of sorts and these have been listed in the form of a type of 'compass card'.

In all voyaging over the horizon the weather would have played a significant part. The 'ships' of the day were relatively small and would only sail more or less before the wind so progress could only be made when the wind was coming from a direction behind the beam. It was probably possible to still make some progress outside this direction, but it would have been limited. This brings into question the ability to forecast the wind direction and strength for two or three days ahead. Even though navigators would make a

The mighty Pharos lighthouse at Alexandria would help navigators to make a landfall on low-lying land.

detailed study of the weather because of its importance to progress, the limits of forecasting were probably restricted to what the navigator could see and the hope that the prevailing conditions would remain relatively stable. While the weather in many oceans can be relatively stable and predictable, the Mediterranean can have quite violent storms arriving at short notice, partly caused by the land masses heating up considerably in relation to the cooler seas. The epic voyage of St Paul when he was under arrest and being taken to Rome, during which the ship carrying him spent fourteen days being carried along in a storm before being finally wrecked on Malta, shows how winter storms can prevail. There was little or no weather forecasting in those days so by and large ships would avoid winter voyages and would try to have options for shelter if a storm materialized.

Trade was the main motive for Mediterranean voyaging and around 1000BC King Solomon built a fleet of ships that sailed with those of the king of Tyre to bring goods back to Israel. There are several references to Mediterranean voyages in the bible and in early AD merchants from the

Mediterranean area were regularly sailing from the Red Sea to India, and it is reported that a couple of centuries later they even went as far as China. It was the Phoenicians, who came from what is now Lebanon, who headed in the opposite direction and are reported to have reached the Atlantic at the opposite end of the Mediterranean by 1200BC. Here it was the silver mines in Spain that were the attraction, but they also looked south with the prospect of heading along the African coastline.

However, the attractions of Africa were tackled from the opposite end and it is suggested that around 700BC Pharaoh Necho of Egypt assembled a flotilla of Phoenician ships at the top of the Red Sea with the objective of sailing round Africa without even knowing how large this land mass was. Already the Phoenicians had been exploring the coasts of East Africa for many years and on this new expedition the plan was to follow the eastern African coastline south into the Indian Ocean. By all accounts this was a leisurely voyage because after months of sailing they found a sheltered bay and went ashore to sow and reap a harvest, and then once re-supplied they sailed on. It took them three years to complete the circumnavigation and return to Egypt. Some credibility is given to this story by reports that they saw the midday sun on their right, i.e. to the north, which for sailors who have always seen the sun in the south must have caused quite a stir.

Although many historians have questioned reports of this epic voyage, there seems little doubt that it was well within the capabilities of the experienced Phoenician navigators, but this was still virtually a coastwise cruise with little or no ocean cruising required.

Navigators from the Mediterranean were growing more adventurous, with the Greeks taking the lead from the Phoenicians. In the fourth century BC 'ships' were turning north after passing the Straits of Gibraltar. Already traders had visited the shores of Brittany and then headed across the English Channel where the quest was to load the tin mined in Cornwall that was an essential ingredient of bronze. However, one of these Greek vessels went on a voyage of exploration and it is suggested that Pytheas circumnavigated the British Isles and even went as far north as possibly the coasts of Norway, Iceland or the Faroes. Certainly in his recounting of the story of the voyage he talks about the land of the midnight sun and of the sea being frozen over so he went well north. Like the Phoenicians when they went south and saw the sun in a different direction, seeing the sun for twenty-four hours a day must have been an extraordinary experience.

We also know that the Romans headed north around 50BC when they invaded Britain and from then on trade became a regular feature. It does seem that trading was the motive for many of these exploratory voyages with new lands offering the prospect of exciting finds. However, when analysing most of these early explorations it does become evident that in most cases the navigators were never very far from land or at least if they were then they had a pretty firm idea that there was land ahead perhaps a day or two away. This gave a degree of certainty about their navigation. Even the Polynesians who roamed far and wide knew that they would almost certainly sight land among the wide range of islands ahead.

Surviving records of ancient exploration must account for only a fraction of the voyages successfully completed by intrepid seamen. There must have been legions of these ancient mariners who returned to their point of departure without ever writing about where they had been, committing the voyage to memory rather than writing it down. An even more open question is how many of these navigators/explorers sailed from their homelands to distant shores, never to return? Apart from the risks and uncertainty of the early navigation techniques and the lack of detailed knowledge of where they were heading, there were the risks of running out of food and water, the risks of storms and shipwreck and in some cases the risk of attack. Exploring was a hazardous undertaking by modern standards and it is hard to picture any modern navigators heading off into the blue without the comfort of weather forecasts, reliable navigation equipment and a sound vessel. However, there was one factor that could have been the motive for exploration and that was faith, and so we come to the Brendan voyages.

By the time of the birth of Christ most of the world's oceans had been explored to some degree with the notable exception of the Atlantic. It was St Brendan who is credited with making the first crossing of the Atlantic, although Thor Heyerdahl would have us think that fishermen from mainland Africa might have drifted across on one of their papyrus rafts. That may have been the case and it would not be surprising to find that the Atlantic was first crossed by fishermen drifting across when winds and storms blocked any chance of them returning back to Europe or Africa. Accidental exploration is always a possibility if the crew does not starve or die of thirst on the way, but there is unlikely to be any evidence of such a crossing, particularly as a new land has not really been discovered until someone comes back to tell the story about it. Accidental discovery is not likely to involve such a return trip. So it is left to St Brendan to lay claim to being the first to cross the Atlantic, but there is a large degree of uncertainty about this.

Brendan was an early Irish monk and saint with a reputation as a traveller or wanderer that earned him the name of Brendan the Navigator. He started out on his voyages around 500AD and is famous for his legendary journey to the Isle of the Blessed. Brendan voyaged to remote islands around Ireland and Scotland to establish monasteries and is reputed to have discovered the Faroes and Iceland. It has been suggested that the land Brendan finally reached was

America. While many historians scoff at such an idea, others have argued that cave dwellings throughout north-eastern North America reflect a strong Celtic influence. Equally Brendan might have reached the Azores and Iceland. There does not appear to be any definitive answer to what Brendan did and what he discovered, but it does seem that he had navigation techniques that enabled him to roam the oceans or perhaps it was simply the power of prayer!

Thor Heyerdahl was one of the first to try to replicate a voyage from the past to demonstrate that an epic voyage from history might have been possible. In 1976, Irish explorer Tim Severin followed this concept by building an ox-leather curragh similar to that reported to have been used by St Brendan to see if the Atlantic crossing might have been possible in such a craft. On his voyage, he encountered various sights that he suggests were really the fantastic sights from the legends of Brendan. The story includes 'mountains spouting fire' (volcanoes), 'floating crystal palaces' (icebergs), and 'monsters' (large sea mammals such as walruses and whales). He also identified a route with places that matched the description given by Brendan, and over two summers sailed the boat from Ireland via the Hebrides, the Faroes (isle of sheep) and Iceland (burning hill) arriving safely in Newfoundland but only

This small craft was used by Tim Severin to try to replicate the ocean voyages of Saint Brendan.

after suffering terrible storms on the way. When a large seaside rock with inscriptions on it resembling Irish letters was discovered in Newfoundland a few years ago it was suggested that the Brendan voyage actually happened. Later maps showed a 'St. Brendan's Island' in mid-Atlantic.

I have to confess to being cynical about replica voyages such as that undertaken by Heyerdahl and Severin. Although the craft were as close a replica as possible, they were equipped with modern devices such as radio, sextants and timepieces for position-fixing plus modern food and drink etc., all designed to remove the risk from the voyage. The original Brendan voyage is reported to have had a crew of sixteen on board, which in a boat of that size must have been incredibly crowded. The replica had a crew of just four. There was possibly a bonus in having a large crew because that would have enabled the boat to be rowed which could have been an advantage in adverse winds, but the details of the original tend to be very sketchy. In sailing in a replica the risk element of sailing into the unknown and not knowing if you can find your way back is largely removed and there are safety back-ups in place so these replica voyages remove so much of the original risk and uncertainty.

It was many years later that the Vikings are reported to have followed much the same route as St Brendan and to have discovered America again. Before that they had set out from their Norwegian homeland and invaded significant parts of the British Isles. Their seaworthy longboats navigated their way across the North Sea and round the north of Scotland which can be pretty

A replica Viking longboat in which oars helped navigation against adverse winds and currents.

hazardous waters and they are reported as having reached the Faroes and Iceland. They voyaged extensively during the 200 years between 800AD and 1000AD and their voyages to Iceland were then extended westwards to first Greenland and then to Labrador and Newfoundland, although it does appear that they had little interest in establishing settlements. It has been suggested that one of the reasons for these voyages of discovery was to find new lands where conditions were not as harsh as those in their homeland, which could account for their voyages and settlements in the British Isles but not for their voyages to Iceland and to the northern part of North America.

The navigation skills of the Vikings have been called into question and some of this questioning is based on the fact that having established settlements in the British Isles where the climate was better than that of their Norwegian homeland, why would they want to continue exploring? The answer from cynics is that they discovered these other places such as Iceland and the Faroes because of their poor navigation skills that allowed them to be blown off course when heading on a more southerly route. There seems little doubt that the Vikings used many of the techniques that earlier navigators had used and it appears that they relied heavily on both previous experience and natural signs along with using the sun and stars as a guiding light. However, the latter may not have been a huge help because in these northern latitudes the skies would often have been overcast, which perhaps supports the theory that their discoveries were by chance rather than by design.

When you look at most of this history of early 'over the horizon' navigation you do have to question how much was accidental and how much was a quest

The Vikings used line-of-sight navigation on voyages that might last for just a few days.

for new lands and exceptional navigation skills. You can picture the huge emigration that took place in the eighteenth and nineteenth centuries from Europe to North America because of starvation, religious oppression and poor conditions in their homelands, but that was a pretty organized affair, buying passages on ships and knowing where they were going. Compare this with those early navigators where there seems to be little evidence of the need to escape from conditions at home and even if there was, why would you sail off into the blue without a destination? Some historians have suggested that it was a sense of adventure that motivated those early voyagers, the quest to see what lay over the horizon, but it takes a lot of faith to just sail off without a destination in prospect and sailing with the wind which could make returning against the wind challenging. The actual records of voyages to discover new lands are relatively few and far between because the art of keeping a log and recounting a voyage was not one of the skills of simple sailors so we only have the information from a relatively few voyages on which to base the motivation and skills of those early mariners. Were they really voyages of discovery using considerable navigation skills or were they accidental voyages: sailors who were blown off course and ended up in unknown lands by accident.

It is hard to know where the truth lies but it is worth remembering that we only tend to have on record those voyages that were successful; those in which the participants returned from their voyages. What has gone unrecorded is the possibly large number of voyages that took place from which the sailors never returned. Shipwrecks, groundings or perhaps starvation might have extracted an enormous toll on those early navigators and while they possibly had considerable skills in maintaining a course, in reading the weather and in detecting the proximity of land, those are no guarantee that a voyage will be successful when you have no charts and little information about where and how you are heading. One interesting fact that emerges from the early voyages that were documented is that most of the successful ones had both sails and oars as means of propulsion. Having just sails does limit the direction of your progress to a great extent because you have to go where the wind takes you and in particular this can make a landfall perilous because running before the wind makes it difficult to stop and make a controlled landfall. With oars you have the possibility of much better control and choice of direction, but against having oars is the need for a larger crew and the consequent need to carry extra food and water to supply them. It should be noted that the Polynesians, the Phoenicians, the Greeks, the Romans and the Vikings all used vessels with both oars and sails on many of their voyages and this could have been an important contributing factor in their success, removing the wind direction as a limiting factor.

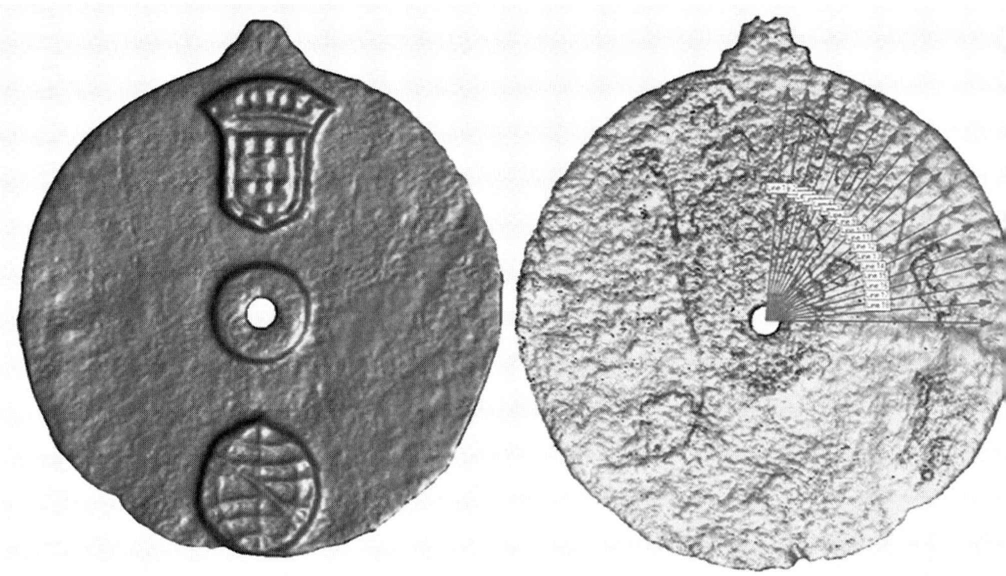

The earliest astrolabe ever found was used by navigators to help determine latitude.

This brings us to Columbus, who changed the world of navigation forever. Columbus was the first person that we know of who set out on a voyage into the unknown as the main function of the voyage. His motive, we are told, was to find a new and shorter way to the fabled riches of the Orient. By the time of Columbus many people were convinced that the world was round but its size was not known so Columbus was setting out possibly on what was the long way round to his destination, but probably convinced that there would be land eventually. In the mind of Columbus it seemed that the question was not whether they would find land but when they would find it.

Columbus had quite a lot in his favour. The Azores had been discovered about 100 years previously, which meant that the Atlantic was a known factor for close to 1,000 miles out. Further south, the fairly consistent winds and currents that would carry ships towards the west had been recognized and Columbus stopped at the Canary Islands before heading out into the Atlantic. By that time navigators had learned how to sail along a line of latitude with a degree of accuracy, maybe not anywhere near as accurate as today but at least to maintain a more or less consistent course west. The compass was available to maintain a reasonable heading which of course could be checked by sun and star bearings so the main problem facing Columbus was not heading west but not knowing when the land might turn up. Columbus was an experienced navigator but the prophets of doom were convinced that he would reach the edge of the world and be carried over into the abyss. In reality it is likely that he would sail as fast as practical during the hours of daylight and then heave-to during the hours of darkness so as not to make an unexpected landfall during the dark.

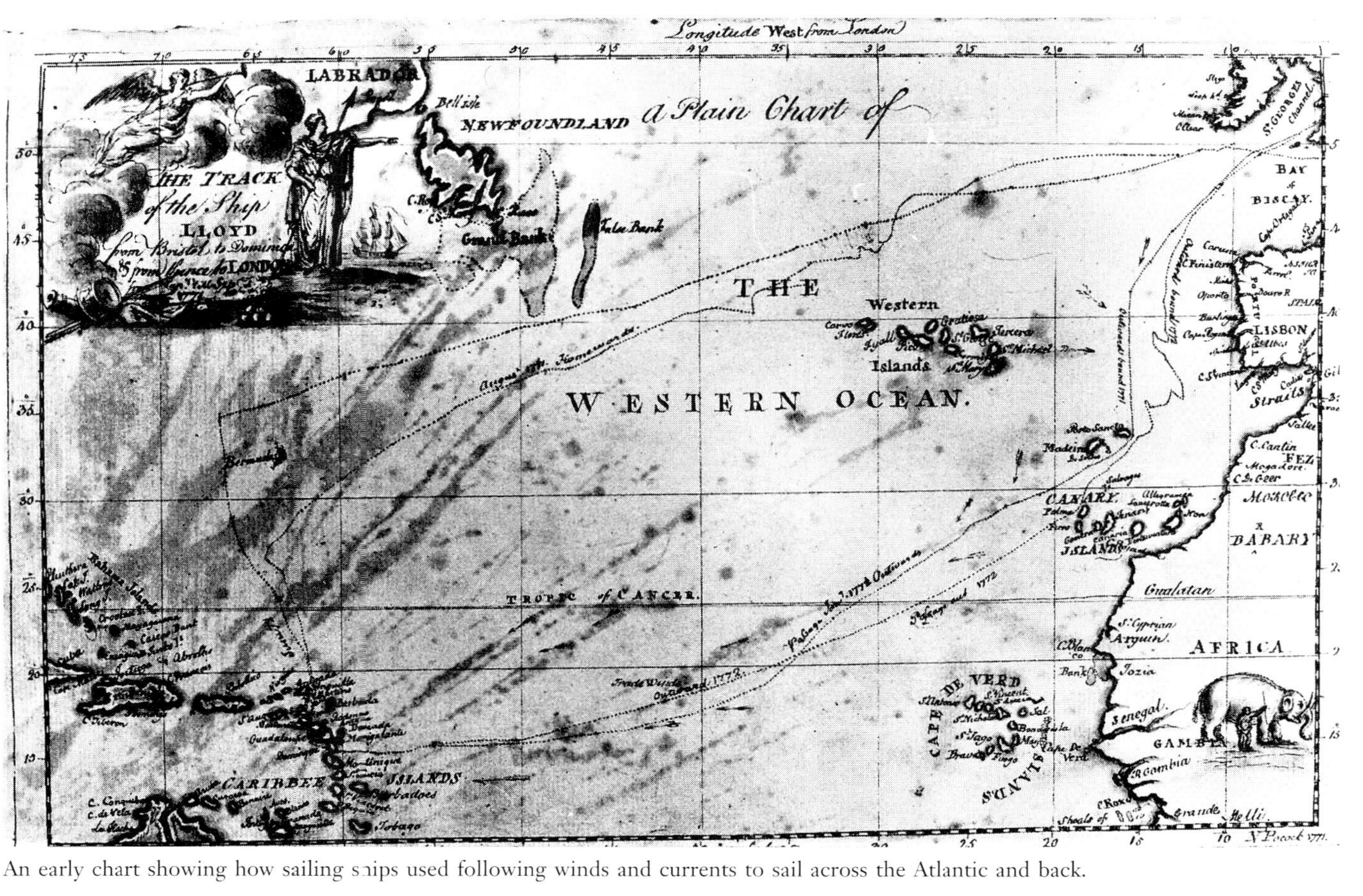

An early chart showing how sailing ships used following winds and currents to sail across the Atlantic and back.

Columbus makes his historic landfall that changed the face of the known world.

As far as we can tell from the records, landfall was made during the night by a lookout on the *Pinta*, the smallest ship in the three-ship fleet of Columbus. Quite how you could sight land in the dark is a mystery and Columbus claimed that it had been sighted from his ship the *Santa Maria* late on the previous evening. This was good timing because by that time in the voyage food and water were running low. We hail Columbus as a navigator for this pioneering voyage and there is no doubt that it was a major discovery, but in fact he did not reach the destination he had been aiming for (there was just the matter of the Pacific to cross before the Orient was reached) and his ship was wrecked when it ran aground on Hispaniola, so perhaps his navigation skills were only moderate. Apart from his discovery of America, however, one of his most important contributions was to return using a more northerly route eastwards across the Atlantic, setting the basis of most Atlantic crossings by sailing ship that took maximum advantage of the prevailing winds and currents. His grounding and the wrecking of the *Santa Maria* demonstrated what a high-risk occupation sailing was and the risk to sailing ships on a lee shore was to be a constant part of navigation until the steamship was developed.

Chapter Three

Soundings

The first attempt by early navigators to actually take measurements as an aid to navigation was the development of the sounding pole. This was the simplest of navigation instruments: just a pole that you stick over the side to determine the depth of water. Its simplicity is such that it is still in use today with yachts feeling their way into an anchorage using a boat hook to probe the depths. Approaching land or shallows was a major challenge for early navigators and knowing the depth of water under the hull of your vessel was one of the basic tenants of navigation almost from the start. The thinking is that if you have enough water underneath the hull, then it is safe to navigate. As most navigators know, this is not quite true because having adequate water under the hull does mean that you are afloat at that moment but it does not necessarily mean there will be adequate water ahead of you for safe navigation. Soundings are important to navigation for many reasons though, and it was the means of sounding that was one of the first 'instruments' developed for navigation.

In the previous two chapters there has been reference to the sounding stick or sounding pole. This has to be one of the most basic of 'instruments' ever developed for navigation and consists of a man in the bow of the vessel equipped with a stick that he prods in the water to try to touch bottom. With the length of the 'stick' probably limited to about 3 metres, touching bottom would leave just enough water to float the vessel and give due warning that it was time to alter course or at least stop and work out a strategy. Using a sounding stick in this way would only give a warning about shallow water coming up and is likely to have been mainly useful in rivers and estuaries where there might be considerable shallows. It could serve as a means to help keep in a river channel, with the 'stick' warning if you were deviating from the channel into shallow water. The only problem here is that the indication of shallow water would not tell you which side of the channel you were approaching; a problem that exists even today when using an echo-sounder in narrow river channels. The shallow water could be on either side of the channel, but at least the sounding stick would give a warning and it might have been possible to use this in conjunction with 'reading' the surface of the water where ripples or changes of colour might help to indicate the main channel.

The effectiveness of a sounding stick would only extend to the length of the stick so a means was found to extend the depths that could be detected or measured by tying a rope to a weight and lowering that over the side. It is known that the Romans used such a method of sounding the depths which could have been used to measure or at least indicate the seabed in depths of perhaps up to 10 fathoms (1 fathom is 6ft, close to 2m but often measured by the span of a person's arms stretched out from fingertip to fingertip). This weighted rope was the origin of the lead-line which is still in use today by traditionalists in which the stone weight on the end of the line has been substitute by a lead weight to give a more compact weight that could slide through the water more easily and reach the seabed quickly. A seaman using the lead-line might measure the depth of water found by measuring the length of line that went underwater in fathoms by stretching the line between his outstretched hands as he hauled it in.

The next stage in the development of the lead-line was to mark the line with bits of fabric tucked into the lay of the rope. Different materials were used for different depths along the line: for 2 fathoms, two strips of leather were used; for 5 fathoms it was a piece of white duck; then came red bunting, blue serge, leather with a hole in it, etc. The aim was to have a line where the different depth indications from the line could not only be seen visually in daylight, but could also be felt in darkness using fingers or lips.

Over the years the lead-line has become increasingly sophisticated and it is surprising how much navigation information could be obtained from using it. In addition to measuring the depth of water, the lead weight had a hollowed-out bottom end and this could be filled with tallow, a grease-like substance that would pick up samples of the seabed such as sand or gravel. This was called 'arming the lead' and knowing from the chart or from experience what the seabed material was could help to give an indication of location. This sort of navigation technique shows how desperate navigators might have become when they had sighted nothing for three or four days and there had been no clear skies for a fix by the sun or stars. Just knowing the consistency of the sea bed would give some indication of where you could or could not be. Combined with the actual depth measured by the lead-line, the position could be more precisely ascertained. Soundings told the navigator more about where he could not be rather than providing a positive fix.

Many of those early explorers such as Columbus would have used the lead-line when approaching a strange coastline as a means of feeling their way into the shore. Rather than use the lead-line directly from the ship, it is much more likely that they would have sent a boat in ahead to take soundings and to

An early version of the Kelvin sounding machine.

find safe water perhaps for an anchorage. A boat under oars would be much more manoeuvrable than a sailing ship if there were dangers and the boat could be tracked from its mother ship as it navigated its way into a strange shore. This was a pretty standard way of navigating until the development of charts that could be relied on by the navigator and today a boat coming into an anchorage might still use the same technique to find its way in, perhaps concerned that the chart detail shown might not be very accurate or not have been updated in rarely-used waters.

When using the depth obtained from a lead-line the navigator would not be so much concerned with the actual depth from a single sounding but the trend of the depths. Was the depth of water increasing or decreasing, suggesting that the ship was moving into deeper or shallower water? That could be a helpful guide for the navigator and shoaling depths would serve as a warning, possibly that the ship was approaching the shoreline or other hazards. On its own a single sounding or a group of soundings might not be very helpful for fixing the position until charts became available. When you knew what the depth might be in certain areas from the chart you would at least know where you could not be because of the depth of the water. It might not be a very accurate way of positioning, but at least the depth could give a clue. Navigation can be about getting one or several clues about where you could be or could not be and by a process of elimination you could narrow down the possibility of the ship's position.

Early harbour or estuary charts often show the soundings on the charts as a series of lines across the channel. This would indicate that the depths were obtained from a series of lead-line soundings, possibly with the survey boat

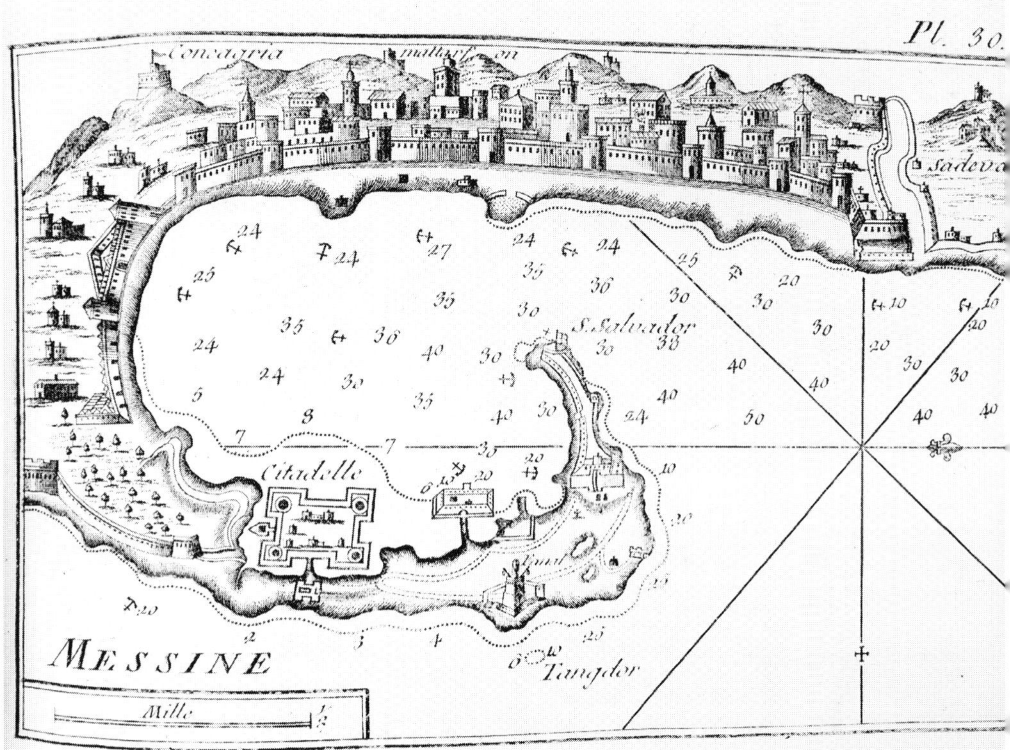

A portolan or early chart of the port of Messina in Sicily showing soundings.

following a mark or transit on the shore. Obviously when the soundings were displayed like this there would have been considerable gaps in the areas of harbour bed covered and it would be assumed that there were no hidden dangers. One method to give more reassurance about the depths in a channel would be to have two boats linked by a line that was maintained tight between the boats. Suspended from this surface line would be a bottom line set at a fixed distance below the surface. If the line could be taken along the channel without snagging, then it would indicate there were no wrecks or isolated rocks along that stretch of channel. We were still using a similar method to check the safe clearance over a wreck in the 1960s.

Using the lead-line as the ship moved along was a skilled bit of seamanship, and the line was swung and then released ahead from the side of the ship so that by the time it touched bottom it was more or less vertical to give an accurate measurement of depth. Then there was the litany of calling the depths with the actual marked depths being called 'marks' and the fathom depths that were not marked being called 'deeps'. So the 'leadsman' might call out 'By the mark 5' or 'By the deep 8'. The leadsman would stand on a small hinged platform fixed to the rails of the ship where he could stand out over the sea alongside to get a clear throw. The markings on the lead-line are a relatively recent

Using lead lines for sounding from a sailing ship when making a landfall.

addition in the long history of the lead-line, probably only used for about the last 200 years.

From its evolution from the sounding stick, the lead-line became a vital piece of navigation equipment for hundreds of years and from the bible, St Paul mentions sailors measuring the depth in fathoms as they made a landfall in Malta. It is thought that the word fathom had been used as a measurement of depth for many years before that and it was a practical measurement of depth with the seaman measuring the length of lead-line with his outstretched arms as he hauled the line in. This would be before the line was marked with the customary marks so the depth could be seen or felt. There are mentions of using the lead-line in many manuscripts and Magellan certainly used it on his round-the-world voyage and John Davis used it when he was trying to discover the North-West Passage. Many of these navigators recorded the sounding on a chart and here you see the beginnings of the modern chart with its soundings shown over the sea areas.

The big disadvantage of the lead-line was that in its standard form it would only work in relatively shallow water. Longer lead-lines with heavier weights were tried, but to get any worthwhile results from these it meant stopping the ship to take the sounding so that the line was vertical when the sounding was taken. It would take a team of sailors to haul the line in and it was probably

Survey sounding from an inshore boat. (*NOAA*)

the arrival of the steamship that led to ships travelling at higher speeds providing the incentive to find better ways of establishing the depth of water. One of the first innovations was the Massey Sounding Fly which was a small propeller attached to the line just above the lead. This rotated as the lead descended and clocked up the distance travelled by the lead. To use it the lead-line would be taken as far forward as possible so that by the time it reached bottom it might be at the stern of the ship and would record the depth when the line was vertical. There were other devices developed to measure the depth in various ingenious ways, some of them using a pressure tube that detected how the pressure increased with the depth, and many of these were used by the fast Atlantic liners to help them make a landfall in poor conditions.

Eventually the standard method of sounding became the Kelvin Sounding Machine which used a fine wire rather than the thick rope as the measuring line; this greatly reduced the size and resistance of the line and gave more accurate sounding. This was used by thousands of naval and trading ships sailing around the world. The demise of sounding machines like this finally started with the development of the echo-sounder in the 1930s. The manual means of sounding endured a slow and painful death and even when I went to sea in 1950, ships were still fitted with the leadsman's platform or chains and we certainly carried a lead-line. In addition to the portable lead-line there was a 'sounding machine' which was one of the Kelvin units on the aft deck and this was like a sophisticated lead-line for measuring depths beyond the reach of the 20-fathom lead-line. The sounding machine was in effect a small winch with the winch drum wound with a fine wire and the end of the wire supporting a lead weight. This weight would be dropped overboard at the stern through a rail-mounted pulley and the amount of wire that would run out before the weight touched bottom was measured by a counter to give the depth of water. From memory this machine could measure depths of about 300 fathoms so could give early warning of the approach to shallow water when making a landfall. Letting the wire run out was easy, but it could be a long, hard slog winding it in. In my time the machine was only used about once a year just to make sure it was still working!

The principle of the echo-sounder was quite simple but, as is often the case, finding a practical solution that would work at sea took quite a time. Back in 1911 a German physicist proposed measuring the depth by setting off a small explosion and measuring the time before the sound came back to the surface. Not a very practical idea on a moving ship, but the idea was refined by firing a cartridge into the water on one side of the ship and measuring the time taken for the echo to return with a hydrophone on the other side of the ship. This was later modified by using the sound of a gong rather than the cartridge. The practical solution was found with transducers, one of which would transmit a short, sharp sound and the second of which was tuned to the same sound frequency to pick up the returning sound. It sounds simple but it took a lot of refinement to create a practical unit that could be fitted to ships and later to boats. This refinement was partly necessary in order to cancel out sounds created by the vessel travelling through the water and finding a frequency that would provide sharp returns from the seabed. The echo-sounder was effectively measuring the speed of sound through the water and the deeper the water, the longer the time between transmission and reception but water can

Using a sounding machine on board a US survey vessel. (*NOAA*)

Lord Kelvin's sounding machine that enabled soundings to be taken in deep water.

have different densities and so those early sounders produced mixed results, but they were certainly much more effective than using a lead-line and the echo-sounder could be used at higher speeds, although above certain speeds aeration around the hull might have produced mixed results.

The major difference between using the lead-line and the depths shown by an echo-sounder is that the lead-line only measures the depth at a single point. There could be a rock close by the point where the lead lands on the sea

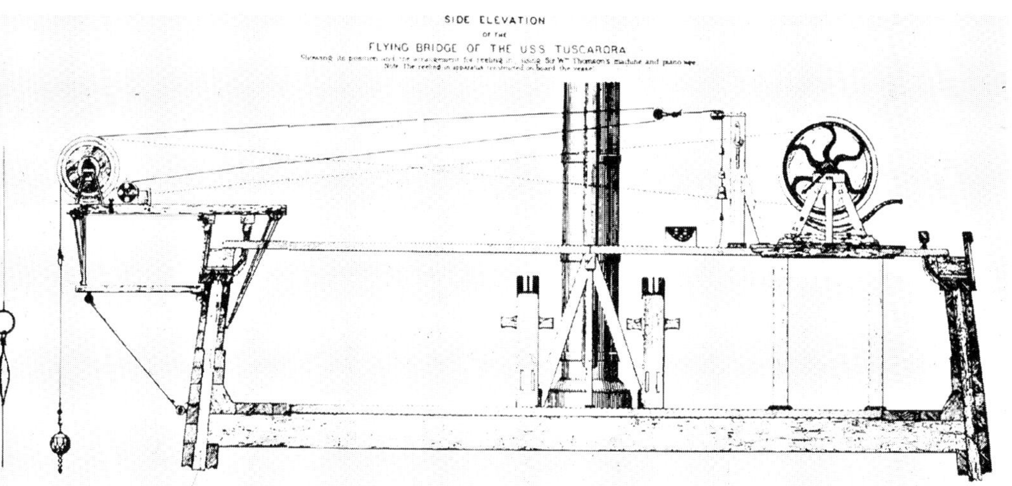

Sounding machines replaced the hand lead line and enabled soundings in deep water.

bed and it would not be detected and many of the early charts were developed using lead-line surveys. These were based on a series of single-point soundings and the assumption was that there were no shallow patches in between the soundings. In most cases this would be a reasonable assumption but there was no certainty and when landing stores at the Eddystone Lighthouse some years ago the ship was fairly close into the rocks with the echo-sounder running when the sea bed recording showed a sudden peak. We explored around it and there was a rock with a depth of just 8 fathoms above it. It was not a real danger and it was unlikely that any normal ship would go that close in but the interesting thing was that it had remained undiscovered all those years. With an echo-sounder you get a continuous trace of the seabed which can produce a more reliable record of what is down there.

However, this continuous trace is still only the depth underneath the vessel which hopefully shows that you are safe at that point. As a navigator you will be much more interested in trends; i.e. whether the depth is getting shallower or deeper, which can be an indication of where you are standing, either into danger or moving away. In good visibility you will probably be aware of this because you may have been able to fix your position from sightings from the land or from sextant positions, but in poor visibility the depth shown by the echo-sounder might be the only clue about your position so it provides vital information. Just as the crew of the ship that St Paul was on were taking sounding as they thought they were approaching land in poor visibility, so the crew of a ship in the twentieth century would rely on the information from the echo-sounder to give the same sort of warning.

The echo-sounder, or fathomer as it was called in America, was developed in the 1930s but the development of the use of sonar for underwater detection was accelerating during the war in the hunt for submarines. The result was that much more sophisticated technology became available after the war, although the basic echo-sounder for shipping had not changed a great deal. Now there was side-scan sonar that allowed objects above the seabed such as wrecks and rocks to be detected and it was systems like this that started to develop much more sophisticated surveying techniques that led to more accurate charts. The bottom-seeking echo-sounder was still the standard for most shipping, but the other beneficiary of the more sophisticated sonar techniques was the fishing industry. The technology was also changing with advances in electronics.

For general shipping the echo-sounder still comprised two transducers mounted in the bottom of the hull: one to transmit and one to receive the reflected signal from the sea bed. Knowing the speed of sound in the water, measuring the time interval between the transmission and reception would give the depth. On the bridge this would usually be shown on a paper trace where a pen would start its journey across the paper at the moment of transmission and make a mark on the paper when the returned signal was received. The result was a trace on the paper showing a continuous read-out of the depth and indicating the trends, getting deeper or shallower as the paper moved down the display.

The echo-sounder trace gave navigators a picture of what lay beneath the surface for the first time.

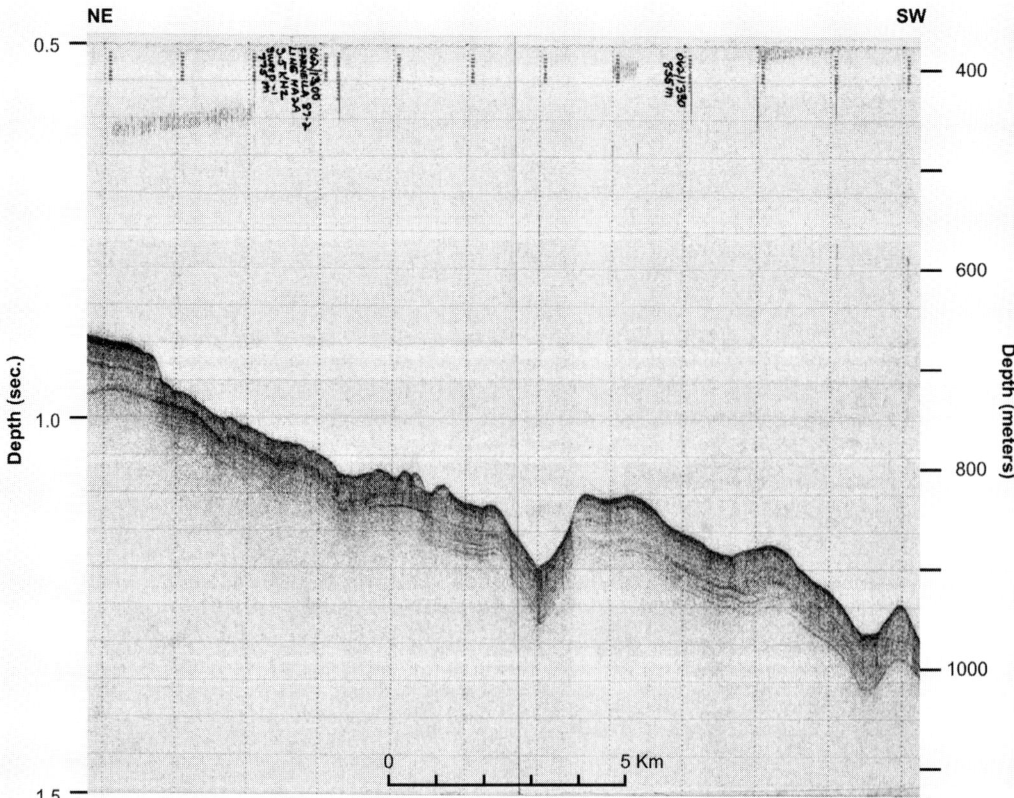

It was a simple electrical/mechanical system that remained the standard type of display for many years. It was too large and complex for small craft and the introduction of compact echo-sounders for boats started when the Seafarer echo-sounder was introduced. This was a revolution in echo-sounders with the paper trace being replaced by a rotation arm with a neon bulb on its end and the depth scale around the perimeter of the display. The transmission would start at the zero point on the scale and the neon bulb would light up and flash when the returned signal was received. It was simple, inexpensive and practical and it became the standard depth-sounder on thousands of small craft. Its only downside was that it did not show trends in the depth unless you studied the display for some time.

Fishermen realized the potential for sonar to detect fish rather than the sea bed and it was fishing sonars that set the lead in the development of sonar systems. These were one of the first to make the transition from the electrical/ mechanical systems to full electronic systems with the results shown first on a cathode ray tube display rather like a radar and later on flat-screen displays. These fishing sonars used transducers that could be lowered through the vessel's bottom and rotated, and as development took place the results were quite amazing. By varying the frequency of transmissions and their length, these sonars could be fine-tuned to detect particular types of fish and their introduction revolutionized the fishing industry. They were particularly used for detecting shoals of fish, but they could even be used to detect bottom-feeding fish and to identify particular types of seabed material that were known to be the areas used by certain fish as a habitat.

Going back to the use of sonar for navigation, flat-screen colour displays were introduced and the use of electronics allowed the depth to be displayed numerically in either metres, fathoms or feet. Corrections could be applied so the sounder measured the depth from the sea surface rather than the depth between the bottom of the ship and the sea bed. This was at a time when the world was changing to metres as the standard measurement of depth on charts and so mariners had to follow suit. For those navigators who had been brought up on a diet of depths in fathoms it was a major change and there were reports that the change led to some vessels grounding because they had not realized that the depth shown on the chart was in metres and not the deeper fathoms. There was considerable rebellion about the change because the fathom related directly to a human measurement, while the metre appeared to be an arbitrary length. The fathom at 6ft was also related to the nautical mile at 6,000ft (actually 6,080ft) but this had little navigation relevance.

The development of sophisticated echo-sounders came at a time when navigators became less concerned about the depth of water. Accurate position-fixing systems would give navigators confidence in their position and there was by now total reliance on the accuracy of the chart information so the depth of the water became less relevant. However, one of the basic principles of navigation has always been to check the position information by every available means so the cautious navigator would use the depth reading to help confirm the position on the chart. If there was a disparity between the position and associated water depth shown on the chart and the depth recorded by the echo-sounder, then this would be a time to check out the accuracy of the information being provided.

While the use of the echo-sounder had been relegated to this checking mode rather than to its use as a basic navigation tool, the use of sonar was taking a new direction. This was in the form of the forward-looking sonar, something that the fishing industry had been using for a long time in their hunt for the elusive fish, but now it was being developed as a means to show what lay underwater ahead of a vessel. The echo-sounder and indeed the lead-line had always had the disadvantage of only showing what was directly under the vessel, but the forward-looking sonar could show possible dangers ahead of the vessel.

It sounds simple to send out a sound ping ahead of the vessel, but in practice it is a complex area. Firstly the transducer pointing ahead is liable to aeration because of the movement of the vessel through the water. Then there is the problem of trying to identify the multitude of returns that come back to the receiver and finally there is the problem of identifying the returns from different depths of water ahead of the vessel. All of these returns have to be sorted out and identified and then displayed on a two-dimensional display. The range might be quite limited because of the complex returns and early ahead-looking sonars were limited to a range of perhaps 200 metres at best. This should be enough for slow-speed navigation which is where this sonar might be used, but longer ranges can be of more benefit. Developers were also limited by what the hull of a vessel could accommodate in the way of a forward-point transducer without interrupting the water flow around the hull.

A forward-looking sonar is something like an underwater radar but the transducer is fixed so that the sound signal can only encompass a limited sector ahead, usually around 20 to 30° which is adequate to show up significant dangers. There are sonars that can be fitted to smaller vessels, but these are limited to displacement speeds if the sonar is to work adequately. The main market is larger vessels that operate at displacement speeds of up to say 15 knots. These sonars are mainly a novelty market at the present stage of development and it is hard to see this changing when there is adequate navigation information available from alternative systems on board, but they could have applications in niche navigation sectors such as in ice navigation.

Sounding has come a long way since the days of the sounding stick, with sophisticated electronics now analysing what lies under the surface of the sea. Today the echo-sounder provides a check but the main sonar market is for those who are hunting things under the water, perhaps fish or submarines and in specialist areas such as wreck detection. Small craft may still use the simple sounding stick in the form of a boat hook when anchoring in strange waters, but today we tend to take the chart as the authority on water depths. However, an interesting development is found with electronic charts where depth and position information found by an echo-sounder and a GPS can be forwarded to the chart developers to provide up-to-date information about charted depths in less frequented areas. In some places this has shown up significant depth changes that have not been shown on the charts so the sounder has found a role as a surveying instrument.

The navigator at sea is in a strange position compared with his compatriots in the air and on land. What really interests him is avoiding the dangers that lie underwater and are hidden from view. While there are instruments that can detect these dangers, the modern navigator tends to rely totally on his charts to show these dangers so that the sounder and its developments now take a back seat in modern navigation techniques, despite having been one of the most important navigation techniques in the past.

Chapter Four

Heading in the Right Direction

Navigation is nothing if you don't head in a steady direction towards your destination. Today the compass is an essential part of the equipment of any boat or ship and we tend to take it for granted, but the compass was a long time in development and early navigators had to find alternatives. As we have seen in Chapter 1, there are many indicators out there that can give the navigator an indication of a fixed direction at least in the short term: what might be termed a visual compass.

The coastline is the obvious one and with most of the early voyages being along rivers, estuaries and coastlines it would be the land that would give the indication of direction. Even today with all the electronic systems available we still tend to steer from headland to headland when travelling along a coastline and those early navigators tended to voyage along coastlines for short distances where they could beach their boats overnight when they lost their visual direction indicators and then continue in daylight the next day if they were on an extended voyage.

Visual direction-finding is still the mainstay of navigation when in sight of land, but it does not make any allowances for shoals and rocks that might lie offshore. These were not a particular problem in the Mediterranean where it is reckoned that most early voyages took place and even if the voyage took the vessel some distance offshore, the coastlines tend to be backed by high mountains that could be visible for a considerable distance. It is an intriguing thought that when voyages were extended out of sight of land, the ability to make a landfall on a low-lying coastline such as the Nile Delta led to the erection of the extremely tall lighthouse at Alexandria. This is estimated to have been over 400ft high which would have made it visible from perhaps 30 miles away, offering a great visual direction clue on an otherwise low coastline. The light from the fire at the top of the lighthouse was thought to be one of the first to give a direction indication at night. This lighthouse was built around 300BC so it represents a significant advance in navigation at that time and it has never been exceeded.

The wind direction was a less reliable guide to direction but in the Mediterranean there are places where there can be steady winds from a known direction at certain times of the year and certain times of the day. Winds like the

Bora which blows from the mountains adjacent to the Adriatic mainly in the winter and the Sirocco which blows north from the North African coast would give a consistent wind direction that could be used as a heading guide. The importance of many of these consistent winds can be seen from the fact that early compass directions that were used in the Mediterranean were named after the winds that came from a certain direction rather than by the names that we know now. So Tramontana was the wind from the north and Sirocco was from the south-east and so on, with all the main eight points of the compass having a wind name.

Wind directions were less than reliable as a guide except in the short term, but the sun was a consistent guide as long as the sky was clear. Even back in 2000BC the daily changes of the sun had been understood as well as the seasonal changes and these acted both as a clock and a direction-indicator. The accuracy in both roles was not high, but an understanding of the hourly changes in the sun's direction could give navigators a useful guide once they had moved out of sight of the land. Once vessels had the confidence to travel overnight on longer voyages then it was the stars that took over the role of providing direction and it should be remembered that in those days the stars would have appeared to be much brighter because there was little or no contamination from land-based lights. It is surprising just how bright and clear the night skies can be when you move away from shore lights and in the usually clear skies of the Mediterranean the stars would have been a useful direction guide. The movement of the stars in the night skies would have been a thing of wonder, and the movements would have been clearly understood so that they could be anticipated and used as a heading guide. In particular it would have been the Pole Star with its fixed location as a north point that would have been identified. It is not the brightest star in the sky by a long way, but it is easy to identify on a clear night and remains as a constant north point.

However, the lack of any consistent heading indicator could explain why most of the early voyages tended to be along coastlines rather than out on the open seas. Navigators would have been reasonably confident about making open sea voyages of perhaps one or two days, but the accuracy of their heading references on the open sea could have made landfalls challenging after a longer time. This would have particularly been the case if they were heading towards an island rather than a long stretch of coastline. Using the wind, sun or stars as a heading reference would have probably given a course accuracy of perhaps 20° which would not magnify into too much of an error over a day or two, but which could be significant over several days. The Polynesians were past masters of using natural indicators such as the prevailing winds and the sun and stars to find a heading and they were finding island destinations, but their skill was in identifying the presence of land from a considerable distance by cloud and wave formations rather than in having direction indicators.

Even when the magnetic compass arrived on the scene the level of accuracy would not have been particularly high and initially might have little better accuracy than that obtained by other means, which might account for the slow uptake of the compass among navigators. By the time the compass was introduced, navigators had already worked out how to do latitude sailing, either due east or due west until land was encountered and then heading north or south along the coast. The latitude accuracy was not particularly accurate either and a latitude line could not be maintained with an accuracy of perhaps 1° at best which would be 60 miles. The big problem when using either a heading reference or a latitude to find a destination would be that once land was encountered as would be expected, which way should you turn to find your destination? Unless the coastline was recognized you could turn left or right to find your destination with little or no indication about which was the right way, meaning that navigation over open sea routes was a pretty hit-and-miss affair. Today this can be overcome by the availability of accurate position-fixing, but even in quite recent times it was common practice to introduce an error into the direct course to the destination so that when a landfall was made it was obvious which way to turn because you had set a course purposely to be on one side of the destination.

It is thought that the magnetic compass was first introduced more than 2,000 years ago and they were initially for use on land to find the way in featureless areas such as deserts. These early compasses used lodestone, which is a naturally-occurring iron ore that is magnetized naturally from the Earth's magnetic field. The magnetic compass using lodestone was not used for navigation initially but for fortune-telling by the Chinese. These earliest Chinese magnetic compasses were possibly used to order and harmonize buildings in accordance with the geomantic principles of feng shui. The peoples of ancient China discovered that if a lodestone was suspended so that it could turn freely, it would always point towards north. It was not for another 1,000 years or so that the properties of magnetism were used to make compasses suitable for navigation and for the Chinese this was during the Song Dynasty in the eleventh century. A number of early cultures used lodestones, suspended so they could turn, as magnetic compasses for navigation. References to such early magnetic compasses can be found in the written records of the Chinese, who began using them for marine navigation sometime between the ninth and eleventh centuries. This is thought to be some years before there was a European reference to a magnetic compass which is thought to be in 1190.

The earliest explicit recorded use of a magnetic compass for maritime navigation is found in Zhu Yu's book *Pingchow Table Talks* which dates between

1111 and 1117. This says: 'The ship's pilots are acquainted with the configuration of the coasts, at night they steer by the stars and in the daytime by the sun. In dark weather they look at the south-pointing needle.' This talk of a 'south-pointing needle' is probably a reference to the fact that a needle has two ends when suspended, so although we talk of the magnetic compass pointing to the north, it could equally well point to the south with reference to the other end of the needle.

These early compasses were simply some form of lodestone either suspended by a thread or more likely attached to a float such as a cork floating in a bowl of water. The rough-hewn lodestone was later replaced by an iron needle that would give a more accurate read-out. Either the suspended needle or the needle floating in water would have worked reasonably accurately on land where they would be on a steady surface, but at sea they were on a moving platform as the vessel pitched and rolled in waves that would have greatly reduced the steadiness of the needle and thus the accuracy of the readings. A considerable advance was made when the magnetized needle was mounted on a platform that was in turn mounted on a pivot so that the needle could rotate around the pivot point and thus be much less prone to the instability of a floating or suspended needle. It is suspected that the Chinese persisted with the floating needle in a bowl right up until the sixteenth century, but it was the Chinese who are thought to have been the developers of the first compass card on which forty-eight directions are marked on a pivoted card that rotates with a magnetized needle as early as 1296 during voyages around the South China Sea.

There are reports of compasses being used in Europe between 1100 and 1300 with 'sailors being guided by a compass needle'. In a later translation of Thomas Neckham it is quoted:

> The sailors, moreover, as they sail over the sea, when in cloudy weather they can no longer profit by the light of the sun, or when the world is wrapped up in the darkness of the shades of night, and they are ignorant to what point of the compass their ship's course is directed, they touch the magnet with a needle, which (the needle) is whirled round in a circle until, when its motion ceases, its point looks direct to the north.

It is suggested that the magnetic compass was a parallel invention in northern Europe alongside that of the Chinese. One quote from an eleventh-century manuscript says: 'An iron needle, after having been in contact with the loadstone, turns itself always toward the northern star (Pole Star), which, like the axis of the firmament, remains immoveable, while the others follow their course, so that it is very necessary to those who navigate the sea.'

In the Mediterranean, the introduction of the compass also included a magnetized pointer floating in a bowl of water that was known as the water compass. While this would give an indication of the direction of north, there were considerable limitations when ships wanted to sail on other courses, which was most of the time. However, the introduction of the water compass did give mariners the confidence to extend their sailing season to year-round operations rather than just when the clear skies of the summer months were available.

In addition to this extension of the sailing season the compass also gave mariners the confidence to undertake more open water voyages such as across the Indian Ocean from the Red Sea to India and across the Bay of Biscay. On these longer voyages the seasonal limitations might be imposed more by the adverse weather conditions rather than by navigation limitations. The water compass was widely used in the twelfth century, but its limitations led to the development of the compass card that would allow courses to be steered much more accurately. Already the water compass had been partially superseded by having the compass needle mounted on a pivot; it was a relatively simple development to fit a circular dial around the needle or, as it developed, the needles, and this was the birth of the modern compass card as we know it today.

It was probably around the thirteenth century that the compass card was developed and the circular form of this would allow navigators to steer a reasonably accurate course on any required heading, although just how accurate that heading might be is open to question. At that time the vessels used for both commerce and warfare were relatively small – perhaps no more than 100ft in length – so their movement in waves would be quite lively, meaning that the movement of the compass card would have been equally lively. We see this today on small craft where the compass card can swing quite a lot in lively seas, even when the movement of the card is damped to reduce the swinging. However, the circular compass card mounted on its pivot was a considerable improvement in providing heading information and it could well have been this development in heading information that gave navigators like Columbus the confidence to head off into the unknown oceans knowing that at least they could maintain a reasonably steady heading in the desired direction.

Looking at pictures of old compass cards, it becomes clear that the cards themselves became something of an art form. They became more and more ornate and were quite beautiful, but you have to wonder whether these ornate cards were the ones that went to sea or whether they were just designed as the ornate ones that stayed on land. These early compass cards were divided

A seventeenth-century compass on which the compass pointer is also the magnet.

into thirty-two 'points' of the compass with the main four being the cardinal points of north, east, south and west. Between these cardinal points the card was subdivided again to give half points and then the space between these half points would again be subdivided to give quarter points. This level of direction accuracy was probably enough for many practical purposes, although there were also some sixty-four-point compass cards. It remains a mystery as to why the compass card became divided into 360°, although it does appear that the Babylonians were obsessed with the number sixty which might account for the significance of 6×60 to make up the 360° card. There is some relationship between the 360° of the compass card and the 360° division of the Earth both east and west to make the measurement of latitude and longitude. The first reference to a 360° compass card comes from the Frenchman Pierre de Maricourt in 1269 but it was not until the nineteenth century that cards with this style of division-marking became commonplace. With a 360° card the markings of one degree are about as close as a helmsman can steer and such a course would give reasonable heading accuracy. Even today,

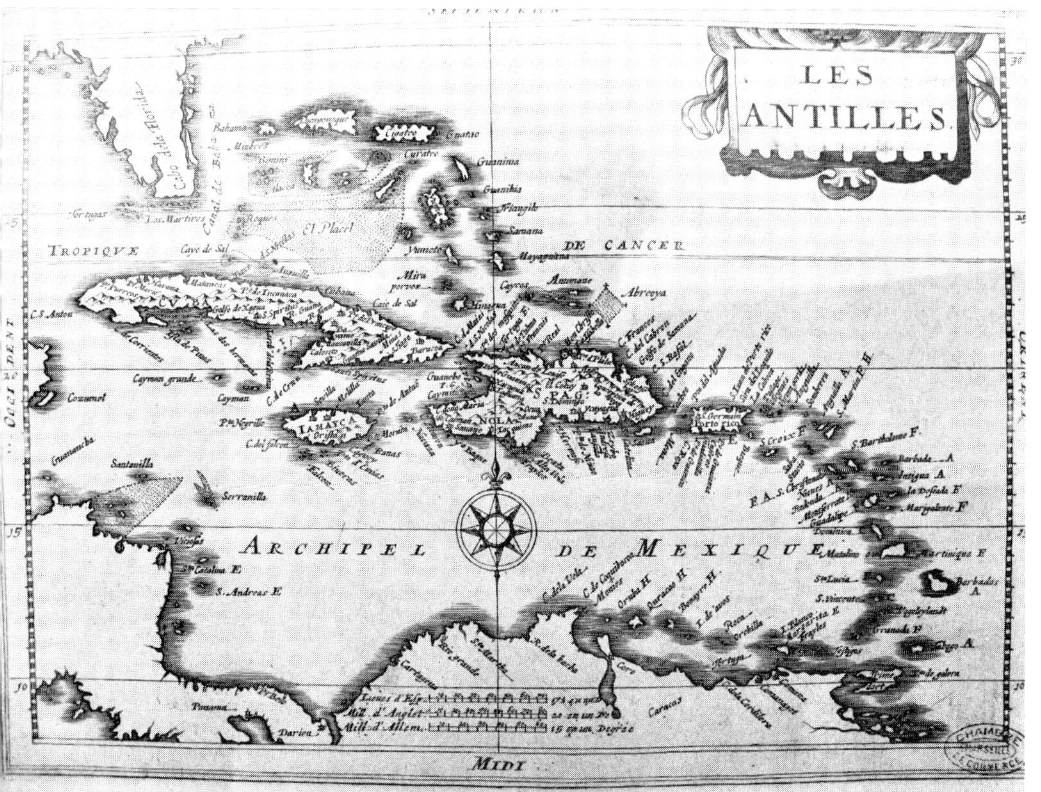

An early chart of the Caribbean with no attempt at showing soundings but with the compass rose near its centre.

compass cards are often marked in both the cardinal points and in degrees and until recently part of the training of a navigator would be to recite the thirty-two points of the compass, rather like a child learning the alphabet.

As for the compass itself, there were steady improvements in the design of the compasses used at sea. Initially the compass card would have just been open in a similar way to the floating needle designs, but the next step would have been to enclose the swinging card to isolate it from the elements. Again that would have offered protection, but on a ship that was moving at sea the enclosure would have interfered with the movement of the card and it was not until the development of the compass mounted in gimbals that the compasses used at sea started to resemble the modern magnetic compass.

That was a significant step forward, but just as important was the development of the liquid-filled compass designed to damp the movement of the compass card and to offer a more steady reading. Not only did the liquid damp the movement of the card, it also reduced wear on the pivot bearing. A basic type of liquid compass was introduced by Sir Edmund Halley in 1690 and from this we start to see all the elements of the modern compass coming together with the liquid-damped compass mounted in a binnacle with the compass itself gimbal-mounted. Gimbals would have isolated the compass card from the movement, vibration and impacts caused by the pitch and roll of the vessel. The first practical liquid mariner's compass is believed to have been patented by Francis Crow in 1813 in Britain and was further developed in the US from 1830 onwards.

The magnetic compass became a vital part of the navigator's equipment and along with the development of instruments to measure the speed of ships this led to the development of dead reckoning as a means of establishing the position of a vessel by calculation when it was not possible to establish this by other means such as bearings from the land or sights of the sun or stars. An accurate heading was required to establish a dead-reckoning position so attention was drawn to making the compass more accurate. Variation error, which was due to the fact that the true North Pole and the magnetic North Pole are not in the same place, was recognized and major surveys undertaken to establish this difference in various places around the world so that corrections could be applied. Then there was the influence of any iron or steel on the ship that could affect the magnetic pattern to which the compass needle was aligning itself, and the means to measure this and establish corrections were found. Known respectively as the variation and the deviation, these two corrections improved the accuracy of the magnetic compass to the point where it could be reasonably assured to be accurate to within 1°.

With wooden ships the correction for deviation was reasonably consistent and straightforward, but once iron and then steel ships were introduced the influence of the ship's magnetism could be considerable. It was Lord Kelvin who developed the sophisticated correction systems such as Lord Kelvin's Balls at each side of the compass and the Flinders Bar at the front of the compass that allowed the compass correctors to remove much of the deviation from the calculations and to improve the compass accuracy.

An early box compass with the facility for taking bearings.

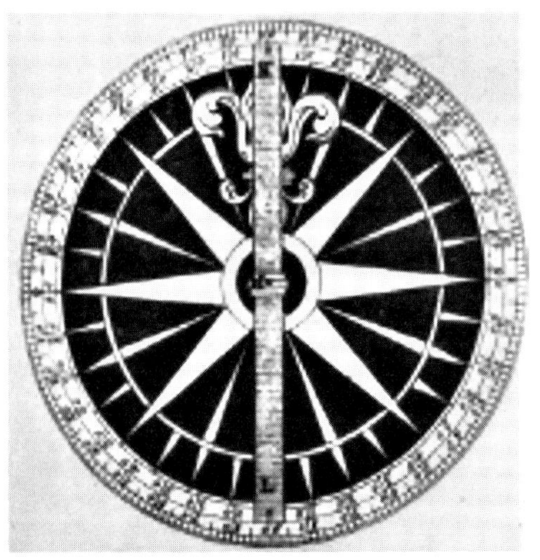

On ships the master compass was usually located on the flying bridge where it was as far removed from magnetic influence as possible. In this open location the compass would be fitted with an azimuth ring that allowed bearings to be taken when navigating along a coastline. Three bearings from shore objects such as a lighthouse or church spire would be used to create the 'cocked hat' triangle in which the ship's position would lie. Many is the time when the navigator would have to brave the cold, wind and rain on the open flying bridge to obtain these position-fixing bearings which were the most accurate positioning prior to the development of electronic systems. Taking bearings of the sun as it was rising and setting was also a good way to check the compass for any errors and the true bearing of the sun at these moments could be worked out from tables depending on the sun's declination or location in relation to the equator. For small craft the hand-bearing compass was used which was a portable compass mounted on a handle that could be used to obtain bearings in much the same way, but of course these magnetic compasses were not corrected, although it was possible to use them in a part of the boat where any magnetic influence was minimized.

Various liquids were introduced as the damping medium in the compass with one of the favourites being water with the addition of alcohol to stop it freezing. However, sailors became aware of this source of alcohol and removed it to drink it so various non-toxic alternatives were found. For the compasses used on fast boats where a firmer damping was required, oil was found to be a good substitute in what were known as high-speed compasses.

The magnetic compass has gone through a huge amount of development over the years, and ships and boats still carry them as the reliable alternative for heading indication that does not rely on an electrical supply. However, the complication of the system and the need for corrections led to the development of first the gyrocompass, then the electronic compass and now we have the GPS compass.

The gyrocompass was patented in 1885 by Marinus Gerardus van den Bos in the Netherlands after the development of small electric motors to power the gyro. It took another twenty years before the practical gyro was made in Germany by Hermann Anschütz-Kaempfe. The gyrocompass had two significant advantages over the magnetic compass: it indicated true north and it was unaffected by magnetic materials on the ship. It was widely used on ships and indeed became the standard heading indicator on most ships, but it was expensive and complex and ships still needed to carry a magnetic compass. The gyro works because when spinning, the gyro aligns with the Earth's axis of rotation but the complications come in adapting this feature into a heading reference that could be used for steering.

When I first went to sea the gyrocompass had a cabin all to itself to ensure that it was kept free from dust and other contamination. Today there are gyrocompasses that operate at the atomic level using the rotation of atoms to provide the heading information. These tiny 'gyros' are fitted into tiny inertial navigation units that not only measure the direction of travel accurately but also, by using accelerometers, measure the distance travelled and thus automatically compute the dead reckoning, taking into account any effects of current, tide or wind to give an accurate location without access to any external sensors. Inertial navigation units were originally developed for use in submarines and were then used in aircraft but now both the cost and the size of these units has dramatically decreased and they can be widely used as a stand-by in the event of disruption of the satellite navigation signals.

The fluxgate compass is what might be termed an electronic compass and it is based on a magnetic core around which are wound a series of coils of wire. The coils are set at angles – sometimes at right angles but more often at 45° – and as the heading varies then a small current is generated in these wires. By computing the amount of current and knowing the coils in which it is generated, the heading can be calculated. These compasses are not highly accurate, but they are relatively cheap and they have formed the heading

Inside a fluxgate compass showing the coils that sense the Earth's magnetic field direction.

reference for a whole generation of autopilots for small craft. Being electronic they can be corrected for deviation by switching to calibration mode and turning the craft through 360°. Another advantage is that the compass unit can be mounted in most parts of the craft, although not near large metal masses such as the engines. The fluxgate compass is what might be termed the poor man's gyrocompass and their performance has been enhanced by linking the output to small gyros. Being electronic, the output allows the heading information to be displayed in a variety of ways such as dials and strip indicators.

The GPS compass is notable for its simplicity. Two GPS antennas are located a short distance apart and by interpolating the two positions generated by these units the heading or direction can be found. The beauty of this compass is that while the GPS can be affected by a variety of errors, the two adjacent GPS receivers will both be affected by the same errors so the relative difference between the two receivers will be immune from these and thus will give an accurate heading reference, accurate to within one-tenth of a degree. These GPS compasses are now reducing in size and they are currently small enough to provide a cost-effective heading reference solution for small craft.

For aircraft use, small liquid-filled magnetic compasses were developed. Aircraft would not normally be subject to the same motions that can affect a ship at sea and so the liquid-filled compass can give a steady reading. Also there is less likely to be magnetic material in the vicinity of an aircraft compass apart perhaps from the engine so reasonable accuracy can be expected. The Creagh-Osborne aircraft compass, which used a mixture of alcohol and distilled water, was introduced for aircraft in 1909 and this led to the development of small pocket-sized compasses for land navigation. The development of aircraft compasses has largely followed that of marine compasses except for the requirement for small size and low weight, although an innovation for aircraft compasses was the grid compass. This has a grid marked on a transparent disc that can be rotated above the compass card. It is rotated to set the required course and then just a quick glance indicates whether the aircraft is on course. One type of grid compass uses a plan of an aircraft as the grid, giving the navigator a quick picture of the heading at a glance.

Aircraft compasses were well in advance of marine compasses in the use of repeater compasses that could give a display suitable for dashboard mounting and, while as with shipping, the magnetic compass is still used as a stand-by, it has been superseded by some of the more advanced types, particularly the atomic gyrocompass that is used in many inertial navigation systems.

The development of good accurate compasses has come at a time when the compass has almost become redundant. Today most heading information can be obtained from the electronic chart that displays the heading vector in relation to the desired track so it is easy to first set the course to the next waypoint and then to adjust the course if the vessel drifts away from the desired track. Compasses are still used as a reference for the autopilot but even that can be controlled from the chart display to maintain the vessel on track automatically. The one thing that the compass cannot allow for is leeway: the angle at which a vessel drifts sideways under the influence of the wind. This mainly affects sailing vessels with their considerable sail area and even though they have a deep keel to help reduce the sideways drift, the leeway can often reach 5° which of course means that the actual course steered will be 5° away from the desired course. The angle of leeway is usually estimated by looking over the stern and estimating the angle of the wake in relation to the vessel's heading and the course steered corrected accordingly. Now with GPS plotting the leeway can be seen and corrected in relation to the track followed.

So it is ironic that the long quest for heading information over the centuries has now become almost redundant, although vessels still have a magnetic compass that does not rely on any outside input to produce a heading. This means that in the event of a total electrical failure there is still a back-up and today that is really the main role of the compass, apart from its use as the autopilot heading reference.

Chapter Five

Speed

Speed has never been quite as important for navigation as have soundings and headings so it took longer to develop means of measuring speed. Perhaps this reflects the fact that in the early days of navigation there was little means of controlling the speed anyway. Your speed was governed by the strength of the wind when under sail over which you had no control, or if you were under oars or paddles there was little you could do about progress except to slow down if necessary. So speed was not a major factor in navigation until the development of dead-reckoning navigation in which the navigator would combine the estimated speed with the estimated heading made good to arrive at an estimated position.

Dead-reckoning navigation started when mariners such as Columbus took to the high seas. As we will see in the next chapter, navigators had worked out ways of measuring the latitude with a reasonable degree of accuracy but for longitude, the east/west direction, their only way of measuring progress was to estimate how far they had sailed each day for which they needed to know the speed. Only then could they get some idea of when they might make a landfall at the latitude along which they were sailing. We don't see much mention of speed as a factor in early navigation and when a voyage was perhaps of two or three days' duration you could estimate roughly when a landfall might be made, both from experience and from having just a rough idea of how fast the vessel was travelling. Certainly the vessels used were not fast, probably sailing at little more than walking pace, so from a walking-pace experience on land a navigator could estimate the speed of his vessel. He might even walk along the deck from bow to stern to get an idea of the speed through the water.

In the age of exploration of the fifteenth century something better was needed to measure the speed of a vessel at sea and one of the earliest mentions of a ship's log, the instrument for measuring speed, is found in the accounts of Magellan's voyages when he became the first person to sail around the world. Prior to this mention of a log for measuring speed it is assumed that the speed was estimated by eye and by experience. Magellan measured speed with a chip log which was also called a ship's log. The term 'log' comes from the very earliest form of measurement of speed when a piece of wood would be thrown overboard from the bow and the navigator would walk alongside it until it reached the stern. The time taken for the log to pass from bow to stern would be estimated and with the distance (the length of the ship) known, the speed could be calculated. This was probably no more accurate than looking over the side and estimating the speed, but the chip log took the measurement of speed a step further.

A further development was the Dutchman's log which, despite its name, is attributed to the Portuguese Bartolomeu Crescêncio, who designed it at the end of the fifteenth century. This was a refinement of the ship's log with a floating object thrown overboard and a sandglass used to measure the time it took to pass between two points on deck. The design of the chip log had also changed and more sophisticated versions used a triangular wooden board that was attached to the 'knot' line by a bridle at each corner. The line would be held on a reel so that it could be paid out easily and a sandglass would be used to measure a fixed time with the speed being measured by the number of knots that were paid out in that fixed time. Over time, the log construction was standardized and the shape of the chip was a quarter-circle or quadrant and the log-line attached to the board with a bridle of three lines. To ensure that the log submerged and oriented correctly in the water, the bottom of the log was weighted with lead. This arrangement provided better water resistance, which in turn gave a more accurate reading. The bridle was attached in such a way that a strong tug on the line would tip the chip and make it easier to retrieve the log.

With the introduction of the nautical mile as a standard unit of measure at sea in the fifteenth century, they began to mark the line at equal intervals proportional to the nautical mile and to the time interval used for measurement. The nautical mile was established at 6,000ft which was a close approximation to the distance of one minute of latitude. When the nautical mile became standardized the actual length was established at 6,076ft which accords more with the one minute of latitude, but the approximation was close enough as far as a vessel's speed was concerned. Initially, the markings were simply knots in the line, hence the reason why speed is measured in knots, but later, like the lead-line for sounding, the marks were bits of cord inserted into the rope with knots according to different speeds. Many ships used knots spaced at 8 fathoms (which is 48ft) apart, while others used a 7-fathom distance. Ships normally used timing glasses set for either twenty-eight or fourteen seconds. Thus knowing the time it took for a fixed distance of line to go out, it was a simple calculation to establish the speed of the ship.

Of course this speed that was measured was the speed of the ship through the water. This could still be considerably different to the speed of the ship over the ground which is the actual distance that the ship would cover across

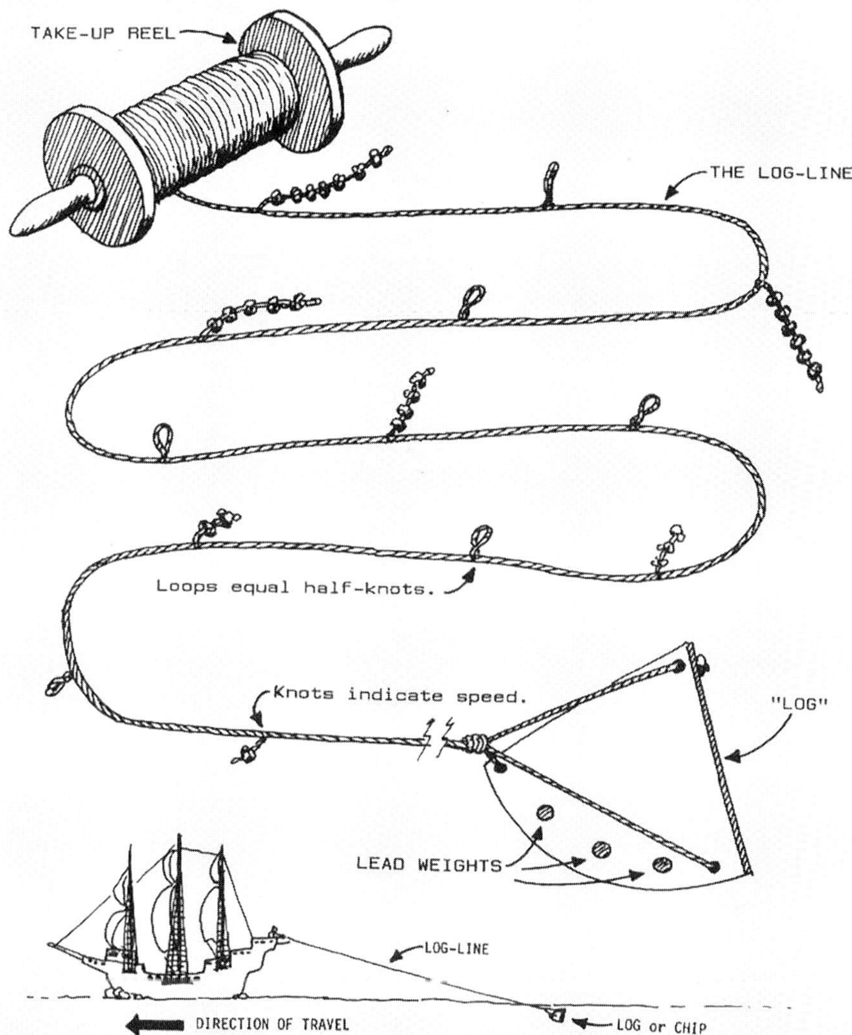

The original log where speed was measured by the distance of rope that went out in a given time.

the surface of the Earth and the speed that would be required in order to establish a new position relative to a previous one. The difference between through the water and over the ground would possibly be due to currents in the water and possibly assistance from the waves in a following sea. The leeway that was mentioned in the previous chapter could also affect the speed over the ground so while mariners could now measure the speed of their vessel with a degree of accuracy they still had to estimate and make allowances for these other factors when trying to establish a dead-reckoning or estimated position. Of course there was always the possibility of errors in the timing glass and in possible stretch in the log line that might affect the result.

The rope log was in use through the sixteenth century and it was later that century, as international trade developed and the need for accurate navigation became more important, that inventors started to look at better ways of measuring the speed of ships through the water. A wide variety of technologies were used ranging from lowering a cannonball on the end of a length of rope and measuring the angle it adopted from the vertical through to systems for measuring the pull on a rope towed behind the ship and to using towed propellers. It was the latter that produced the most reliable and accurate results and a number of what became known as 'taffrail logs' were invented or developed. The name came from the way the log was mounted on the stern railings of the ship and these taffrail logs were used to measure the distance travelled rather than the speed, which was the important figure when calculating the dead-reckoning position.

The taffrail log was essentially a propeller that was towed behind the ship. It was fitted with a counter that would measure the number of rotations of the log 'propeller' and translate this into distance. On the earlier logs this counter was fitted to the outboard end of the line with the 'propeller' fitted behind it so that the log had to be pulled in to get the reading from the counter. Later special ropes were developed that would rotate with the propeller so that the counter could be mounted on the taffrail to allow continuous readings. This type of log, which was the basis of the famous Walker log, continued in production right through to recent times, although its installation switched to use on yachts rather than ships. When I went to sea in 1950 we were still using these towed logs and as an apprentice it was my job to read the log at the end of each four-hour watch, although sometimes the rope would be found hanging limp in the water when a shark had come along and bitten off the rotator. This was fishing on the grand scale with the rotator acting like the spinner used for catching mackerel, although of course there was no hook on the log rotator.

There were a number of variations on this towed log. One had the rotations of the propeller connected to a small bellows that then transmitted impulses to a connected counter. Another used electrical impulses in much the same way. Another design used a rotator much like an anemometer used for measuring wind speed. However, it was the brass rotator that stood the test of time. This had to be constructed with considerable accuracy to produce reliable results and although the propeller rotating on the end of a line was the design that lasted, there were also experiments with speed or distance

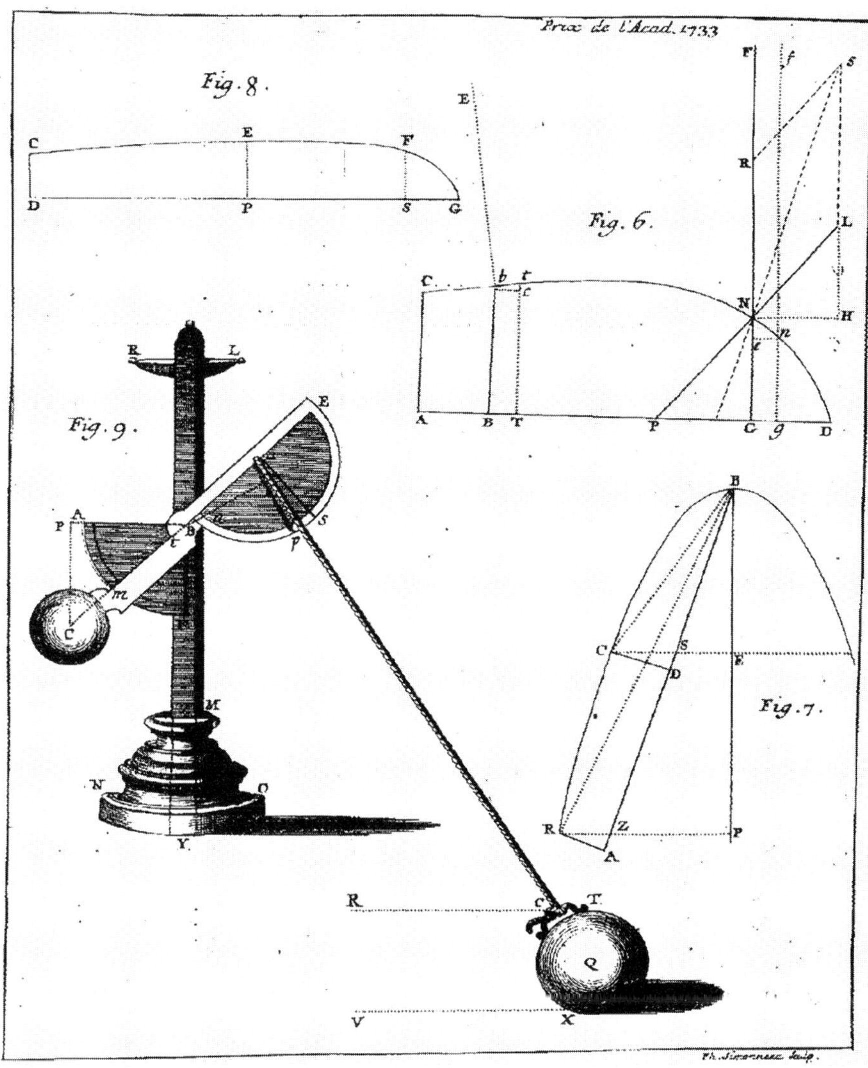

A cannonball log where the angle of the rope supporting the heavy ball gives an indication of the speed through the water.

measuring devices that were actually attached to the hull of a ship. Much of this development of mechanical logs took place at the end of the seventeenth century and the early eighteenth century. With the advent of steamships fitted with paddle-wheels the speed of revolution of the paddles was used as a measure of speed and this was a method favoured by mail steamers on short routes where the paddles were maintained at much the same height in the water all the time. When propellers became the norm much the same system was used, but with propellers often varying in immersion and difficulties when the ship was pitching in rough seas, the accuracy of propeller revolutions as a measure of speed was not reliable.

Attention turned to developing devices attached to the hull of a ship to measure speed at the beginning of the twentieth century, and the one that stood the test of time was the Chernikeeff log. Developed by a captain in the Russian navy, this log comprised a rotator on the end of an arm that could be lowered through the bottom of the hull so that the impeller was about 15in below the hull. The rotation count was transmitted by electrical pulses to a read-out on the ship's bridge, so for probably the first time there was instant speed information available to the navigator. The Chernikeeff log continued in use until the end of the last century when it was replaced by electronic devices.

A competing log was the Pitot meter log developed in France by Henri Pitot in 1730. This was simply a tube with its open end facing forward in the direction of travel with the speed obtained by measuring the pressure generated in the tube. While not very popular for use on ships because marine growth could affect the readings, the Pitot tube became the standard means of measuring speed on aircraft.

The demand for accurate speed and distance measurements for vessels at sea accelerated after the Second World War, spurred on partly by demand for more accurate navigation as the speed of ships and boats increased but also by advances in electronics. For ships the Doppler log was a major innovation because for the first time here was a log that could measure the speed over the ground rather than the speed through the water, at least in relatively shallow water. The speed over the ground was a much more accurate navigation reference because it eliminated any errors that might occur from applying the effects of current and leeway to the speed through the water and so was an accurate portrayal of the distance travelled rather than an estimation.

The Doppler log sends out a sound pulse rather like an echo-sounder, but instead of measuring the time it takes to return after being reflected from the sea bed it measures the change of frequency of the signal that occurs in the reflected signal which is a direct measure of the speed of the ship. Doppler logs for ships were reported to have an accuracy of 0.1 per cent which was highly accurate, but the downside was that the log was only effective in relatively shallow water when the signal could strike bottom and in ocean waters it would measure the speed in relation to the water as the signal was reflected from small particles in the water. For the navigator it was important to know which speed was being measured, of course.

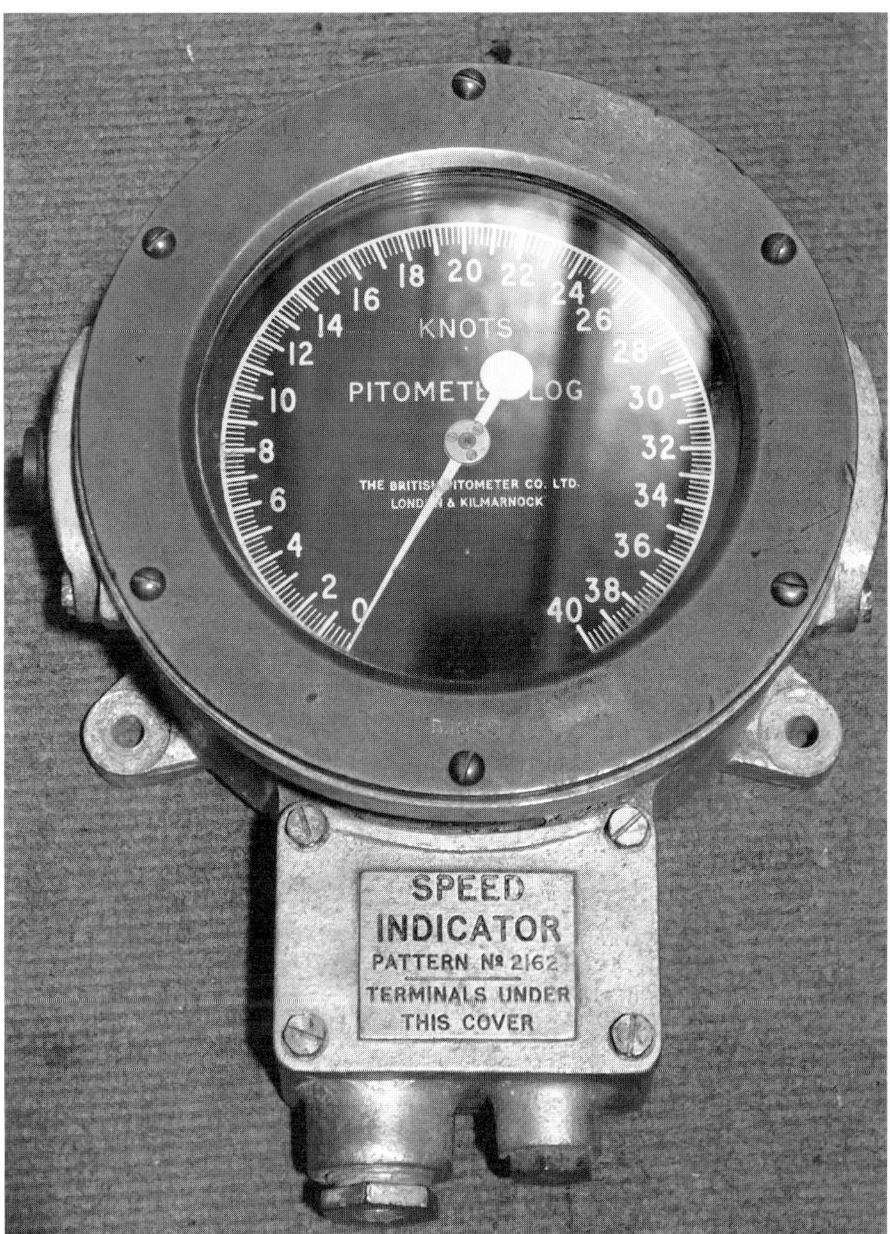

The display head of a Pitot meter log that was used by many large ships.

One advantage of the Doppler log was that the transducer in the hull was virtually flush with the hull. A number of small craft logs had been developed using a variety of paddle-wheel or impeller designs that rotated at a speed dictated by the speed of the vessel. The electromagnetic log used a very different principle with two electrodes mounted on a plate attached to the hull and the water flowing past these electrodes would generate an electrical current that would be proportional to the speed of the water flow. This was a simple effective solution to measuring the speed through the water, but it had the disadvantage that marine growth on the plate could quickly render the log ineffective. This type of simple log was mainly aimed at the small craft market.

Over the years there have been many innovative attempts to develop logs that can measure the speed of a vessel either through the water or preferably over the ground. It was a vital part of navigation when ships were navigating in cloudy or foggy conditions when it was not possible to fix the position by sextant or visual bearings and the navigator had to rely on his dead-reckoning calculations. Log readings tend to underestimate the speed rather than overestimate it, so the cautious navigator would often add a bit more to the speed registered so that if anything he would be ahead of his expected position, which would be a safety feature until he could get confirmation by soundings

The electro-magnetic log where the fitting in the hull of the vessel measured the speed of the water flowing past.

or other means. Like other instruments, today the log is almost redundant as the speed over the ground can now be obtained with considerable accuracy by calculation from consecutive fixes from the GPS. However, there are still two areas in which the log can be useful and one is when the GPS system goes down, of course, and the navigator has to resort to more traditional navigation means to find his way home. The other is for sailing boats where the speed through the water can be a vital indicator of the performance of the yacht under wind power and the speed over the ground may be of less importance. So the log still remains a useful tool for the navigator, even in the modern highly-automated world of navigation.

Chapter Six

Fixing the Position

Fixing the position of a vessel out on the open ocean must have been a challenge for the early sailors. The only clues they had were the record or estimation of the distance that had been sailed and the direction in which they had sailed. However, how do you define the position in what was then the middle of nowhere? Along the coasts there are headlands and other features that can provide a reference, but out of sight of land there is nothing but the sun and the stars and it was these that the early sailors turned to for clues about where they were.

This still begs the question about how you record a position on the open ocean and in those early days when it was still considered that the Earth was flat, the concept of a grid that shows latitude and longitude was a long way in the future. The navigation was achieved simply by following a steady course guided either by a wind from a steady direction or by the sun and the stars. As we have seen, the movements of both the sun and the stars were understood from the early days of navigation and rather than fix a position, navigation was achieved simply by heading in a fixed direction until the expected land was sighted. This was the basis of navigation for a long time and it was not until there was a method of establishing longitude that positions could be recorded in terms of latitude and longitude on the chart with any degree of accuracy.

History has shown that navigators at sea are very adaptable, using the information that is available and finding ways to adapt this to meet their requirements. Because they could measure their latitude with reasonable accuracy or at least consistency, they would follow along a line of latitude when navigating across the open sea. They might not know what that line of latitude was, but it was the consistency that was important and so a certain direction was maintained.

The invention of a geographic coordinate system goes back to the third century BC with the credit going to Eratosthenes of Cyrene. This was improved upon by Hipparchus of Nicaea 100 years later who also developed an improved system of determining latitude using measurements from the stars in addition to the sun. Hipparchus was way ahead of his time when he developed a way of measuring longitude using simultaneous timings of lunar eclipses, but that was a method for use on land rather than for use at sea.

When developing a coordinate system on which to base latitude and longitude measurements a variety of prime meridians was used, one being located west of all known land at that time so it was out in the Atlantic. Later the prime meridian was moved east not too far from where it is located now and it was not until the second century AD that latitude was measured from the Equator. So there was a lot of variation in the establishment of latitude and longitude grids but what is amazing is that more than 2,000 years ago the need for and working out of systems to plot positions was well established. In time the Equator became the standard for 0° of latitude but it was not until 1884, after the International Meridian Conference in the US, that the Greenwich meridian was established as the zero reference for longitude, bringing all navigators into agreement about how to record positions around the world and incidentally also having a standard for time.

When the mathematicians and scientists of history were studying the world and its shape and size they came up with measurements and figures that gave an estimate of size which in turn enabled navigators to have some idea how far they needed to travel to reach a certain destination. At some stage in the estimation of the size and shape of the Earth the decision was made to divide the circumference of the Earth into 360° both in the latitude and longitude, although the reason for choosing this figure is not clear, rather like the reason for choosing 360° for the compass card. When the actual size of the world was finally established this division of the Earth into 360° segments proved to be a wise choice and it meant that each degree of the division was equivalent to 60 nautical miles (close enough), which in turn meant that one minute of arc on the Earth's surface was equivalent to 1 mile. In fact, to be accurate one nautical mile established as a minute of arc is 6,076ft but the correlation between the measurement of distances at sea and the division of the distances on the latitude and longitude scales surface of the Earth is direct.

The work of the mathematicians and astronomers more than 2,000 years ago is amazing and set the scene for the future of celestial navigation. They worked out the way the sun changed its declination, its orbit north or south of the Equator as the seasons changed over the year so that navigators could work out their latitude from the altitude of the sun. They realized that what was taking place in the heavens with the movement of the sun, stars and planets could be translated into calculations on the surface of the Earth. Probably even more challenging was the way in which they developed spherical trigonometry, the ability to work out the lengths and angles of a triangle on the curved surface of the Earth so that measurements taken from the heavens to fix the position related to the Earth's surface. This is like normal trigonometry on a flat surface where the triangle can be completed by calculation if two sides or angles are known but with the complication of the curved surfaces. This is the basis of all celestial navigation and what those ancient mathematicians worked out is still in use today to work out latitude and longitude from sextant angles. It was probably recognized that time was an important element in these calculations, but they had not developed any reliable means of measuring time accurately enough for position-fixing and we had to wait nearly 2,000 years for that to happen.

One of the earliest tabulations of the day-to-day positions of the heavenly bodies was *Ephemerides*, compiled by the German astronomer Regiomontanus (born Johannes Müller von Königsberg) and published by him in Nuremberg in 1474. This work also set forth the principle of determining longitude by the method of lunar distances, i.e. the angular displacement of the moon from other celestial objects. This method, which was destined to become the standard for a time during the nineteenth century, remained impracticable for more than three centuries because of the inaccuracy of existing lunar tables and because special knowledge and tedious computations were necessary in its use. Meanwhile, during the sixteenth and seventeenth centuries, working from translations of Portuguese and Spanish manuals, a flourishing school of instrument-makers, chart-makers and teachers grew in England. This group rapidly improved the theory of navigation and compiled tables of increasing accuracy. In 1675 the Royal Observatory was established at Greenwich with the specific object of providing sailors with astronomical data of the required precision. In Paris the *Connaissance des Temps* (*Knowledge of Time*), the first national almanac, was founded in 1679. It contained tables for the crude determination of longitude from observations of the occultation or eclipses of Jupiter's moons by Jupiter, first seen by Galileo in 1610. (Galileo himself had advocated the preparation of such tables for this purpose but the method, although sound in principle, could not be made practical aboard sailing ships.) In 1755 Johann Tobias Mayer, a German astronomer, published remarkably accurate tables of the motion of the moon. To make them useful to navigators, however, it was necessary to prepare from them an ephemeris of the moon for every noon and midnight. The fifth British Astronomer Royal, the Reverend Dr Nevil Maskelyne, supervised this task and the results were published in the annual *Nautical Almanac*, which was inaugurated in 1766.

While the mathematicians struggled with longitude, the focus of early position-fixing was on measuring the latitude and one of the first instruments developed for this was the astrolabe. This allowed navigators to measure the inclined position in the sky of a celestial body, day or night. It could be used to identify stars or planets and to determine when local time was known. While the astrolabe is effective for determining latitude on land or calm seas, it is less reliable on the heaving deck of a ship in rough seas, so the mariner's astrolabe was developed.

The astrolabe comprises a series of discs or pointers that were engraved with the positions of heavenly bodies and it dates back to the third century BC, reflecting how much was known about the movements of the sun and stars at that time. It was effectively an analogue calculator capable of working out several different kinds of problems in spherical astronomy. The mariner's astrolabe was not developed until much later when celestial navigation was being developed and it has been suggested that it was used by navigators for coastal navigation from the fifteenth century onwards and it is reported that it was used by Columbus on his Atlantic venture for determining his latitude. The oldest-known astrolabe found in a wreck in the Arabian Sea has been dated at around 1500 and has its edge inscribed in 5° sectors, suggesting that an altitude could be measured with an accuracy of 1° or 2°. This would allow latitude to be obtained with an accuracy of between 50 and 100 miles. The mariner's version was first developed in Germany and this was a greatly simplified version where most of the astronomical data was removed and there was a pointer with pinhole sights that could pivot around a 360° scale on the outside. Even with this simplification, the astrolabe was still challenging to use in rough seas and mariners were looking for a more practical solution to finding the altitude of heavenly bodies to establish latitude.

By the seventeenth century the astrolabe was being replaced by the cross staff which had been developed years earlier. This was a very simple solution for measuring altitudes and comprised a wooden stick along which wooden discs could slide. The end of the stick was held up to the eye and then the bottom of a disc was aligned with the horizon and the top of the disc with the sun or star. A scale marked on the stick would then give the altitude of the heavenly body. Three of the crosspieces or discs were often used which would be effective for different altitudes and avoid having a long stick that would be hard to manage on a moving ship. The cross staff gave greater accuracy in measuring the altitude because of the length of the stick compared with the compact size of the astrolabe, but even then the accuracy would probably be only within a few degrees. For sun observations it was usual to have a piece of tinted glass to look through and it was suggested that a correction be applied to the reading because the sighting was not at the eye but slightly below it.

A further development was the back staff which allowed a longer stick to be used to give greater accuracy and this was also the first time that a mirror was incorporated into the viewing system; something that became an inherent part of all future means of measuring altitude. With the back staff the stick was equipped with two sighting pieces, one below the stick and the other above, and the mirror was attached to one end. In use the observer faced away from the sun or star with the lower sight at his eye. He would look past this to

Using the cross staff worked well on land but was challenging on the moving deck of a ship.

the mirror which was aligned with the horizon and he would sight the sun in the mirror, adjusting the back stick to line up with the sun. The altitude would then be obtained by adding the marks on both sticks together.

John Davis writing in the sixteenth century commented on the challenge of obtaining altitudes of the sun and stars and he developed the Davis Quadrant, which started to look something like the modern sextant although much larger. Again a mirror was used that had a slit in it to allow the horizon to be sighted and the observer faced away from the sun. This time it was the sighting glass that moved on a scale and because this scale was enlarged it meant that for the first time not only degrees could be measured but multiples of minutes. So this meant that the accuracy was being improved, but it still took some time to take a sight of the sun and the instrument was quite unwieldy.

This was followed by the Hadley Quadrant introduced in 1731 which is recognized as a milestone in the development of navigation comparable with the advanced compass of Lord Kelvin and John Harrison's chronometer. Hadley is credited with the development, although there were other similar inventions at the same time. Hadley's Quadrant was the forerunner of the modern sextant, using two mirrors with one fixed and one moveable in angle. It was the top mirror that was moveable with the movement controlled in angle by mounting it on an arm, the lower end of which moved against a scale on the lower arc. That sounds very much like a basic description of a modern sextant, but the frame was made of wood with the scale on an ivory insert. It is reported that the quadrant could be used to measure altitudes with an accuracy of one minute of arc which gave the potential to establish a position with an accuracy of 1 mile which was certainly accurate enough for ocean navigation and even for making landfalls. Of course the Hadley Quadrant, which was in reality an octant, so-named because of the range of angles it could measure, was gradually developed into the modern sextant as design and construction techniques were improved and as the wood frame was replaced with more stable metal frames.

The technology of the sextant relies on the principle that when a mirror is rotated the reflected image moves through twice the angle of the mirror rotation. You sight through a telescope at the horizon mirror which is split with one side open and one side mirrored so that the sun or star can be seen alongside the horizon. For sun sights tinted shades were introduced to filter the sun's rays and a variety of refinements were introduced over the years. Initially the angle was measured on a vernier scale that allowed very accurate measurements to be made, but of course the accuracy depended on the skill of the manufacturer in etching the scale on the silver insert. Another major step forward with the development of the sextant was the introduction of the micrometer for measuring the angle and this in turn depended on the ability to machine the worm-drive gearing of the micrometer drive to a level of accuracy consistent with measuring angles to within one minute of arc. I am always amazed by the skill that can produce an instrument that can measure to such a level of accuracy and yet be tough enough to be used in the rough and tumble of the small craft that are making ocean voyages. Modern sextants are precision instruments and as a navigator you are trained in how to handle your sextant and to treat it with respect because the accuracy of your position will depend on the accuracy of your sextant. I sailed with the mate of a ship that was torpedoed during the war and when they took to the lifeboats he made a sextant from one of the tins that were used for preserving the biscuits in the lifeboats. Because there was no chronometer, this 'sextant' could only measure the altitude of the sun at noon but that enabled the lifeboat to maintain latitude which in turn enabled the crew to eventually reach shore.

So we see the ability to measure the altitude of heavenly bodies increasing over the years so that latitude could be established with considerable accuracy and this led to navigation techniques that took advantage of this. When setting out on say an Atlantic crossing from northern Europe, a navigator would initially head south around Ushant and the end of the English Channel and across the Bay of Biscay. Compass direction would be accurate enough to make a landfall on the northern coast of Spain and then it would be coastal navigation further south until the ship reached the area of the favourable trade winds, named because of their consistent direction and strength and creating good following winds for crossing the Atlantic. This crossing would then be made using latitude sailing before making landfall in the Caribbean when the winds and currents would be favourable to sail from island to island before landfall on the American coast. It might be a long route as far as distance was concerned, but it could be achieved with the navigation skills available at the time without undue risk and in moderately good and reliable conditions.

Latitude could be found quite easily by taking the altitude of the sun as it passed through the meridian and then applying a variety of corrections. The main one was for the half-diameter of the sun because it was the altitude of the centre of the sun that was required, not its lower limb. There was also the height of eye or dip correction to apply because the sums only worked if it was assumed that the observer was at sea level. Other corrections are for refraction and parallax, the latter correcting for taking the sight at the surface of the Earth rather than from its centre. Eventually the latitude could be found by applying the declination, the position of the sun in relation to the Equator, which would be a factor in determining the calculated latitude. Although it is easiest to take the sight for latitude when the sun is at its zenith or highest point, the clouds do not always cooperate and it is possible to take what is known as an ex-meridian sight before or after the zenith point and to calculate the latitude from that. The approximate time of the meridian passing could be calculated so that the navigator could be ready with his sextant and then record the reading when it reached its peak. Taking the noon sights became a routine ritual on board a ship at sea, although it did not always occur at noon because the ship's time would be changed an hour at a time as the ship moved east or west so noon would rarely occur when the sun was at its highest.

So latitude sailing has been a feature of navigation for centuries because it is relatively easy to establish the latitude. Over the years the accuracy of the latitude has increased dramatically from the perhaps 100 miles accuracy when using a back or cross staff to the half-mile accuracy when using a modern sextant. The beauty of calculation is its simplicity, but when taking sights of the Pole Star as a means of determining latitude it is even easier and there are fewer corrections to apply. To capture the Pole Star needs careful timing because it is quite a weak star in comparison to many in the night sky and so at twilight it appears late and the sight has to be obtained while there is still a visible horizon. It is the same at dawn when both the star and the horizon are visible for just a short period in good conditions. The Pole Star is visible over most of the northern hemisphere, although near the Equator it tends to be too high for a reliable sight and further north particularly in the winter it is too close to the horizon, but in the main it provides a reliable guide to latitude and has been used for this purpose almost since man started to navigate on the high seas.

There is no equivalent star in the southern hemisphere and many of the familiar star patterns found in the north start to disappear once the Equator is crossed. Early navigators tended to operate in the northern hemisphere where they had the reliable Pole Star, so it must have been quite a challenge when they headed south on their exploration voyages and had only the sun to provide a latitude reference.

So latitude has been relatively easy to establish but what of longitude? In order to establish a position you need two position lines, a position line being a line along which the vessel must lie. With two position lines the location of the ship is where the lines cross, so obviously where the longitude line crossed the latitude line would be the location of the ship. The longitude could be

Some of the early navigation instruments used to establish latitude.

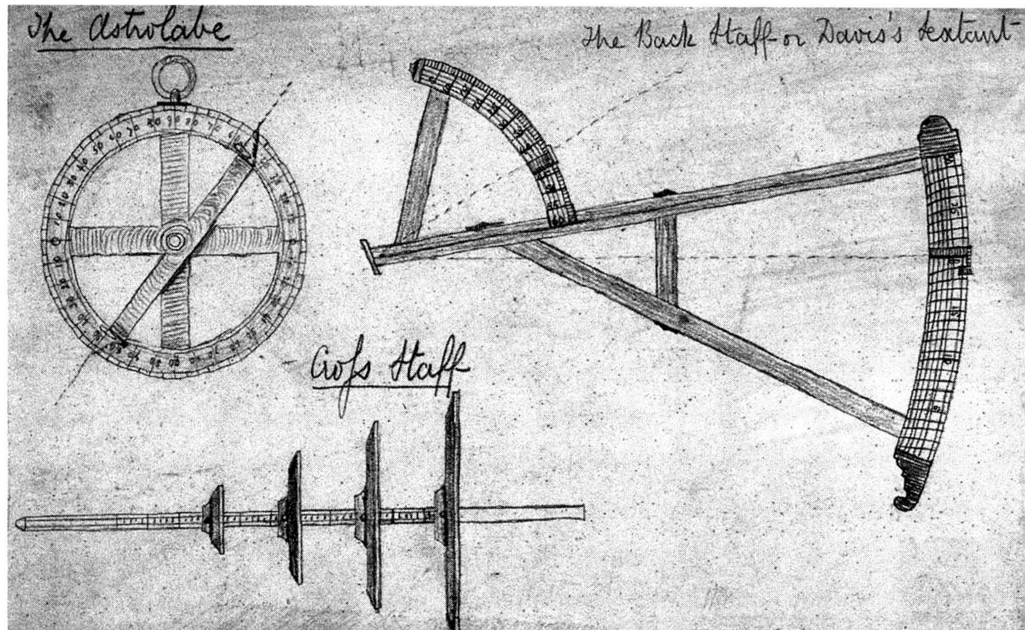

established by dead reckoning, combining the distance sailed with the direction sailed but the accuracy of dead reckoning deteriorates with time so it would become unreliable after a few days, particularly with the less than accurate means of measuring direction and speed. So the quest was on to find a way to measure longitude and to establish reliable ships' positioning.

It has long been known that the Earth made a full revolution through 360° every twenty-four hours at a uniform rate so if the time difference between the meridian of one place compared with another could be found, then the longitude would be known. It was established that the time difference between an eclipse of the sun, moon or planets could be observed in one place and then another; this would then establish the longitude of an observer. This was a bit of a hit-and-miss method and would depend on waiting for a suitable eclipse to take place. The best way to establish longitude was to have an accurate clock that could measure the time difference so that if such a clock was maintained on Greenwich Mean Time relating to time on the Greenwich meridian when the sun would be overhead at noon, then the difference in time when the sun was overhead in the observer's location would indicate the longitude.

We have talked about finding longitude using eclipses of the planets and their moons, but this was not a practical solution at sea. There were proposals to use the magnetic dip as a solution. This was based on the fact that not only does a magnetic needle point to magnetic north when suspended, but it will also adopt a downward angle depending on the angle of dip in the location. Because the angle of dip varied from place to place it was thought that this

Measuring lunar distance at sea was a challenging method of establishing position.

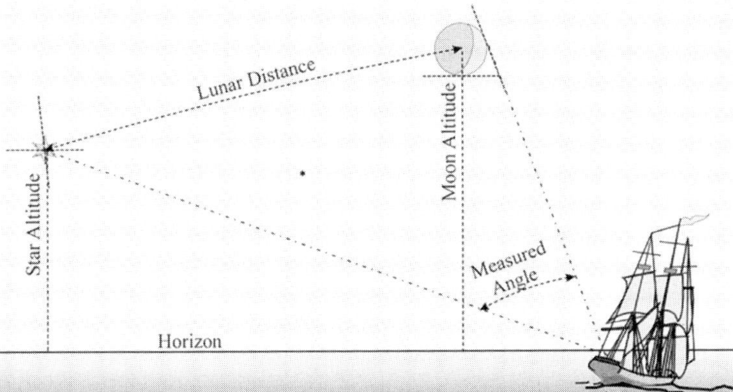

might offer a solution. Another possibility was the change in the magnetic variation. These measures show the level of almost desperation to find a solution to establishing longitude with good accuracy and in the seventeenth century it was reckoned that 50 per cent of ships that put to sea on ocean voyages never returned. Much of this total would have been accounted for by storms because there was no weather forecasting in those days and hull and rigging failures were another possibility, but for ships on the North Atlantic routes just making a landfall was hazardous. There were extensive shoals and persistent fog on the American side and rock-bound coastlines in Europe that presented a serious danger at the end of a voyage when the longitude was more or less guesswork.

The requirement to establish longitude for accurate positioning at sea had become so acute by the eighteenth century that the Board of Longitude in Britain offered large sums to anybody who could solve the problem, with the sums on offer increasing depending on the accuracy of the solution. Matching sums of money were on offer in other countries as well. Supposedly accurate clocks for measuring the time needed for longitude were developed as far back as 1669 by Christian Huygens in the Netherlands using both spring and pendulum systems, but once again their use at sea became problematical. The pressing need for an accurate clock to establish longitude was emphasized when part of the British naval fleet led by Admiral Sir Cloudesly Shovell hit the low-lying rocks of the Scilly Isles in 1707 because of his unsure position-fixing. The Board of Longitude was established just six years later, but there was little progress in finding a solution. This was at a time when in Britain there was the development of the skills of instrument-makers and this led to the development of mathematical instruments similar to the astrolabe. This skill of the instrument-makers led to improved versions of the quadrant and the sextant, but attention was also turned to making improved clocks and watches that could be used at sea.

John Harrison of 'Longitude' fame started making clocks around 1729 and his pendulum clocks designed for use on land were highly accurate to within one second over a month. After six years of work Harrison made his first chronometer for use at sea and this was followed by other versions that proved much more accurate, being only five minutes of longitude out on a trans-Atlantic voyage in rough weather. The longitude problem had been solved by 1767, but it was many years before the chronometer came into general use because of the high cost of the instrument and initially it was mainly used by naval ships.

It was the middle of the nineteenth century before the chronometer came into more general use, spurred on by the increase in the speed of ships such as the mighty clipper sailing ships and the advent of steamships on the Atlantic

Using an octant where the long moving arm would give a more accurate reading on the angle scale at the bottom.

routes. Accurate positioning was needed when ships travelling at 15 knots were making a landfall in challenging weather conditions, but it should be remembered that the chronometer itself did not establish a position; it had to be used in conjunction with sun or star sights taken by sextant so clear skies were still necessary to obtain a position. The introduction of the *Nautical Almanac* with its tables for the calculation of 'sights' helped in the establishment of accurate astronomical position-fixing. It then became the normal practice to take a sun sight in the morning and evening and the meridian sight at 'noon' which gave two position lines, and by advancing the early-morning sight by dead reckoning to the time of the noon sight, two position lines were obtained and the position fixed. For star sights taken at dawn and dusk when both the stars and the horizon were visible. The Marcq St Hilaire method, named after the originator in 1875, was the common system in use. Here the position is found by taking the dead-reckoning position and then working out from the sextant sights how far away the ship is from this assumed position, which means you then know where you are. This is a clever technique that has now stood the test of time.

So finally navigators now had a means of fixing the position of a ship with an accuracy of around a mile in good conditions which was adequate for making a landfall and this was the case right up until the advent of electronic navigation systems. While the basic tools of the ocean navigator remained the same, there were notable advances in the technology, particularly with the chronometer. The chronometer needed to be checked for accuracy at every possible opportunity and the 'time ball' was established in many ports whereby a ball on a mast would drop precisely at midday, allowing the navigator to compare this accurate time with what his chronometer was showing. You did not alter the chronometer but merely noted the error so that it could be applied when a sight was taken. The error might be plus or minus but a good chronometer would have a fixed rate of error, say one second per week, and so even without

An advanced version of the sextant developed by Admiral Coutinho for air navigation.

the ability to check the error from the time ball the cumulative error could be calculated by applying this steady error. Chronometer timing became available over radio links so that the instrument's accuracy could be checked at sea and later electric chronometers were introduced that did not need the daily winding routine of the clockwork chronometer. With the radio 'time ball' it then became possible to automatically apply the corrections to the chronometer so it was maintained at GMT the whole time with no errors having to be applied. Since the advent of satellite navigation systems that rely on time measurement, extremely accurate timing down to nanoseconds has become available but, like so many aspects of navigation, just when technology had made advances with long-sought-after accuracy the need for this particular measurement no longer exists.

Fixing the position of a ship had reached a considerable level of accuracy and sophistication, but still everything depended on having clear skies in order to get a sight. Just when navigators had the accurate timepieces and good sextants to fix the position, it all started to be overtaken by electronic systems. Like so much navigation technology that had been developed over centuries such as compasses and sounding systems, position-fixing by the

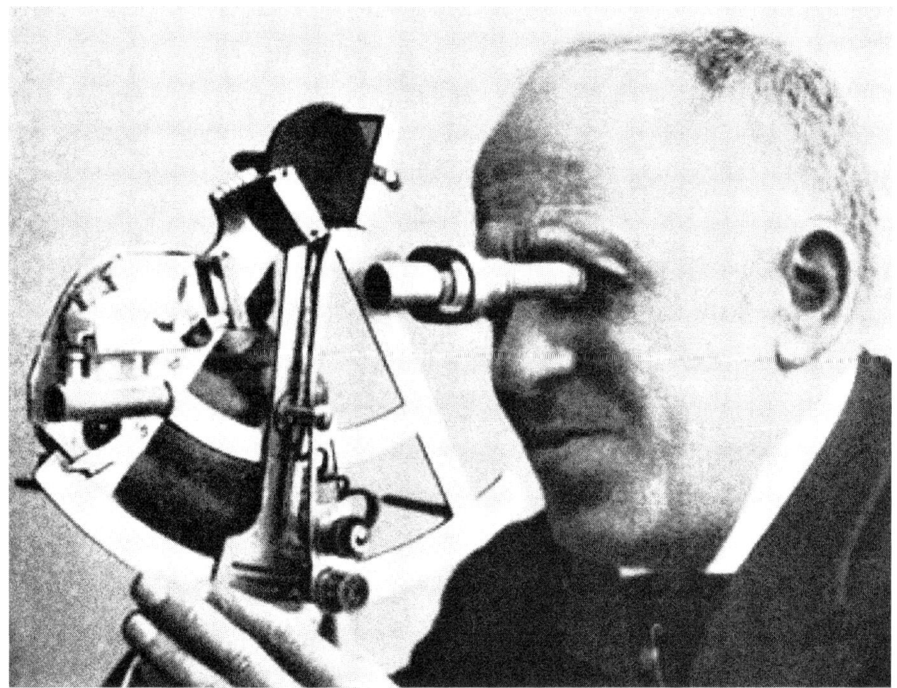

Admiral Coutinho with the modified sextant he used for ocean crossings by air.

observation of heavenly bodies, and just when it reached maturity, it was being cast aside by technical advances that brought in a host of electronic systems offering constant availability even in fog and with an accuracy that would have challenged even the best 'sight' system to match.

Fixing the position of a ship at sea or an aircraft in the sky has always been a challenge. We will look at the challenge of making a landfall in a later chapter, but in the open ocean any natural clues about position can be hard to find and it is amazing that navigators have crossed the oceans for hundreds of years with so little information about where they were. It is small wonder that the number of shipwrecks through grounding has been so high, particularly during the time when navigators could only make headway with the wind behind them. That would make it difficult to stop when the water became

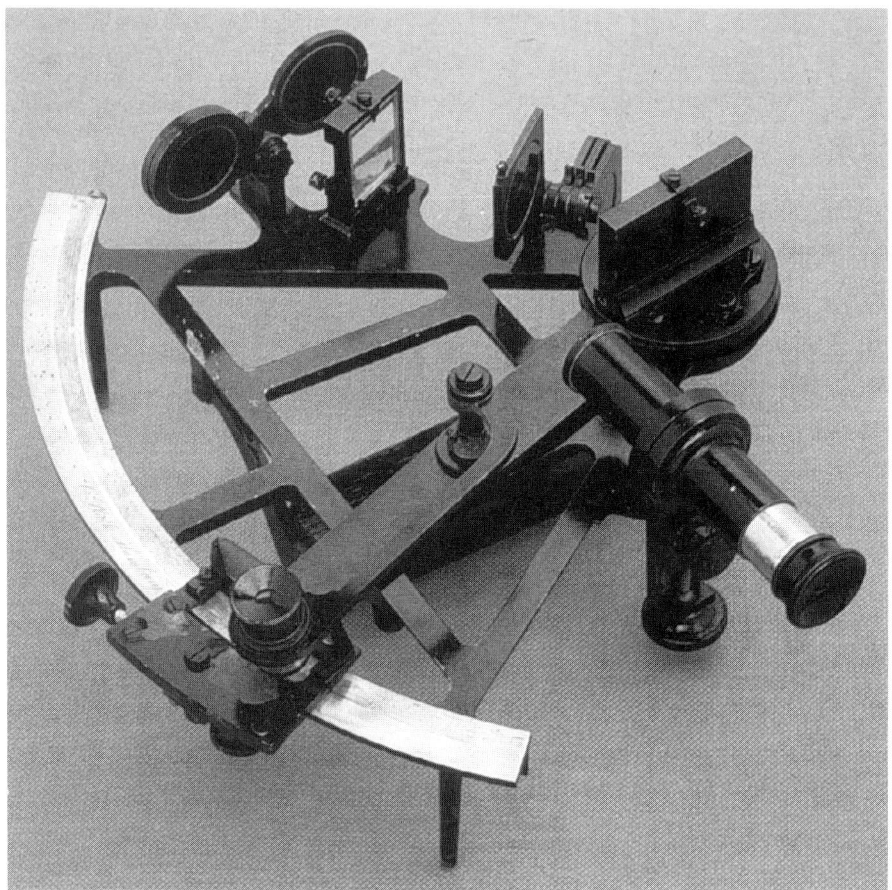

A vernier sextant that was used before the introduction of the micrometer sextant.

shallow or when breakers or land were sighted ahead. The oceans are also littered with shoals and rocks even in mid-ocean where you can find rocks like Rockall that just poke their tops above the waves, lying in wait for the unwary navigator. On the American coast the very low-lying Sable Island and its shoals were a graveyard for shipping until lights were established on it, and even then this is an area where fog is prevalent so it still remained a threat.

So it is easy to see why navigators clutched at straws and any information that would help them establish their position. Finding out what the sea bed consisted of seems like a very remote way of fixing positions, but it was just one of the many clues that would help the navigator establish where he was or, equally importantly, where he wasn't. As we said earlier, fixing the position is a bit like detective work. You have a number of clues with which to work and it is only by assembling all the clues that you can come up with a solution. The development of electronic systems has gone a long way towards taking the guesswork out of position-fixing, but at the point where we end this chapter even many of the electronic systems would not offer the 100 per cent certainty that a navigator would like and he is left with niggling doubts about his position. In fine weather that is not so much of a problem, but it is when the fog comes down and the many clues about position start to disappear that the uncertainties start to creep in. With the electronic systems some of these uncertainties start to disappear, and we have to wait for the satellite systems to start getting the certainty that the navigator has always sought.

Chapter Seven

Charts and Pilot Books

It is hard to picture navigating without a chart in front of you. The modern chart contains a wealth of information that acts as the guide for the navigator about what is below the surface of the sea as well as covering all the land features that might be useful to a navigator. Yet for thousands of years navigators sailed the oceans without charts and even when they did come into use they were little more than maps, showing mainly the land boundaries rather than what was underwater.

The use of charts for navigation came quite late in the history of navigation. This was partly due to the lack of any surveys taking place to map out the underwater features but also because many of the early navigators wanted to keep their information about coastlines, shoals and rocks secret because they had significant commercial value. Even having appropriate material on which to lay out a chart was a challenge before the days of suitable paper and so it is thought that rather than creating charts of where they had been to provide a record for future voyages, the early navigators kept records or notes. These were often made up after a voyage had been completed and this could well be the origins of the modern log book. However, rather than just an hour-by-hour record of the voyage, those early records are thought to have contained many diagrams of coastal features.

Much of the information gained from voyages was probably passed on by word of mouth rather than committed to paper. The first written aid to coastal navigation came in the form of a pilot book, or periplus, of which examples survive from the fourth century BC, although some may have preceded this date. These pilot books recorded the courses that needed to be steered between various ports, but as this was before the development of the magnetic compass these courses were recorded more in terms of the wind directions relating to the consistent prevailing winds. In addition to these 'courses' these pilot books also described the various headlands, landmarks, anchorages and currents that might be experienced along the routes. In addition, port entrances were also described so these pilot books were very much like the modern pilot books today, combining a wealth of information that was adequate for navigation and to find port entrances.

We have seen how the Polynesians used a form of chart or pilot made from wooden strips and alongside these rudimentary chart forms there is no doubt that this information was supplemented by word of mouth. The first graphic form of information would have been sketches that formed part of the pilot book such as a sketch of a harbour entrance. These would have been more like maps than a chart as we know it today because there is no record of any form of survey being carried out to show the underwater features. Even in the fifth century BC maps were being drawn that would have shown coastlines and Herodotus's map of the known world from that time shows the Mediterranean shoreline quite accurately, but there is nothing showing in the areas of sea that were on the map. Reliable sea charts showing depths were still a long way off and even when they were developed they tended to show courses from point to point rather than the underwater features. The introduction of the magnetic compass was the trigger for this generation of charts and the accuracy was some way off from modern standards because of the difficulty in establishing positions by latitude and longitude.

Distances that were quoted in the early pilot books tended to be measured in terms of the distance sailed in a day and units such as leagues were used. A league is a land measurement that is the distance a person could walk in one hour, but for sea use it became 3 nautical miles, although different countries had leagues of different lengths. Eventually the nautical mile was established as the standard unit for measuring distances at sea with its direct relationship to the division of the Earth's surface into degrees, minutes and seconds.

It was not until the Middle Ages in the thirteenth century AD that we find charts being developed more as we know them today. The pilot books that had been developed as the navigator's guide evolved into the Portolano or portolan chart, the harbour-finding manual. An early Portolano for the whole Mediterranean Sea, *Il Compasso da Navigare* of 1296, gives directions across the water to the nearest half-point of the compass which is around 6°, probably as close to a course as a helmsman could steer with the fairly rudimentary compasses then in use. The information contained on that Portolano was the result of gathering information from a wide variety of sources over the years and for the first time it was displayed on what was thought to be the first marine chart. This was a single volume that covered the entire Mediterranean and it was one of the first to put north at the top of the chart rather than east which was the usual practice of land maps at the time. These charts were mostly compiled in Genoa, Venice and Majorca, and they had a scale of distances.

The main aim of the portolan was to allow the navigator to set a course from port to port across the Mediterranean. For this there was a colour-coded pattern of rhumb lines which crossed the north/south meridians at a constant angle. To set a course between two ports, the navigator would join the points on the chart indicating these ports with a straight line and then find the rhumb line most nearly parallel to it. From there he would trace the rhumb line back to its wind rose which would allow him to read off the required heading. As the voyage progressed with the speed and thus the distance sailed being estimated by dead reckoning, the navigator would then know roughly where he was along the line and for this type of navigating the portolan was adequate. It should be noted that there were no details of the water depths or any other dangers in the sea areas but then the Mediterranean is largely clear of dangerous rocks and shoals, although there were many small islands that would have provided a guide rather than a danger. There is no record of any underwater features or soundings on any charts of this era.

In a compact sea area such as the Mediterranean the portolan worked reasonably well as a guide to navigating, but when sailors ventured out onto the more open waters of the eastern Atlantic things changed. The Portuguese, under the leadership of Prince Henry the Navigator, were venturing south along the west coast of Africa, and here they encountered difficulties with navigation when they assumed that the charts used in the Mediterranean could simply be extended. Over longer distances the rhumb lines could not be used when on the surface of the curved Earth. With the more advanced methods of locating positions developed by the Portuguese astronomers and mathematicians these were represented by latitude and longitude rather than bearing and distance and new ways of portraying the line to be followed had to be developed.

What was required was a practical method of representing the curved meridians and parallels onto the flat surface of the chart. This could be done for an area as large as the Mediterranean without too much distortion coming into the reckoning to vary the heading or distances, but for larger sea areas some distortions are inevitable. On certain types of chart projections distances can be shown accurately but directions cannot, while on others headings are displayed in their true sense but the distances start to vary considerably from the reality. This is the penalty that comes from trying to display what is a three-dimensional curved surface on a flat paper chart. The navigator accepts the second type because the risk of lengthening the voyage is preferable to that of missing the destination.

In 1569 the Flemish cartographer Gerardus Mercator published a world map that was based on a new type of projection. A projection is where the map-maker sets out to portray the curved surface of the Earth on a flat sheet of paper, which means that the areas on the map or chart have to be distorted in order for them to be shown as flat. It is converting a three-dimensional model into a two-dimensional display. There are many types of projection

A sixteenth-century chart of the Mediterranean accurately showing all the coastline and islands.

that were developed around this time but the Mercator projection was the one that was best suited to ship navigation and it began to be widely adopted. Today virtually every chart except that of the Polar regions uses this form of display. Taking the chart as having north at the top, on a Mercator chart the meridians of longitude are represented by equally-spaced vertical lines and the parallels of latitude are represented by horizontal lines. These parallel lines of latitude are closer together near the Equator than near the poles and this uneven spacing of the parallels compensates for the increasing exaggeration of the east-west distance between adjacent meridians at higher latitudes. If you think about the Earth as a sphere, then it becomes obvious that the distance between the meridians of longitude get closer together as they extend north and south until they meet at the poles. On the Mercator projection these meridians stayed the same distance apart while the lines of latitude get wider apart as they went north and south.

The Mercator projection takes some getting used to but there is a lot of logic in it for navigation. When measuring distances on the chart it is the latitude scale that is used and the measurement has to be taken off the latitude scale at around the same latitude as the distance required. One thing that does confuse people is that the shortest distance between two points on the Earth's surface is what is known as a great circle, an arc that if extended into a sphere would intersect with the centre of the Earth. This is the line that ships want to follow when on east-west courses and it shows on the Mercator chart as a curved line with its apex towards the poles. These aspects of the Mercator chart only become relevant when a ship is on an ocean voyage and for many practical purposes such as small-scale charts of bays and harbours, courses and routes can be plotted with straight lines and the latitude scale is pretty well consistent for the area covered, although it is only at the Equator that the latitude and longitude scales are equal. A big bonus of the Mercator-based charts is that bearings from the land and courses can be measured directly from the compass rose on the chart.

The early charts or portolans made no attempt to show depths of water, although where rocks were known to exist, usually by having a ship wrecked on them, then some sort of warning mark might be shown on the chart. You have to remember that even right up to the nineteenth century the means of fixing the position at sea was still very rudimentary and certainly not accurate enough to think about using a position to relate to a depth of water. Even the compass was not particularly accurate so that positions fixed by bearing could be quite vague. So we don't see depths shown on charts until quite late in their development. On harbour charts the depths might be shown in much more detail and here, close to land, the location of soundings could be established quite accurately in relation to the land using land surveying techniques. The

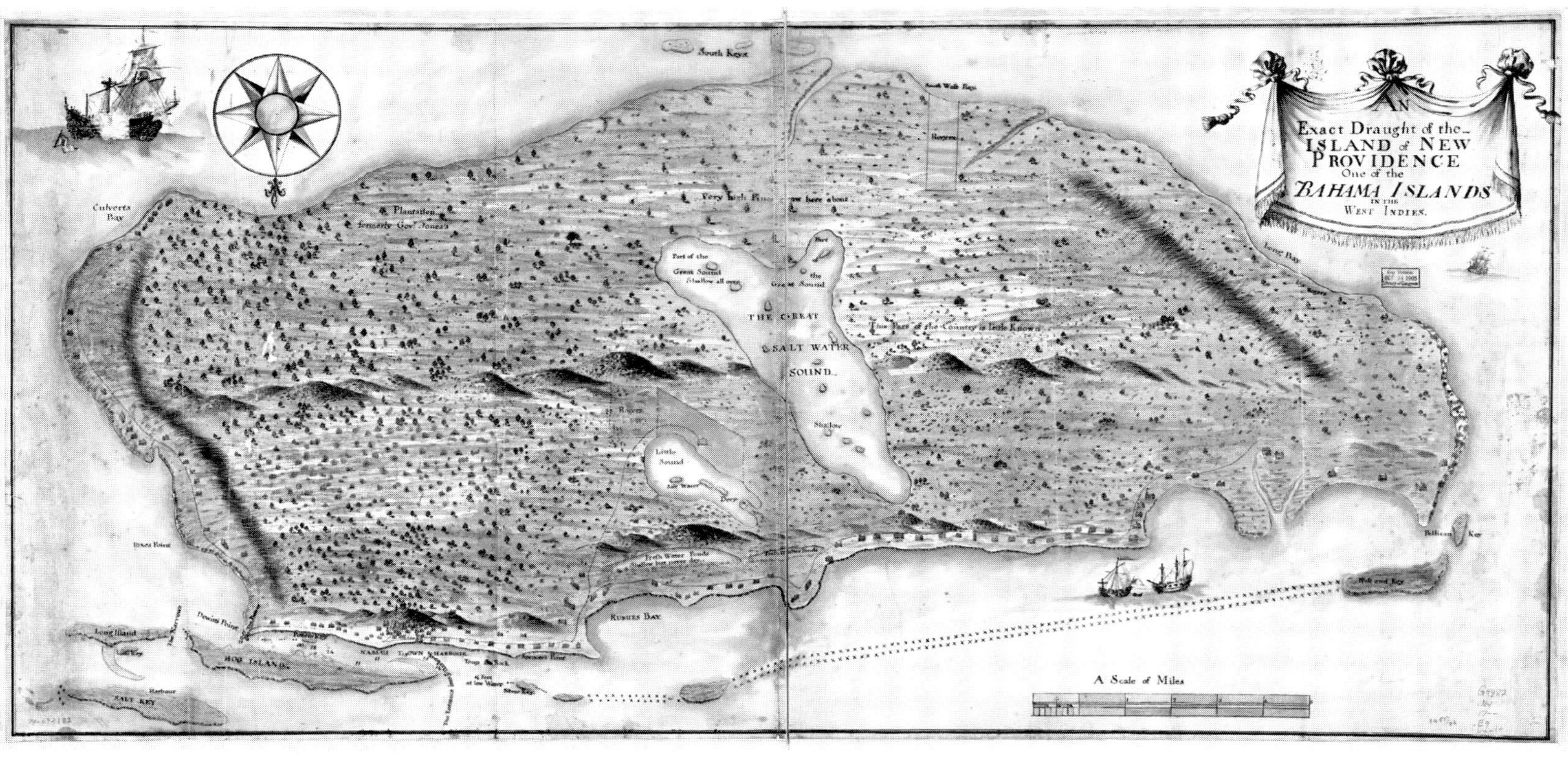

An old chart of the island of New Providence in the Bahamas.

water depths in harbours were also essential for safe navigation in the harbours of course, and in regions where the tidal rise and fall was considerable such as in northern Europe it became necessary to establish chart datums to work to a common sea level when measuring depths.

Those early portolans tended to cover the areas favoured by the Mediterranean venturers and extended over the Mediterranean, down the coast of Africa and later to span the Atlantic with much of their development encouraged by Henry the Navigator. It was the Dutch, at the end of the sixteenth century, who recognized the importance of charts to maritime trade and they continued as the main provider of nautical charts to the merchant shipping fleets for the next 100 years. Still though, there was little attempt to show underwater features except when there were shoals such as in the Dover Straits and off the coast of Holland. Ships of the time had a relatively shallow draft so ocean depths were of little relevance, although what the sea bed consisted of was important as we saw in the chapter on 'Soundings'.

In both Holland and Britain navigation schools were established and interest in surveys and charts expanded. The first charts in Britain were printed on vellum, but it was the Dutch who printed the first charts on paper in 1584 and these covered the ports and coasts of much of western Europe. Produced by Lucas Waghenaer, they were some of the first to show soundings and other underwater features and much of the information for these early charts came directly from seamen. Waghenaer was the first cartographer to show chart features by symbols such as buoys and beacons and by using a ' + ' to denote a rock, a symbol that is still in use today.

Around 1660 there was a revival of interest in Britain in maritime matters, the Royal Observatory in Greenwich was established and a naval officer was charged with carrying out a survey of the British coasts. This seven-year project resulted in the publication of Great Britain's Coasting Pilot in 1683 and comprised around forty printed charts plus views of the coast and sailing directions and these formed the basis of the charts used by navigators for the next 100 years. This set the pattern for survey work and for charts and only a few years later a similar project was completed for the French and Spanish coastlines, although on a smaller scale. The French also carried out and published surveys of some of their overseas territories including the Saint Lawrence River, making these the first charts to be published in North America.

Murdoch Mackenzie published his 'Treatise on Maritime Surveying' in 1774 and his charts mainly of the Thames Estuary reflected the first use of position-fixing using horizontal sextant angles of known points on shore that could be plotted with the newly-invented station pointer. This was the

A German chart of the Strait of Gibraltar which shows the Mediterranean as a battleground.

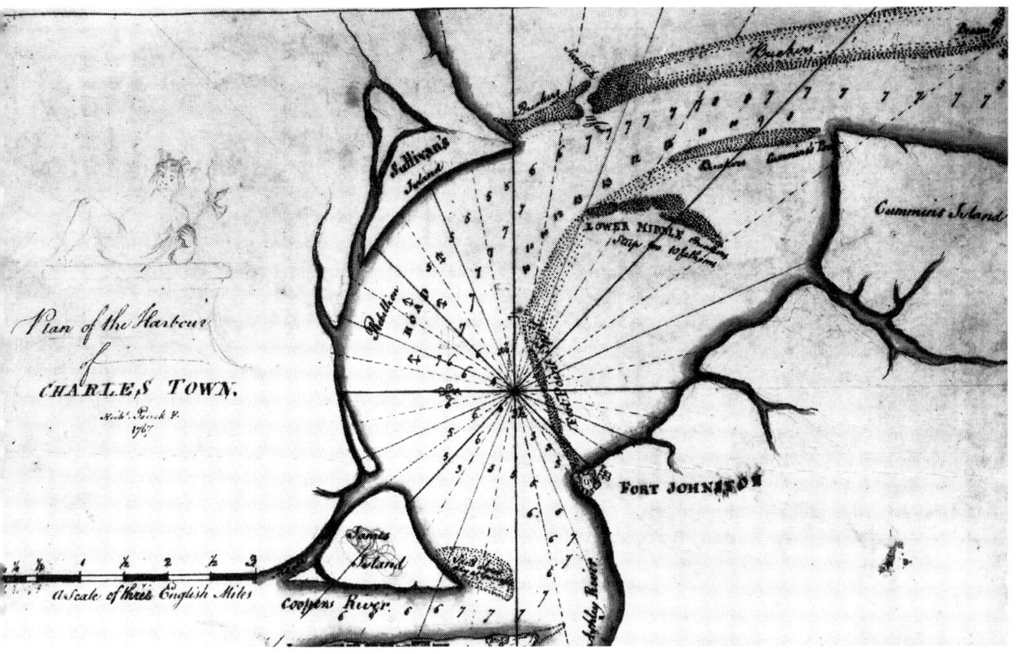

A 250-year-old chart of Charles Town harbour in the US which has many similarities to modern-day charts.

method of accurate position-fixing for survey work that was still in use in the 1960s. It was around 1800 that the British Admiralty formed their embryo Hydrographic Department that became the model of chart production and accuracy right up until the present day. In the US their equivalent was formed in 1807 and today produces a similar range of detailed charts.

Soon these organizations were operating on a worldwide basis and there was an exchange of information between the various hydrographic authorities so that each was able to offer a full worldwide portfolio of charts. Position-fixing was still a challenge, as was taking soundings in deeper water, and many of the charts in use today still use lines of soundings that were taken by means of a lead-line. Modern survey work is carried out using much more advanced technology such as multibeam echo-sounders that can cover a swathe of ocean at a single sweep and of course position-fixing is now done by the accurate GPS satellite system, but there are huge areas of ocean to survey and limited resources with which to do it.

The modern paper chart is a masterpiece of information display. Getting all the navigation information onto a single sheet of paper is always a challenge and the modern paper chart shows a wealth of information pertaining to the safety of navigation. However, the chart is only as good as the information available and there are still undiscovered shoals and dangers in more remote parts of the ocean. The liner *Queen Elizabeth* hit a rock in Long Island Sound that had an incorrect depth above it shown on the chart and the cargo ship *Muirfield* also struck an uncharted rock in water depths charted at over

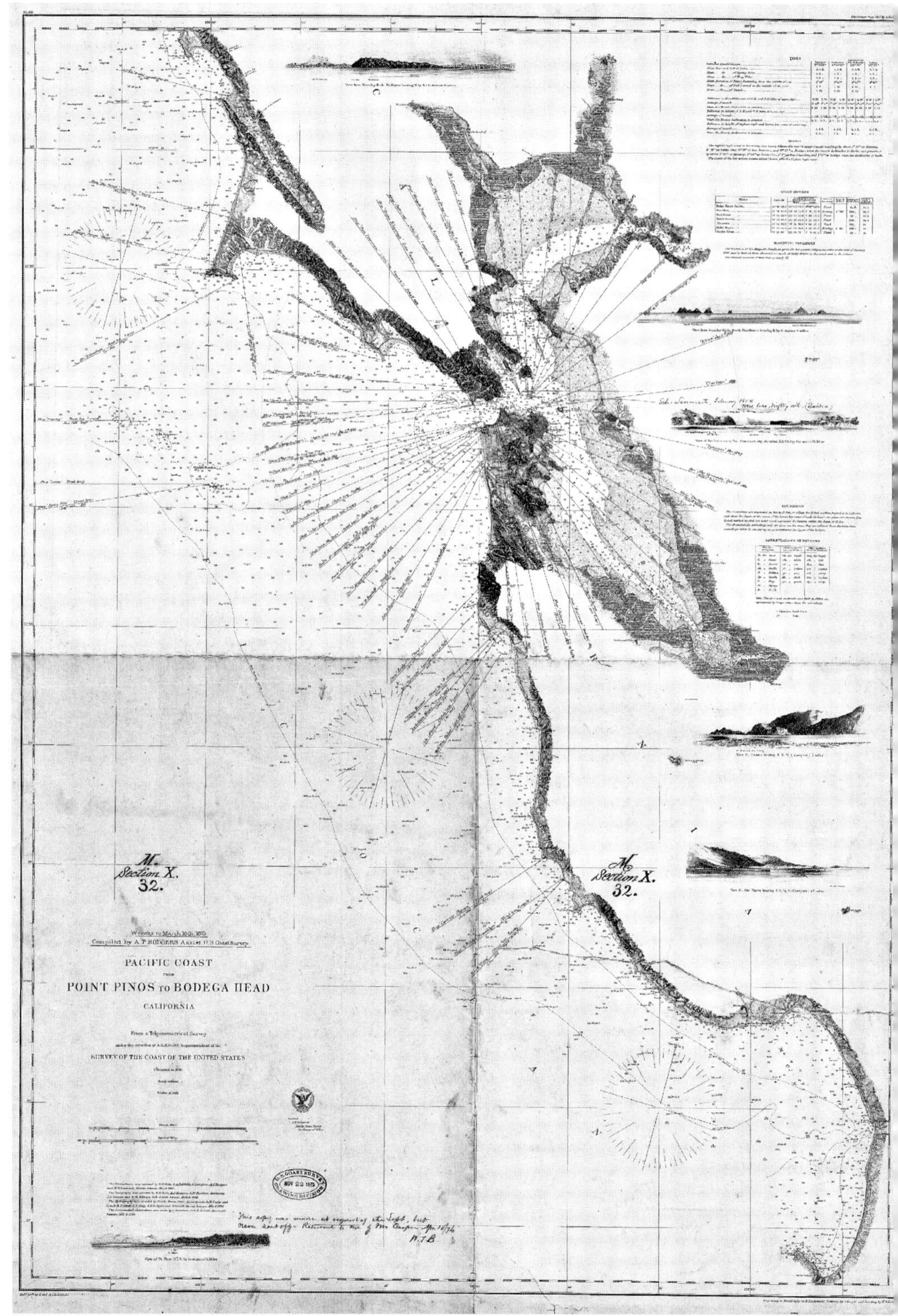

A 150-year-old chart of the US West Coast that compares with modern charts apart from the use of colour.

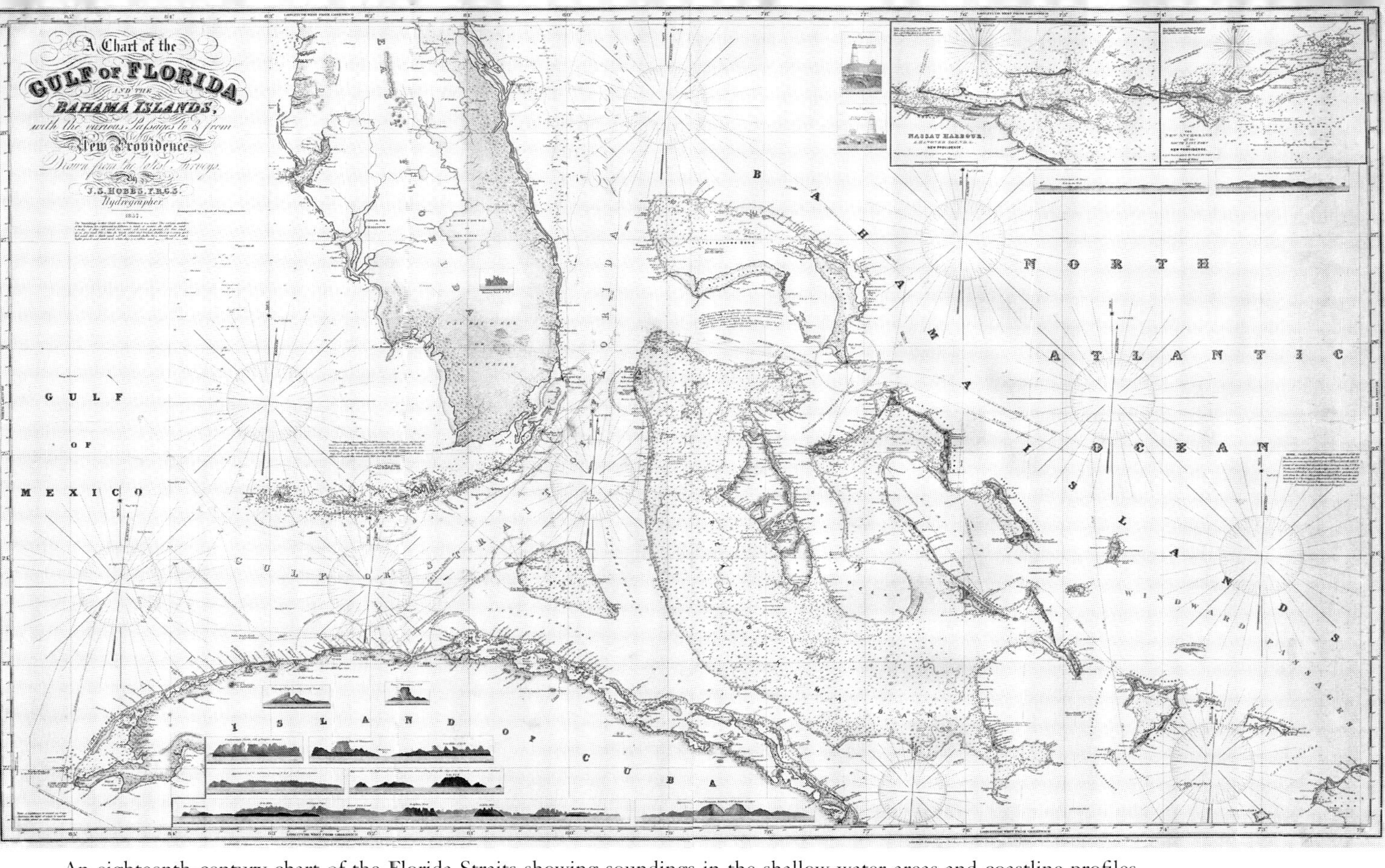

An eighteenth-century chart of the Florida Straits showing soundings in the shallow water areas and coastline profiles.

5,000 metres! As the *Mariners' Handbook* states: 'No chart is infallible. Every chart is liable to be incomplete.'

The past fifty years have seen dramatic changes in charts. It is not only the switch from fathoms to metres as the unit for denoting water depths and the use of colour contours, but the introduction of electronic charts. Approximately forty years ago electronic plotting screens were introduced that allowed electronically-obtained positions such as those from Loran and Decca Navigator to be displayed on an electronic screen. The screens allowed you to plot a proposed route on the screen using latitude and longitude positions, and then the course would be automatically plotted so that you could see where you were in relation to where you wanted to be. There were no chart features such as the land and shoals and all the other normal chart information displayed, partly because it was not available in electronic form but mainly because the positions given by Loran and Decca Navigator were not accurate enough to use at this level of detail. For a full chart display to be viable, the position of the vessel that is displayed has to be shown with a consistent degree of accuracy, otherwise a lot of false and potentially dangerous information could be displayed.

One of the first full electronic displays developed did use Loran C as the position-fixing system. This was a differential form of Loran C that offered a much higher level of accuracy with errors of probably around 10 metres which made the full electronic chart viable. This differential Loran C was established in New York harbour primarily for use with the Staten Island ferries so that they could operate more safely in fog on this important route. I went on trials on one of these ferries and saw an electronic chart for the first time and it was quite eerie to see the plotted position of the ferry moving across the surface of the chart. With that pioneering electronic chart, the chart was a fairly basic representation of the normal chart features but it was more than adequate for the requirements of navigating the ferry.

With the advent of GPS position-fixing which was made available as a public service in 1983, the possibilities of using GPS as a means of position-fixing for these charts became feasible. GPS had been under development for quite a time before this date, but in anticipation of its availability for the general public work had been going on to upgrade the electronic plotting displays into full electronic chart displays. The plotters had all the basic requirements and what was required was to convert the paper chart into electronic form so it could be displayed in relation to a vessel's position. Here there were two options: raster or digital charts. Raster charts were simply a scanned copy of the paper chart that would convert it into a form that could be displayed on an electronic screen but such a system lacked flexibility in the way that the chart information could be displayed as what was shown on the screen was simply a section of the chart. In those days the displays were quite small and mainly in black and white so the resulting raster displays were a poor substitute for the paper versions of charts. It takes a lot more effort to develop a digital chart because every point on the paper chart has to be converted into an electronic version that is characterized by its particular use on the paper chart. The big advantage of a digital chart is that it can be expanded or contracted without losing details and it is possible to add features and customize the chart to meet the requirements of different levels of navigation. If you expand a raster chart you simply get a blown-up version of the original which, if taken to extremes, could mean that a single sounding number could occupy the whole screen.

It was pioneering work carried out in Italy by Navionics and C-Map that led to the world's first true electronic charts in 1983, the same year that GPS became publicly available. Navionics pioneered that first one which by today's standards was very basic, but they had opted for using digital charts which was later seen as a major step forward. It was an interesting development that these two companies actually produced the charts as well as the hardware to operate them, but they were also offering the charts to other electronics

Pages from a ship's log book of 1828.

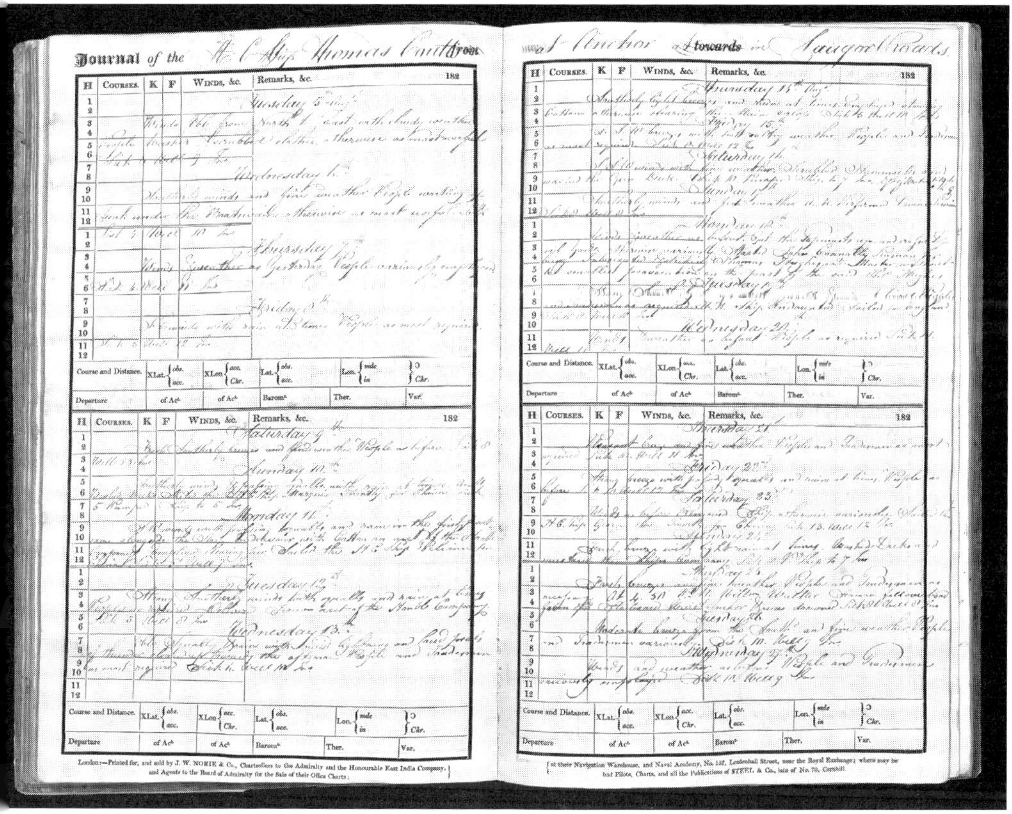

companies so that they could produce their own hardware. This approach meant that an electronic chart system actually comprises three components: the chart software, the operating system software and the hardware that houses the package. These early electronic chart systems were aimed at the small craft market where there were no regulations regarding charts that had to be carried and the way in which they were used; this allowed the electronic charts to be developed in a free way to suit the end user.

After a few years the various official hydrographic offices around the world realized that they were being left behind in electronic chart development and they started to produce raster versions of their official charts that could be used on electronic chart systems. In this way they hoped to cash in on their 'official' status, but of course the digitized charts that were in production were also based on the official charts under a licence system. The market became awash with electronic chart hardware and various chart systems, each claiming to have advantages over their rivals, but gradually the digital chart systems won the day because of their obvious advantages over the rival raster systems, one of which was the relatively easy way that the charts could be updated. There were bitter court cases in some countries before various hydrographic offices realized that they had to reach agreement with these new developing companies regarding the use of their charts.

One of the big advantages in favour of digital charts and the one that probably won the day for the development of approved systems for shipping was the ability to incorporate warnings of shallow water and danger areas. It became possible to set a water depth warning that would sound an alarm if a ship strayed into shallow water, but equally important a warning would also sound if a route was plotted that strayed into the shallows or other danger areas such as wind farms and oilfields. There was also a downside for the unregulated market for small craft electronic charts when manufacturers introduced systems that would plot a route automatically. All you had to do was enter your departure point and the arrival point and in theory the software would plot the optimum route between the two. It sounds a very simple and time-saving system, but unless you check the route thoroughly yourself you could find the plotted route leading you into trouble. In particular in my experience they take no account of traffic routing systems so you could find yourself in trouble with the authorities if you follow the route blindly, and the charts you use need to be fully up to date to avoid wind farm and oilfield developments. This auto-routing is another step along the way to fully automatic systems and these problems demonstrate some of the perils that could be found with such developments.

Today the electronic chart has become official and dedicated specifications have been developed so that systems being used for ships have to meet the specifications in order to get approval. Not only do the charts have to come from approved suppliers, they have to meet certain standards, not only in their production but also in their updating capability which can now be done over internet links. Today the electronic charts for ships use large colour displays, although many of the land features that were so important in the past have now been simplified. The use of these charts and positioning using GPS meant that many of the older paper charts were in error regarding their position according to GPS criteria and a whole new survey standard was introduced with GPS which is WGS 84. This survey standard is now accepted worldwide for both paper and electronic charts. Using this standard put many remote islands and other features out of position as far as paper charts were concerned and there was considerable confusion during the transition period but this is now largely resolved. Progress with the electronic chart over the past twenty years has meant that ships can now officially throw away their paper charts and rely solely on the electronic systems. Along with the introduction of GPS, this represents one of the most fundamental changes in navigation throughout its history and today even small boats have the facility of electronic displays and accurate charting.

The electronic charts systems for shipping are heavily regulated but those for smaller craft remain largely unregulated and this has allowed a free-for-all in the market with some of the developments opening up whole new possibilities as far as the display of the charts and information is concerned. It is now possible to click on a feature such as a buoy or even a sounding and find out more information about it. Information about harbours and marinas is also included so that the electronic chart for small craft has become both a chart and a pilot book. You can access satellite picture overlays and even 3-D representations. The paper chart is becoming redundant in many navigators' eyes, but for others it still provides a vital back-up should the electronics develop a fault or even fail.

The pilot books that were once the mainstay of the navigators' information package are also disappearing. From its origins in history the pilot book became an essential companion to the paper chart, containing instructions about how to sail the coastlines of the world and with pictures of what the shore might look like as well as port and harbour details. The sketches of the coastline and approaches to ports and harbours would be vital to navigators making a landfall to help identify where they were. Like the paper chart, the pilot books were a masterpiece of condensing information into a useable and compact package for use at sea. Pilot books are still available for official sources but today they are supplemented by a variety of informative privately-published versions that are aimed at the yachtsman. The ultimate pilot book is the *Ocean Passages of the World* that is published by the British Admiralty. This gives advice and recommended courses across the oceans of the world for both sailing and steamships according to the seasonal weather conditions and ocean currents.

For everything involving charts, both electronic and paper, and pilot books the information contained in them might be useless if it is not kept up to date. Shipping these days is tending to work to fine limits as far as the depth of water is concerned, and in ports and harbour the draft of a ship and the depth of water available might be almost the same. In some ports the ships are almost navigating in the soft mud of the harbour bottom in order to maximize the depth available. In a fast-changing world it can be a real challenge to keep things up to date with the surveys that are involved becoming increasingly expensive and challenging. This does tend to mean that surveys tend to be limited to the main sea areas and waterways and there could be considerable doubt if you stray off the beaten track into waters that are not frequently visited. Like the charts that are the result of surveys, the methods of surveying are also changing and in this specialized branch of navigation survey techniques have moved on from the lead-line to sophisticated multichannel sounding systems that can cover a wide swathe of seabed in one pass.

Charting the seas and oceans of the world has been a long and often painful process that has had to combine mathematical discovery with painstaking practical survey work. The difficulties are compounded by the constantly

An excerpt from a log book of 1771. Log books were a vital means of recording progress and events for future reference.

changing nature of much of the seabed and with the dredging of ports and harbours and even the open seas to allow ever larger ships to navigate safely. Every time a ship sinks, the surveyors have to be out there checking that the wreck is not a danger to other shipping and the buoyage has to be adapted and moved to cope with shifting sandbanks. The work of the nautical surveyor is never done and it is a tribute to their dedication over the centuries that ships can sail the seas in safety.

Chapter Eight

Buoys and Lighthouses

The concept of marking both headlands and dangers to shipping to help navigators is almost as old as navigation itself. As we have seen from the earlier chapters, the early navigators would find their way along coastlines in the early stages of taking vessels out to sea and it seems likely that they would have marked significant headlands in such a way that they could be readily identified when approaching them. So perhaps a tower would have been built on a headland as an identification mark. Such a structure may not have been entirely for identification purposes and the location might have had some religious significance and the tower had been established there for this and had also proved useful as a navigation mark. Certainly this is borne out around the UK coasts where so often a conspicuous church tower or spire would be close to the coast and would make a useful identification mark. Such churches were often marked on charts and in the late 1950s such coastal churches were used to help position navigation buoys accurately.

Whatever the reason for their establishment, conspicuous buildings on headlands represented what were probably the earliest of identifying features at sea. These were not lighthouses because there was no fire or other means of illumination at the top, but they were marks that stood out. At that time navigation was carried out in daylight only so there was no need for lights, but it is suggested that the Greek Themistocles built what might have been the first lighthouse at the entrance to Piraeus Harbour in the fifth century BC. This was a simple stone tower with a place for a fire at the top and around that time there are reports that suitably located structures capable of holding a fire at their top were established as guides for ships entering harbours at night. These fires would have also served as a daytime guide for port approaches because the smoke from the fires would have been visible from a long way off.

As navigators became more adventurous they had to make landfalls as they came in from sea. With navigation being rather vague in terms of the course and distance covered it would have been helpful to have had a means of identifying a location as early as possible when coming in from seaward. This may have been the motive for the building of what is still the most grand lighthouse ever built, the Pharos of Alexandria. Unlike many other parts of the Mediterranean coastlines, the coasts in the region of the Nile Delta, which was part of a very important trade route, were low-lying and would have been hard to identify when coming in from seaward. Apart from being a monument to Alexander the Great, the Pharos would have been a wonderful landmark for navigators to pick up from seaward. With a height reported to be 480ft it would have been possible to see it from 30 miles out at sea on a clear day even without its smoke and probably much the same at night. This monumental lighthouse was completed in the second century BC at huge cost and as a lighthouse it has never been equalled. However, it could not stand up to the forces of nature and it was destroyed more than 1,000 years later by earthquakes.

The Colossus of Rhodes was a bronze and iron statue built at the harbour entrance to the port of Rhodes in 280BC and some descriptions of it suggest that it was equipped with a fire at its top, but whether this was for a role as a lighthouse is open to dispute. This statue was also destroyed in an earthquake but this time just fifty years after it was built.

The Romans, perhaps inspired by these two large structures, built several lighthouses. At La Coruña at the north-western corner of Spain they built the Tower of Hercules, a massive structure high on the headland. It was rebuilt towards the end of the eighteenth century with some height added and it stands today but not as a working lighthouse. Other Roman lighthouses were built at Dover in England as a guide for the Dover Straits and another at Genoa in Italy. Although pictures of these lighthouses generally show them with smoke or flames at the top suggesting that a fire was maintained, the sheer logistics of taking the large amount of combustible material up the tower would have been considerable and you have to wonder how many of them were actually lighthouses for night-time use or just high towers to identify a port. Before the development of clearly-defined ports, mariners were guided by fires often built on hilltops or headlands and keeping such a fire going at night would have been a much easier proposition with access by horse and cart. Since raising the fire would improve the visibility, it is suggested that placing the fire on a platform became a practice that led to the development of the lighthouse. It is thought that lighthouses were established more to identify port entrances rather than to act as a warning against reefs and shallow waters. A lighthouse at a port entrance would also serve as a lookout tower.

One of the oldest working lighthouses in Europe is Hook Lighthouse in County Wexford, Ireland. It was built during the medieval period, in a sturdy circular design. From the Middle Ages there is the 40ft lighthouse tower offshore at the entrance to the Gironde estuary on the Atlantic coast of France. Some 100 years later a second one was built alongside it and this had richly-furnished apartments; perhaps a forerunner of the conversion of many modern lighthouses into residential apartments when they were no longer used as lighthouses. This French lighthouse was heightened in the late eighteenth century and it became the tallest lighthouse in France and one of the tallest in the world. The Cordouan Lighthouse was one of the first to be fitted with a specially-developed Argand lamp (a type of oil lamp) and parabolic mirrors that revolved, making it one of the earliest flashing lighthouses so that it could be clearly identified from seaward. It was also one of the first to be converted to use the Fresnel lens that concentrated the beam of the light into a horizontal plane and so intensified the visible light. This became the basic system for lighthouse use for the next two centuries, although the type of lamp moved on from oil to electric.

In Britain serious lighthouse-building started at the beginning of the eighteenth century and many of these were privately owned with the owners collecting light dues from passing ships. Eventually Trinity House, which was the government-approved body responsible for safe navigation, bought out these private lighthouses and operated them under one umbrella. This was at a time when there was a considerable increase in sea trade, particularly on the trans-Atlantic routes, and the demand for lights to allow ships to make a safe landfall was seen on both sides of the Atlantic.

While most lighthouses were built on land and were of the simple tubular masonry tower type which was relatively simple to construct, there was a growing demand to establish light on dangerous outlying rocks. This was seen in the Scilly Isles which was a landfall point for many trans-Atlantic ships and a lighthouse was built on the westernmost island of St Agnes. This provided a warning for shipping making a landfall but there were more rocks further out to seaward and eventually this led to the building of a lighthouse on the most seaward of these rocks, the Bishop Rock. When you consider its location, wide open to the Atlantic with nothing between it and America, building a lighthouse on this rock would have been a challenge even with today's technology.

Trinity House decided to build a lighthouse and work started in 1843 on an open steel pile structure that would allow the waves to pass through and under the light but this was washed away before completion. Work started on a stone tower in 1841 and this was completed eight years later with the stones all dovetailed together and into the rock which was just 40 metres long. Thirty years later the tower was reinforced with more stones added at the lower level and the lighthouse has withstood the might of Atlantic storms ever since, which is quite remarkable. This lighthouse not only gives a warning light and a fog signal to ships making a landfall, but it also marks the end point of Atlantic record attempts by the liners challenging for the Blue Riband of the Atlantic.

The same type of technology was used to build a number of lighthouses on isolated rocks, among them the famous Eddystone Lighthouse which is built on an isolated rock near the entrance to one of Britain's major naval ports, Plymouth. Here the engineers got the design right at the fourth attempt. The first was built in 1699 and marks the start of attempts to build lighthouses on isolated rocks, but it was destroyed in a storm. The second caught fire and it was only at the fourth attempt that the engineers got it right, using much the same technology as was used for building the Bishop Rock Lighthouse. The challenge of building these lighthouses on isolated rocks that were a danger to navigation was seen in stark reality when it came to building a lighthouse on the Bell Rock off the Scottish coast. This rock is underwater even at low tide so an advanced engineering solution had to be found to lay the foundations and this was back in 1810 when marine technology was not very advanced. The need for these lighthouses on isolated rocks and the contribution they made to safe navigation was clearly demonstrated by the challenge that the builders faced in constructing these masterpieces of engineering.

Lighthouse-building in North America followed a slightly different tack with most of the inlet harbours along the East Coast having a tall lighthouse at their entrance. This is mainly a low-lying coastline and, like the Pharos, the tall lighthouses enabled navigators to identify the location of an entrance from a considerable distance out at sea. Many were painted with distinctive candy stripes in various colours to help identify them. The first lighthouse in America was the Boston Light, built in 1716 on Little Brewster Island in outer Boston Harbor. Lighthouses were soon built along the marshy coastlines of the East Coast from Delaware to North Carolina where navigation was difficult and treacherous. Many of these lighthouses were built of wood as it was readily available but due to the fire hazard, stone towers were increasingly built. The oldest of these stone towers was the Sandy Hook Lighthouse, built in 1764 at the entrance to New York Harbor.

Finally there were lighthouses that were built mainly in the water of river estuaries that would serve as a distance-marker to help identify the various channels in an estuary. This type of estuary lighthouse would often be constructed using screw piles that were simply 'screwed' into the sands. Construction of one of the first began in 1838 in the Thames Estuary which was the Maplin Sands Lighthouse, but the first of these screw-pile lighthouses to be built and lit was the Wyre Light off Fleetwood. Also in estuaries you might find leading lights: two lighthouses which when lined up showed the optimum course to steer into the harbour. These are found at the entrance to some major ports such as Rotterdam where very deep-draft ships have to stay within a narrow dredged channel. More sophisticated versions of leading lights have three lights on towers to give a more precise indication of the course to follow and more importantly indicate very quickly if the ship is drifting out of the channel.

Lighthouses have had a very important role to play in the history of navigation and, as we saw with the Pharos of Alexandria, the height of the structure was thought to be important so that it could be seen a long way out at sea. However, high lights proved to be something of a double-edged sword because while the light might be visible over a long distance, when it was placed high up it could disappear into low cloud or fog and so lose its effectiveness. This was seen at Beachy Head on the English Channel where the initial lighthouse on this high chalk headland was located at the top of the cliff. Later a new lighthouse was built in the sea just off the headland in order to keep the light at a lower level, even though this meant delivering supplies and personnel to the light by boat rather than by the easy route overland.

Bright lights in lighthouses were also important to extend the range of visibility. It was reckoned that it would take 400 tons of coal a year to fuel an ancient lighthouse and even when replaced by candles and oil lamps, maintaining the light was both expensive and difficult. We have talked about the Argand light used in France which was a type of oil lamp, but a real advance was made with the introduction of gas lights. One of the first gas lamps installed at the Baily Lighthouse off Dublin was reckoned to be thirteen times

A sheltered waters' lighthouse like a house on stilts.

more powerful than the most brilliant light then known. Ireland was ahead of the game when the lighthouse at Wicklow Head was fitted with Wigham's patent intermittent flashing mechanism, which timed the gas supply by means of clockwork. Then this was combined with a revolving lens in the Rockabill Lighthouse, the world's first lighthouse with a group-flashing characteristic that was produced to help mariners identify it from seaward.

A major development came from Sweden when the AGA company used acetylene gas as the illuminant. This burns with a very white flame and the company invented a system whereby the gas could be used to create flashing light characteristics and also a daylight timer so that the gas would last a long time with the light switched off in the daytime. With many lights installed in remote locations, this allowed for unmanned lights and these AGA lights became the standard type of light used to illuminate buoys.

Electric light became the norm with generators supplying the power both for the light and for the fog signals when mains power was not available. Today we see lighthouses using extremely bright LED lights that consume minimal power and this technology is now transferring to buoy lights.

After more than 200 years of development, lighthouses are now largely unmanned with reliable remote control and monitoring systems taking over. The service is just as reliable as when heroic lighthouse-keepers manned the lights, but it is also modern technology that is starting to make lighthouses redundant. The advent of modern GPS position-fixing means that navigators no longer need lighthouses to the same extent as before and we are currently in a transition period when lighthouses and modern electronic position-fixing operate side-by-side, but the writing is on the wall and most navigators will confirm that they cannot remember when they last took a bearing of a light-house to establish a position. However, the lighthouses do provide the navi-gator with a reassurance about their position and there is still something very comforting to see the loom of a lighthouse light appearing over the horizon at night, but there was also the fright when you heard the fog signal of the lighthouse which meant you were close to danger.

A lightvessel does much the same job as a lighthouse but it is moored at sea to provide a warning or position reference in areas where it is not possible or practical to build lighthouses. Being a member of the crew on a lightvessel is one of the toughest jobs at sea because the vessel is out there in all weathers, storms and calms, and the motion of most lightvessels in rough seas has to be experienced to be believed. The first lightvessels were built at the beginning of the nineteenth century and they were constructed from wood. Later versions had either iron or steel hulls with a modified shape to help reduce the rolling, but the lightvessel remained on station when all the other ships

A fixed structure light tower replaces the Frying Pan Shoals lightvessel.

were running for shelter in bad weather. Some lightvessels, notably US ones, were self-propelled but most were dead ships apart from generators for the light and the fog horn.

The first British lightvessel was placed on station at the Nore in the Thames Estuary in 1736 and shortly after more vessels were placed out in the North Sea to mark the many sandbanks in the area. The notorious Goodwin

An early unmanned lightship or light float used to mark a significant danger.

Sands in the Dover Strait were marked by lightvessels near the turn of the century and by using lightvessels it was possible to give ships early warning of these dangerous shoals compared with the weaker lights on buoys and often obscured lights from the shore. Being close to the shipping lanes, many of these lightvessels were involved in collisions with ships as the ships were set down on them by the tide and this added to the dangers for the crews.

The first US lightvessel was established at Chesapeake Bay in 1820. By 1909 there were fifty-six on station at locations around the coast. The Nantucket Lightvessel was one of the most hazardous stations and it was located many miles offshore to mark these extensive shoals with ships using it as their preliminary landfall after an Atlantic crossing. Frequent fogs added to the dangers and the lightvessel was in collision several times, sometimes with a loss of life. The situation became worse when the lightvessel was one of the first to be fitted with a radio beacon with ships homing in on the radio beacon in order to locate the lightvessel in fog. It must have been a frightening experience on the lightvessel when the deep whistle of an ocean liner was heard in the fog and to hear it getting closer and closer.

The role of the lightvessel was a vital one for shipping, their flashing lights giving a warning of the shallows close by when there might be little else to give a clue about the position of the ship. Navigators were warned not to use bearings from a lightvessel because it might be on the end of 100 fathoms of chain and would swing with the tide so its location was not precise. Nowadays lightvessels are a dying breed and few remain. They have largely been replaced by very large circular buoys moored on station that can carry a

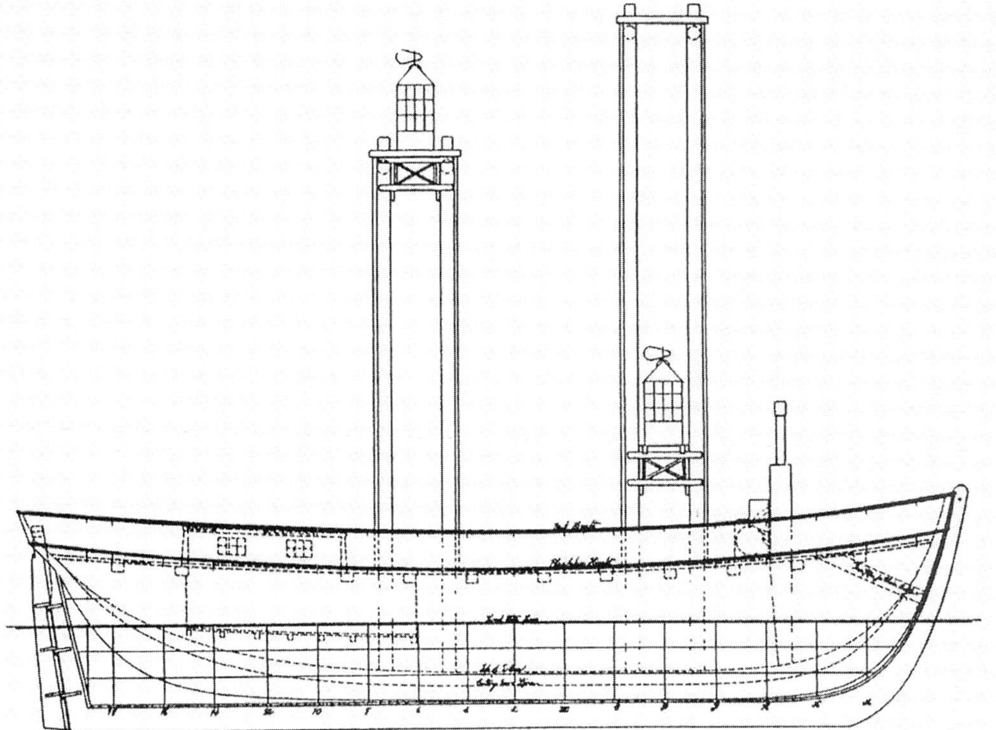

Plans of America's first lightship with twin lights.

matching bright light but have no crew on board. These buoys are monitored remotely from the shore.

Both exposed lighthouses and most lightvessels had fog signals to give a warning to shipping when the visibility was poor. Lighthouses tended to have either high-pitched reed signals or, in the past, set off explosive bangs at regular intervals, while lightvessels tended to use the deep grunt sound of the diaphone (similar to a foghorn) that replaced bells and gongs. Between the world wars a number of underwater bell systems were established that had a much longer range than most air fog signals but these were largely discontinued with the advent of radar for ships after the Second World War. To aid those using radar the Racon (short for radar beacon) was developed that would return an identifying signal back to the radar of the ship when it was pinged by the radar signal. Racons were fitted to many strategic lighthouses and lightvessels and the use of sound fog signals was gradually abandoned as ships were fitted with enclosed bridges where the fog signals could not be heard.

The marking of shoals, rocks and channels by buoys goes back as far as the use of lighthouses as navigation marks. Early buoys were used to mark channels in harbours and comprised mainly barrels or similar floats that were moored in position by a rope attached to a sinker. These were daylight-only marks and a few were coloured to help identify them, but the local knowledge of a pilot would know which buoy was which. Even smaller channels up tidal creeks were often marked by withies, a stick stuck into the mud at the side of the channel. Such a marking system is still in use today, but it requires a withy on each side of the channel to be useful otherwise you don't know on which side to pass.

It is thought that a very basic form of channel-marking buoy was used in some of the ancient harbours in pre-Roman times. If buoys were being used then, this suggests that some form of surveying had been done in order to establish where the channel and shallow water lay, which was probably a very basic form of surveying and navigation. Rather than fixing the position when a sounding with a sounding pole was taken, a buoy would have been laid to mark the deeper water areas.

Buoys are mentioned in documents of around 1300 relating to navigation around the Mediterranean with buoys in the river at Seville in Spain. Later buoys were used to mark the channels and shoals in the River Maas in Holland. These early buoys were made literally from anything that could float and they were anchored by ropes tied to stones. Some 200 years later buoys were being made from hollow barrel-like structures that were much larger to make them visible from a distance and it is reported that many of the German and Dutch rivers bordering the North Sea were marked by buoys and there were even special ships built designed for servicing the buoys. When Trinity House was formed in Britain in 1514, the Thames Estuary was being marked

Servicing a beacon that marks a fixed shoal area.

by buoys and indeed buoys became a commonplace feature of many ports to allow safe navigation. None of these buoys had lights of any sort so safe navigation was limited to daylight hours and of course this would have to be combined with favourable winds.

Like shipbuilding, the construction of buoys turned to metal and they were fitted with top marks and were painted in different colours to help identify them. To give warnings in fog, bell buoys were developed on which the bell was rung by the movement of the buoy in the water. Later whistle buoys were developed, again using the motion of the buoy in the water to force air through the whistle. These fog signal buoys relied on the movement of the buoys in waves to be effective, but were not much use in the calm seas that often prevail during fog. It was in the late 1800s that the first lights were installed on buoys, but it was many years later that these were developed into a reliable navigation tool that finally allowed shipping to enter harbours with winding entry channels during the hours of darkness. These first lighted buys used acetylene gas and gas-powered buoys using the reliable AGA lights are still in use but are being replaced with battery-powered electric lights, mostly charged by solar panels.

Establishing lighthouses, buoys and other marks as warnings to navigators has been one of the most challenging engineering tasks imaginable. Trying to build a lighthouse on a rock that only just breaks the surface of the sea and is exposed to the full force of the ocean's storms required engineering of the highest order. Similarly but perhaps less dramatic, trying to design a buoy that will stand up to the ocean's storms and shine its light in such a hostile

An early acetylene US buoy with an acetylene-powered light.

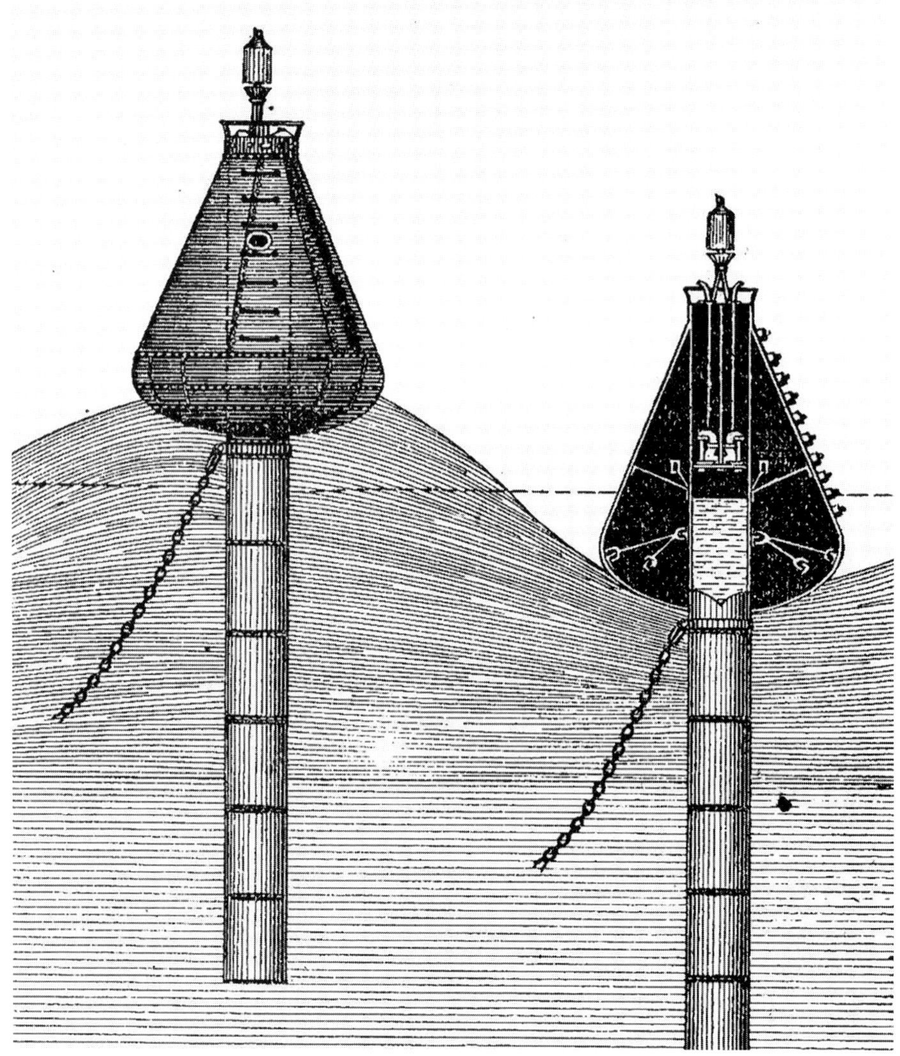

Early plans for a wave-powered whistle buoy that gives a warning in fog.

environment is another challenge. The installation of lights on these navigation markers has also been a considerable challenge, but ships tend to keep going both day and night so the lights were vital to safe navigation. These lights with their different flashing characteristics along with the coloured navigation lights of ships means that a navigator at night has to understand the code of the various lights at night rather than the more visual navigation that is used in daylight.

It has been a long journey in the history of navigation to give navigators good warning by both day and night of the dangers that lurk around the coasts and in harbour areas so that navigation can be carried out safely. It is interesting to see how these marks have changed navigation, partly taking away the need for the vessel to fix its position and instead to mark the dangers that lurk both above and below the surface in such a way that the navigator has due warning of the dangers. Lighthouses, lightvessels, buoys and beacons have played a vital role in improving safety at sea by giving mariners early warning of the dangers of the shoals, rocks and land and despite all the advances in electronic navigation, these sea marks still play a vital role in navigation but you have to wonder if their days are numbered. It is a recurring theme in the history of navigation that just when a technology that improves the quality and safety of navigation has reached maturity, along comes a new technology that may render the tried-and-tested solution obsolete. In this case it is satellite navigation which, if the charts are correct, allows the ship to pinpoint its position so that it does not need the marks and warnings issued by these fixed marks on the shore and marking of the shallows. As a navigator you may want to put total faith in the electronic satellite systems, but from a personal point of view there is nothing quite as reassuring as sighting a mark that pinpoints the unseen dangers to navigation. That first sighting of the loom of a lighthouse over the horizon that heralds the expected landfall is one of the best sights to be seen by any navigator.

Chapter Nine

Making Landfalls

Out on the wide waters of the ocean your world is limited by the horizon and you are likely to be more concerned about the weather than about dangers to navigation. For the navigator it has always been the approach to land that has been the challenging time; the time when he has to make the change from the relatively safe ocean waters to the potential dangers of the land. Not only does the environment change but the techniques to cope also have to change and it is during the transition from one type of navigation to another that there can be increased risks. Making a landfall is probably the most challenging time for a navigator and it has been the same throughout the history of navigation.

Those early navigators were probably very sensible in not venturing out of sight of land because the land was their reference for navigation and they wanted to keep it in sight so that they knew roughly where they were, using what might be termed mental navigation. Once you go out of sight of land then you have to make a landfall, you need to be able to identify the coast that has come into sight and you need to know that coastline well enough to know which way to turn to find your harbour. It sounds simple and it should work well when you have been able to fix your position accurately enough out on the ocean so that you make a landfall where you know the coast and can identify it and be aware of any off-lying dangers. Making a landfall by sight requires reasonable visibility and when there is fog about then the dangers of making a landfall increase dramatically and you are entering a high-risk area where grounding or worse could be imminent. That first sight of land can be a very welcome sight and that applies today just as much as it did 1,000 years ago when navigators were heading into the unknown. That first sight of the loom of a lighthouse when you see the beam of the light reflecting off the clouds before you actually see the light or that first glimpse of high land as it appears over the horizon on a clear day are some of a navigator's most welcome sights, even when you know where you are with the benefits of modern electronic systems.

I know from personal experience what it can be like. When we were trying to set a new record across the Atlantic in *Virgin Atlantic Challenger II* we had to make our landfall at the Bishop Rock Lighthouse which was the official finish line. Some 20 miles out and I was watching the radar for the first signs

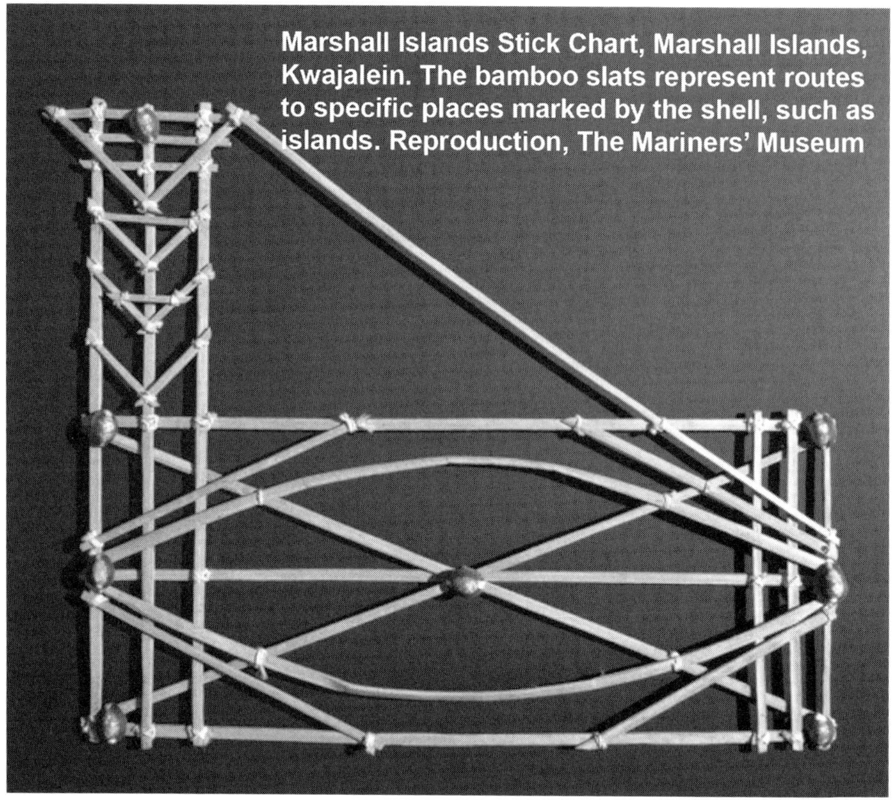

The Polynesian system that helped them to make landfalls on distant islands.

of the Scilly Isles and the Decca Navigator was indicating we were on track. Then this huge thunderstorm came over which blanked out the radar, upset the Decca so that positions were unreliable and cut visibility down to less than 2 miles. This was crunch time and the world was watching us so after 3,000 miles of ocean and being awake for three days and three nights I was suddenly faced with disaster on the final stretch. In the absence of any other guidance we had to stick to our planned course and you can imagine the relief when the lighthouse showed up among the rain just 2 miles away. This demonstrates how, even with the best of equipment, you are still at the mercy of the elements and can take nothing for granted when making a landfall. I have made many landfalls in my long career at sea, but that was the most dramatic because we did not have the luxury of time to slow down.

I feel sure that the navigators of old must have felt the same sort of pressure when making a landfall either on an unknown coastline or when the conditions were far from perfect to see what lay ahead. I can put myself in their position when there was a following wind to push them along and they desperately wanted to know what lay ahead in order to make a safe landfall. You heave-to at night just trying to hold your position so that you don't get taken by surprise when breakers loom out of the darkness and with daylight you rely on the lookout up the mast to detect the first signs of approaching land. It might be breakers on the shallow water or perhaps the land itself or even a change in the colour of the water, but nothing is certain until you have got that positive fix and know where you are in relation to the dangers so that you can plan your next move. Before the time of reliable charts you might not even know where the dangers lie so it is a challenging time for any navigator and even today when you have positions at your fingertips you still want the reassurance of that visual sighting of the land.

Some of the most challenging landfalls were made by the Atlantic liners in their heyday. Imagine steaming towards the land at your full speed of perhaps 30 knots because it was so important to keep to your schedule. The liners' reputation lived or died through keeping to schedule and this put enormous pressure on making a safe landfall so that they could then plan the rest of the route into harbour. Visibility may be poor because the Atlantic in winter is not noted for its good weather and clear skies and they could not afford to slow down. This was in the years between the wars when electronic navigation was not available and the chances of getting a fix in the past two days might be only 50 per cent because of poor weather. The visibility might be less than perfect so you can get some idea of how important it was to get that first sighting of the flashing light of a lighthouse. I am sure that aircraft had similar challenging navigation difficulties when making a landfall after an ocean crossing when they desperately needed to sight the land below and there was low cloud. Do you go below the cloud to get a fix or do you stay above the cloud and hope there will be a break before you run out of fuel? Many of the significant headlands along the West Coast of Ireland had large numbers painted on them to help identify them from the air during the war when planes were flying across the Atlantic.

Making landfalls when coming in from the ocean will be a challenging time for navigators but at the same time those who are navigating along a coastline will find it challenging when they go out of sight of the land and have to return.

This is the dilemma of navigating and demonstrates the considerable gap in technique between those who navigate along the shoreline and those who navigate on the oceans. For the early navigators the shoreline represented a link with safety and with the security of the known world. To lose sight of the land was a voyage into the unknown. Once that link with the 'unknown' had been broken and navigators ventured out onto the high seas, it was the return to the shore that represented the challenge because it could be into unfamiliar waters where danger could lurk below the surface of the sea.

So how did those early navigators cope when virtually the only information available would have been what they could see? Sight was such an important factor in early navigation and it remains important even today when electronics have taken much of the uncertainty out of the equation. What you could expect to see and what you might actually see would depend a great deal on the type of coastline where you were making your landfall.

The Nantucket Shoals are a major hazard to shipping when making a landfall after an Atlantic crossing.

Making landfall in poor visibility was a hazardous occupation until electronic position-fixing systems became available.

High land and cliffs might give you a strong visual clue about your position when making a landfall, whereas with offshore shoals and low-lying land you would have to depend largely on interpreting the surface of the sea and colour and changes in the wave patterns, but nothing was certain. The experienced navigators would perhaps have a good idea about what type of coastline to expect when making a landfall gained from experience while navigating along the coastline but even then the big challenge would be to know on which part of the coastline you were making the landfall.

For hundreds of years a ship coming in towards land at the end of an ocean voyage would most likely have been following along a line of latitude before making the landfall. Latitude was the only type of position line that could be measured out on the ocean so latitude sailing was the common technique used to make an ocean crossing. So it seems likely that a navigator would select the latitude that would provide him with a landfall point of his choosing. Coming across the Atlantic from west to east on a return voyage to Europe, the choice of landfall points might be the Spanish and Portuguese coastline if the voyage was heading to the Mediterranean or perhaps the long coastline of Ireland if heading for somewhere in Northern Europe. The English Channel would have been the destination for many voyages and here the navigator might want to attempt a landfall point between the sentinels of the English Channel, with Ushant to the south and the Scilly Isles or the Irish coast to the north. This might be a more challenging landfall because neither of these points might be sighted and the ship could sail on into the Channel and make a landfall further to the east. Sailing along a latitude was a useful navigation technique, but in those early days the accuracy of measuring the latitude was not good so the measurement might be up to only 5° accurate which would equate to around 300 miles so the choice of a landfall point would have to take this into account.

What the navigator would probably choose to avoid was making a landfall somewhere in the Bay of Biscay. With the poor sailing characteristics of the ships of those days a ship would struggle to sail in any direction of about 90° each side of the wind direction. This means that if a ship sailed into the Bay of Biscay it could become embayed and struggle to be able to sail out again. Sailing into a bay – either large like the Bay of Biscay or small like those along many coastlines – could put a ship in danger especially in strong following winds so the experienced navigator would choose his landfall point with care. Another factor he would have to consider when selecting a landfall point is which way to turn to reach the destination once the landfall was made. With the limited accuracy of the positions obtained from the sun the chances of making the landfall exactly at the desired place were small, which meant that unless they recognized the place where the landfall was made they might not know which way to turn along the coastline in order to reach their destination. The solution was to set a course either to the north or south of the chosen landfall and then they would know which way to turn. This is a technique that was still in use until quite recently by small craft even when, say, crossing the English Channel so that when you sighted land you would know which way to turn to reach your destination.

Early navigators when making a landfall on the coastline of America or the Caribbean islands were faced with a different challenge. Here much of the land is low-lying and in many places there are extensive shoals offshore so that sighting the land and getting a position from it might not be possible before the ship was entering the areas of shallow water. This presented the navigator with a real challenge and taking soundings was the only way to get early warning of shoal waters ahead. Indeed, the sounding line was one of the most important pieces of equipment on board when making a landfall and while the normal rope 20-fathom lead-line was useful when entering harbours, navigators making a landfall wanted warning of shallowing water in deeper depths, say up to 100 fathoms, to give early warning that they were approaching the shore. This would particularly be the case when visibility was poor and the skies overcast so there would be no other clues about the approach to land.

An early fog signal that gave warning of land during fog.

When you look at the challenges of making a landfall it is small wonder that there were so many ships lost in grounding incidents in those days. The tally of shipping accidents was very high and of course the absence of any means of communication meant that many ships just disappeared without trace. It is safe to assume that a high proportion of these shipping casualties were the result of trying to make a landfall in adverse conditions, and for hundreds of years since Columbus made his epic voyage across the ocean making a landfall has been probably the most high-risk part of navigating the oceans.

Even when you find the coast and manage to establish where you are, the navigator is still faced with the challenge of getting to the destination port. You may find the coastline at the end of an ocean voyage, but you need to recognize where you are on that coastline and with the early charts available that would not always be easy. Those early navigators that were mentioned in the first chapters would sail from headland to headland and in many cases those headlands might be identified by a building on the headland. Today we have lighthouses and even beacons built on headlands that can allow the navigator to know which is which, but early navigators might have to rely on memory. One of the early means of identifying a headland is found in drawings of a coastline that show a horizontal view of what the coast looks like from the sea. We still see these drawings in relatively modern pilot books and they have been a rich source of information for navigators throughout the centuries, although they can often have limited value because they only show the coast from one viewpoint at sea and the view of a coastline can change considerably depending on the time of day and the prevailing light.

When first sighted a coastline might be just a faint haze on the horizon that will gradually become clearer as the ship approaches the shore. Out at sea you may also see cloud formations on the horizon that can easily be confused with land. I had one occasion coming in towards Land's End on the south-west tip of England when we were still 100 miles or more offshore according to my calculations, but I could see what I thought was land ahead. It looked so

Virgin Atlantic Challenger II making landfall at the Bishop Rock Lighthouse after her record-breaking Atlantic crossing.

eadlands were the guide for early coastal navigators.

ome of the earliest boats were dug-out canoes used for river navigation.

The *Kon-Tiki* vessel went with the winds and the currents rather than being 'navigated'.

A Polynesian navigating 'chart' that was used for inter-island navigation.

he backstaff was one of the first tools for measuring the elevation of the sun, moon and stars.

he Vikings were pioneers of ocean navigation.

The lead line for soundings that took over from the sounding pole and was used by navigators for hundreds of years. (*Mariner's Museum*)

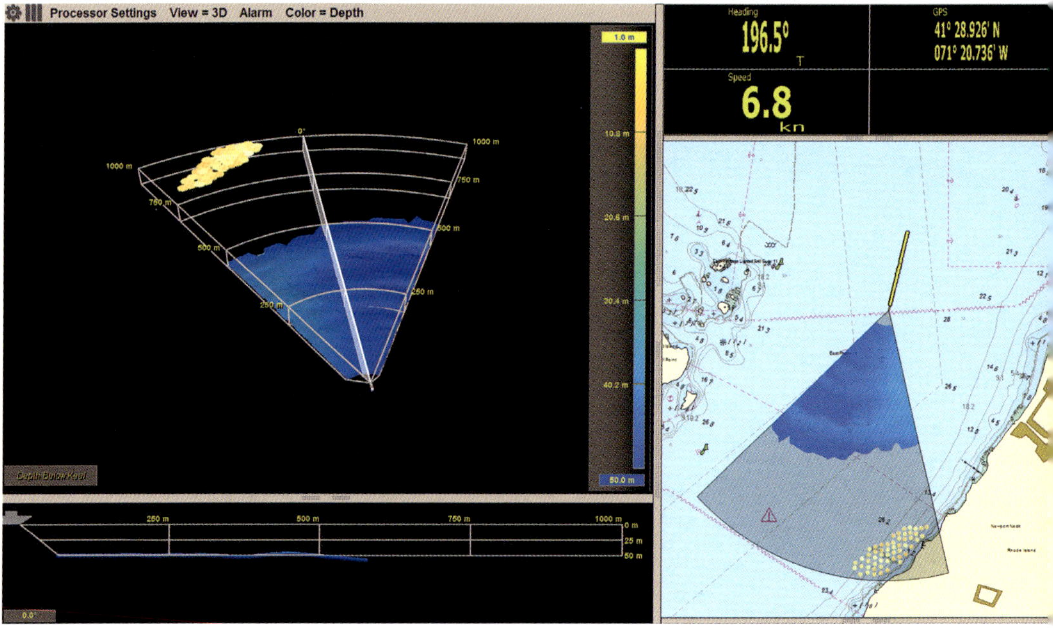

Forward-looking sonar gives navigators an underwater view of what lies ahead. (*FarSounder*)

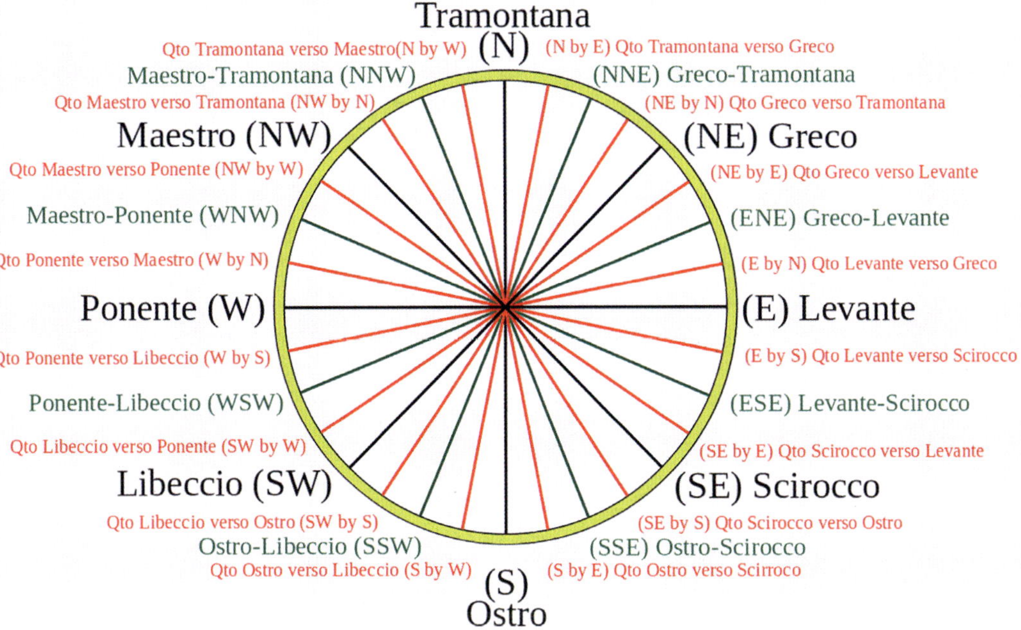

The direction of the wind was vital to navigation and this diagram shows the names of the winds from different directions in the Mediterranean.

An early Chinese magnetic compass.

The bridge of the liner *Queen Mary* where the magnetic compass takes pride of place but is flanked by gyrocompass repeaters.

The Walker log where the speed of rotation of the impeller measures the speed. This was widely used on both ships and smaller craft.

An advanced bubble sextant that was used for air navigation before electronics.

Using a sextant at sea. (*US Navy*)

A more modern version of
the octant with brass inserts
and a vernier scale.
(*Smithsonian*)

It requires considerable
skill to use a sextant in a
small boat.

German chart of 1583 showing the Portuguese coast with many inshore soundings marked.

colourful old chart from 1504 by Portuguese cartographer Pedro Reinel of the Atlantic showing
ts of North America as well as the islands of the Atlantic.

Alligator Reef lighthouse in the US; a tall lighthouse used on a low-lying coastline.

A lighthouse can help identify a landfall headland by day and night.

The Bishop Rock Lighthouse, a significant landfall mark off south-west Britain and built on an isolated rock.

The liner *Olympic* collides with the Nantucket Lightvessel in fog.

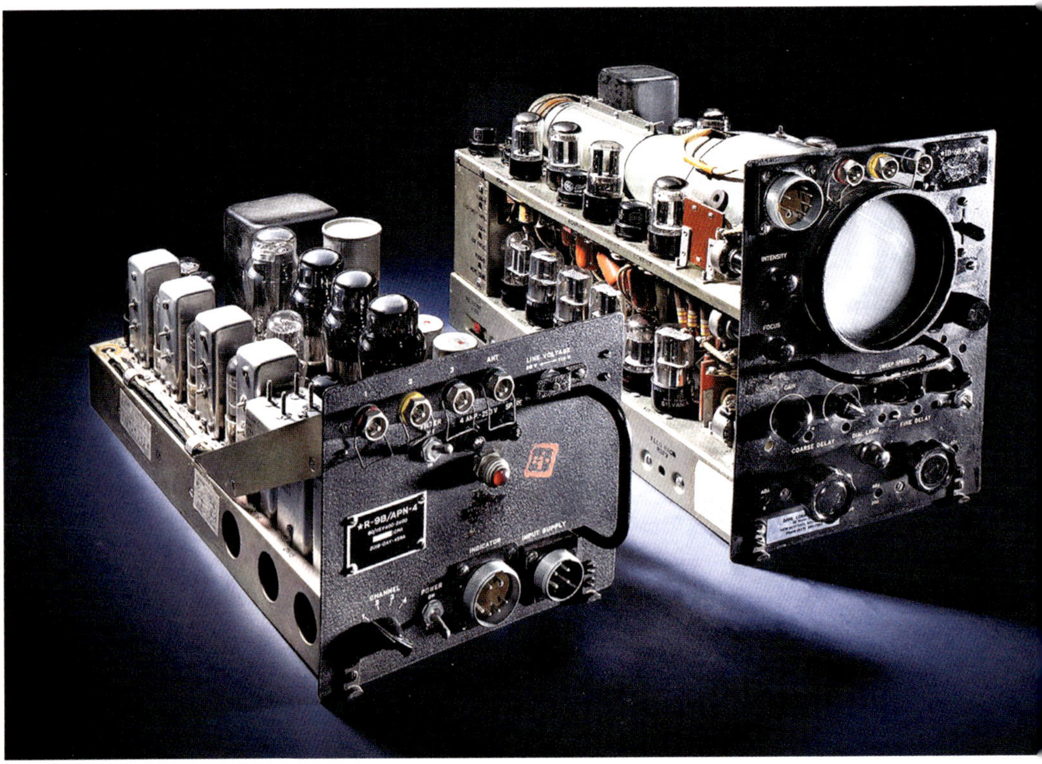

An early inertial navigation system that was an expensive position-fixing solution.

The classic marine Decca Navigator receiver that required special charts to plot the position.

modern inertial navigation module that uses atomic sensors instead of gyros and accelerometers.

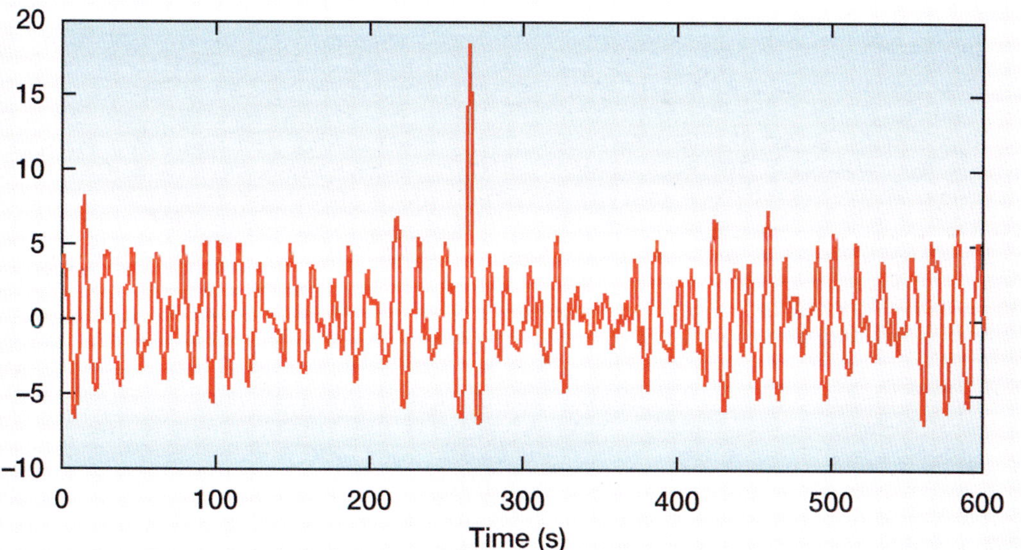

wave-recorder trace of a major rogue wave measured at an oil platform.

The bridge of a modern ship where the focus is almost entirely on the electronic systems.

The International Ice Patrol keeps a check on icebergs to prevent another *Titanic* disaster.

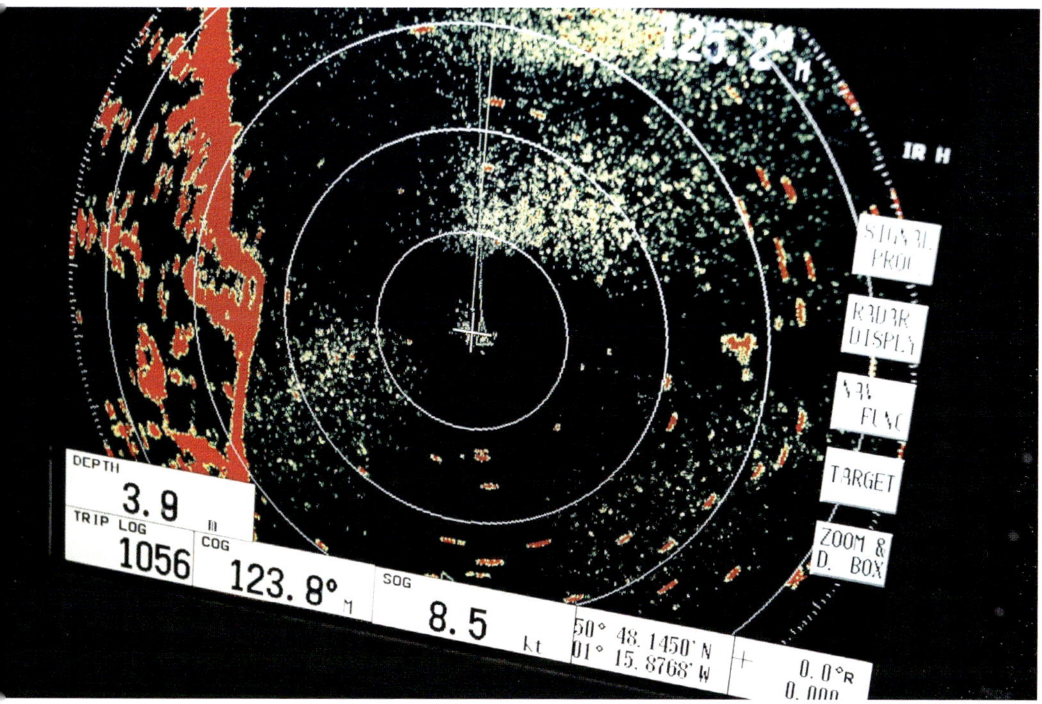

in clutter on the radar display can hide small craft targets.

diagram illustrating the various components of the GPS position-fixing system. Other satellite stems are similar.

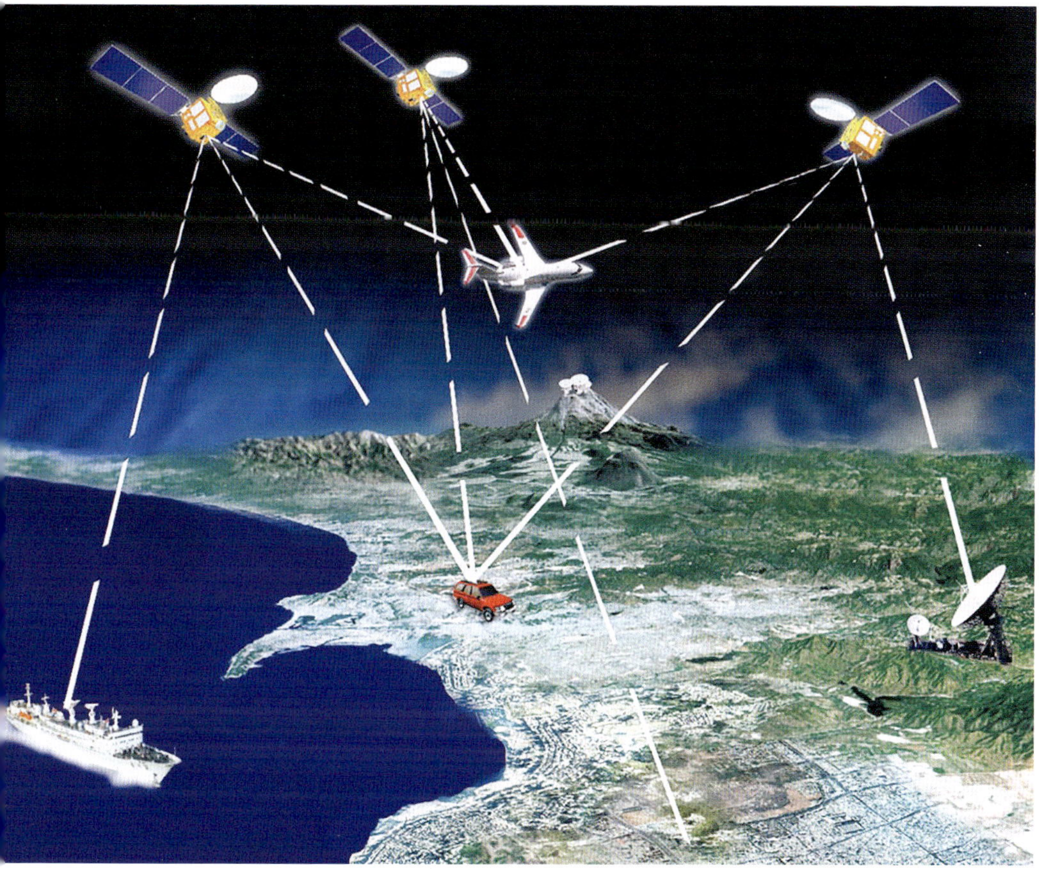

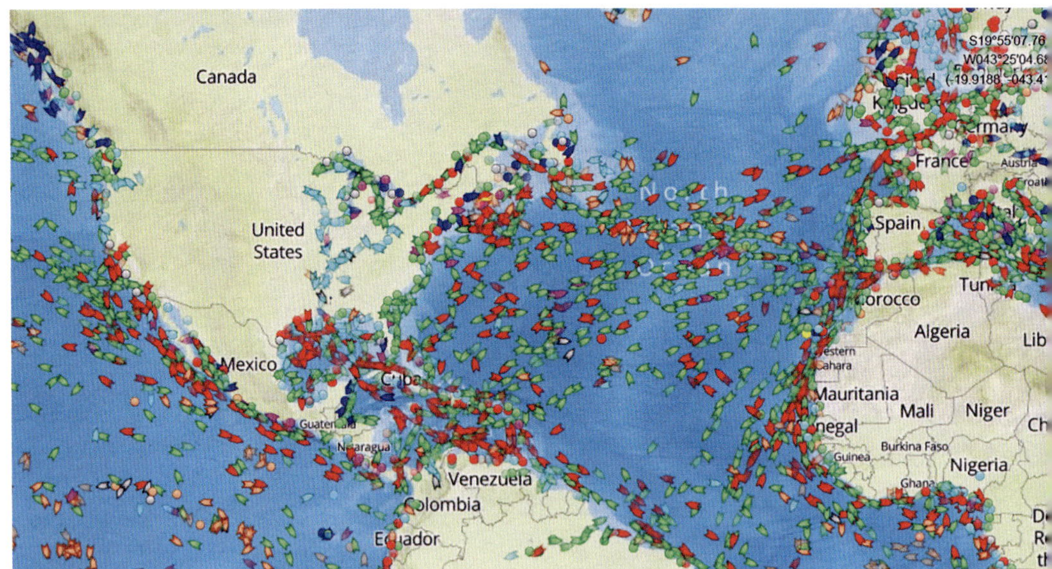

A plot of AIS returns on the Atlantic showing the high density of shipping on the main ocean routes.

The cockpit of a modern airliner is highly complex, but it allows navigation to be almost automatic

realistic that I was frantically checking out my electronic navigation because according to that there should have been no land in sight. It took some time to realize that the 'land' I could see was indeed a cloud formation, but it does show how easily mistakes can be made when making a landfall and without the electronic help I would have been convinced that we were making a landfall. It is easy to make what you think you see fit what you expect to see.

Then of course there is the challenge of making a landfall in the dark, which without any electronic help would have been a high-risk operation. With a position estimate established by dead reckoning only as far as the latitude was concerned, the cautious navigator would heave-to during the hours of darkness when his calculations suggested that he might be close to land and wait for daylight when things should become clearer. Before lighthouses were established there would be very few lights on the shore that might give any indication of land, and this is where soundings might give the navigator that vital clue about his approach and allow him to sail on during the night.

Before the introduction of various electronic position-fixing systems a navigator could fix his position along a coastline by taking bearings of known objects such as headlands, lighthouses, church spires, etc. These bearings would be plotted on the chart as position lines, lines along which the position of the ship should lie. Where two or more of these position lines crossed, that was the position of the ship. There were also techniques where the position could be fixed with reasonable accuracy by taking consecutive bearings of the same object and then taking the distance covered by the ship during the time between the bearings. This was known as a running fix and was one of many techniques developed to fix the position from identifiable objects on the shore. The sextant could also be used and horizontal sextant angles of known objects could be plotted with a station pointer that could be set to the recorded angles. This was the accurate plotting system used by surveyors and for buoy-laying prior to the introduction of electronic systems.

When plotting a course along a coastline then it was possible to plot the position of the ship along the coast to the destination port, but this all depended on having an accurate chart of the coastline on which the under-water features and significant objects were all recorded. These accurate charts did not come into being until the middle of the nineteenth century so before that the navigator was still relying on having perhaps an indication where dangerous shoals and rocks lay along the coastline and he could still be sailing in fairly treacherous waters when sailing close to the shore. The technique before accurate charts became available was to keep offshore as far as possible where safer waters could be assumed to lie, but to keep the shore in sight as a reference for positioning. History has recorded the development of the

The wreck of the tanker *Argo Merchant* after she went aground on shoals on the US East Coast.

accurate timepiece by Harrison as perhaps the major improvement in navigation for shipping, but the introduction of accurate charts probably did more to save lives at sea and prevent shipwreck. It was around 1850 that the British Admiralty had a major fleet of survey vessels to produce accurate charts, not only of the British Isles but also of other sea areas frequented by British ships so that for the first time ships making a landfall could rely on having charts that could be used with confidence when making the transition from ocean to coastal navigation.

Once there were accurate charts available it was possible to use soundings of the depth with a lot more confidence when making a landfall. Single soundings could help to pinpoint the ship's location or when you had a depth reading at least indicate where the ship could not be by studying the charts. As we have said before, navigation can be like detective work and a more precise location could be obtained from soundings by taking three or four soundings at fixed intervals, say about every 5 miles, and then plotting these on a strip of paper, using the chart scale to judge the intervals between the sounding plots. Knowing the course the ship followed, this strip of paper could then be placed on the chart in the hope that it would show a matching line of soundings on the chart that would be a good indication of the ship's position. There were also local areas of deeper water surrounded by shallower water that could give an indication of position by soundings. The Hurd Deep in the English Channel was one, and off the American coast the significantly deeper water of the Fundian Channel might have helped navigators to establish a position before making a landfall. It was all detective work with clues here and there to help the navigator establish his position or, equally importantly, to tell him where he wasn't.

Accurate charts were only one factor in making a safe landfall and even when positions in the ocean could be obtained with adequate accuracy because of the chronometer, this still required clear skies to sight the sun or stars. Crossing the North Atlantic in winter could well mean that no position sights were available for days on end so this still left the navigator with the challenge of making a landfall. Accurate charts might help to establish a position using sounding, but in fog or poor visibility this would only be a rough guide indicating the nearness of land. Just when a navigator needed accurate positioning there was very little to come to his aid in these conditions except his skill and experience and possibly prayer. It was not until the 1930s that a solution was found other than using dead reckoning and this must have been a major development of the time: the radio beacon. Here for the first time was a way of fixing a position with reasonable accuracy in any weather conditions. The range from the beacon transmitter might be only 50 to 100 miles and the accuracy perhaps no better than 5 miles but that was a huge improvement over many dead-reckoning calculations. The radio beacon was a major development in making landfalls and was the first use of electronics in navigation. Being introduced at a time when the speed of ships was increasing and keeping to schedules was becoming important, the radio beacon must have come to the rescue of many navigators desperate to get a position fix in adverse conditions.

Two other factors would also come into play when making landfalls. Along coastlines on both sides of the Atlantic and in many other parts of the world, tides had to be considered. With tides it is not just the regular rise and fall of the water levels but also the currents that these rises and falls produce. The Mediterranean is practically devoid of tides so those early sailors would have had a relatively easy life with negligible currents and a rise and fall of only a foot or two. It must have been quite a challenge when the Roman sailors headed north to find that they had to cope with tidal currents of sometimes up to 3 knots or more and the associated overfalls and turmoil that can be associated with these currents. Probably one of the reasons why they were successful in their explorations was the fact that they could navigate under oars or paddles as well as sails, which would give them a lot more flexibility in the direction they could make progress. It would have been the same with the Vikings in their explorations of northern waters, and the use of paddles enabled them to navigate through the narrow channels of the Scottish west coast. Using paddles or oars would have needed a larger crew which might have limited the duration of their voyages to a few days at most because of the need for food and water, but it had the benefit of not being reliant on the often fickle nature of wind propulsion.

While the nature and effects of the tides were perhaps understood by the earlier navigators, it was those surveyors who started compiling accurate charts around 1850 who also turned their attention to assessing the tides. This allowed the charts to have tidal flow and direction arrows added which would have been a tremendous help when making a landfall, particularly when this was being based on dead reckoning. Tidal flow still has a significant effect on navigation these days and the information developed by those early surveyors, who would have anchored their ships often in exposed waters to measure the tidal flow, was a vital addition to navigation information.

The other significant factor that might come into play when making a landfall was leeway. Leeway is the sideways drift of a ship or particularly a yacht when the wind is on or nearly on the beam. This causes the ship to be set sideways from its intended course and a navigator has to allow for this by steering a few degrees up into the wind to counteract the sideways drift. There is no easy way to measure leeway except to look over the stern of the ship and to try to estimate the angle between the ship's head and the way the wake is angled away from this heading. For a sailboat or ship the leeway might be about 5° because often the hull is designed in such a way to reduce this sideways drift, but it can also be a problem for powered ships and boats because they tend to be flat-bottomed and so more prone to this sideways drift. Coming in towards land or when navigating along a coastline the leeway could become a significant factor in assessing the position of a ship by dead reckoning and generally it was up to the skill and experience of the navigator to make the correct adjustment to the course.

I know from personal experience about the effect that leeway can have on the course made good when I had my first shipwreck. I was a young apprentice on a 6,000-ton cargo ship bound from Liverpool to Newcastle around the north of Scotland. She was a light ship, i.e. no cargo on board, so she was riding high in the water with a draft of only about 12ft. That night it was blowing a whole gale from the west and it was a mixture of rain and snow so visibility was down to almost zero with the addition of the spray flying about. Our course was planned to take us up through the Minch which is a wide channel and we must have been making a lot more leeway than estimated because instead of picking up the Skerryvore Lighthouse we ended up going inside it and hit the rocks among the islands. With no radar or electronic systems on board we did not know where we were and because we were not

Making a successful landfall is always a moment to cherish for a navigator.

where we expected to be, our distress message was vague about position. However, the lifeboats from the shore found us the next morning and we were rescued, while the ship became a total wreck and still lies on the seabed. The ship had a freeboard of about 30ft which must have acted just like a sail so that the wind was pushing us sideways a lot more than the officers on the bridge estimated. We were trying to make a landfall on an isolated lighthouse in poor visibility and this just shows how quickly things can go wrong when you are estimating your position in adverse conditions so leeway can be a significant factor and that incident was only a little over sixty years ago.

Here was a case of trying to make a landfall at an isolated lighthouse and we were only less than 100 miles from our last fix. There were no radio beacons to come to our aid in that area so this was dead reckoning gone wrong. Trying to make a landfall on an isolated point – perhaps a lighthouse or maybe a small island – has always been a challenge for a navigator who does not have the assistance of modern electronic aids to navigation. If you don't sight it when you expect to you will not know which way to turn to try to find it. You can offset the course to at least know on which side the landfall should be, but then you will not know when to turn unless you can assess your speed accurately. It is the navigator's dilemma and those skilled Polynesian navigators in the Pacific thousands of years ago partially solved this problem by making their destination islands 'bigger'. Their landfall might be low-lying islands that might only show up perhaps 10 miles away, but by looking for the distinctive clouds that often assembled over the islands they could be seen for perhaps three or four times that distance. The wave pattern created by the seas around the islands would also give a clue and throughout the centuries navigators have always been looking for these subtle clues, maybe not about giving a position but knowing that the changing conditions of sea and/or sky could give a clue about the proximity of land. Soundings were always the primary clue with the material on the seabed perhaps narrowing down the area over which the ship was sailing, but nothing was definite about a landfall until land was sighted and the land identified. Today with modern electronic systems a landfall is no more challenging than other types of navigation and it is a routine operation, but still there is much the same anticipation and excitement that must have heralded landfall for the past 5,000 years.

Chapter Ten

Electronic Navigation

The concept of using electrical or electronic signals for navigation is more than 125 years old, dating from the time when it was proposed that a powerful microwave beam transmitted from the shore would be able to be picked up by shipping in fog when lights were not visible. It was proposed to build a 'sort of radio wave lighthouse'. It was a long time before such a vision became reality, but by the turn of the century ships were being equipped with a radio transmission system that could transmit Morse code messages. For the first time ships did not have to be in visual contact to be able to communicate and over the years radio has been responsible for a tremendous reduction in the loss of life at sea. It did not make navigation any easier, but it did allow ships to let the outside world know when they went aground and so greatly increased the possibility of rescue. Although not directly affecting navigation, the availability of radio links did allow ships to receive weather information which was at a time when weather maps were starting to be generated so at least ships could get storm warnings when they were within radio range. Like most things electronic though, it was mainly the passenger ships on the Atlantic run that could afford the expense of radio communication equipment and for most shipping it would be a couple of decades before radio became commonplace.

Despite the prophecy of radio wave lighthouses, it was not until the 1930s that the concept of radio beacons was developed. Radio beacons were the first attempt at using electronics for navigation and the concept was very simple. You fit significant lighthouses or lightvessels with a radio transmitter that sends out a coded signal that allows it to be identified. On board the ship the signal could be picked up by a receiver through a special antenna that could locate the bearing of the transmitter. Two versions of antenna were used: one which was basically a ferrite rod antenna where you rotated the antenna itself to find the bearing, and another which was a double-loop antenna that was fixed and the bearing could be measured through the relative strength of the signal in each loop. The double-loop type was used widely on ships, while the more compact but less accurate ferrite rod type tended to be a portable unit used on small craft. The radio beacon transmitters were generally arranged in a pattern of transmitters at adjacent navigation marks with each transmitter sending out its signal in rotation which allowed the user on board the ship to take a series of bearings from the different transmitters. These would be relative bearings where the ship's heading had to be applied to convert it to a compass bearing and these bearings could then be plotted on the chart to produce a position fix. In taking a bearing the user rotated the antenna until the signal was at its weakest which was easier to identify than when it was at its maximum.

The accuracy of a radio beacon bearing would be in the region of 2 to 5° depending on the conditions and the experience of the person taking it, but this was adequate to provide a fix when coming in from the ocean and making a landfall. The range would be anywhere from 50 to 100 miles so this would give adequate warning about approaching land or dangers and of course the accuracy would improve as the vessel neared the transmitter. The only way that range could be obtained was by plotting the bearings of two or more beacons and no range was possible from the transmission from a single station so mariners were warned not to follow the bearing of a single station in order to make a landfall because of the risk of hitting the station sending out the signal! There was an attempt to equip lightvessel radio beacons with a secondary beacon with a weak signal that could only be picked up at shorter range so that this would give ships a warning when they were getting close.

Radio DF sets were widely used on yachts as a means of position-fixing when the visibility was poor or when making a landfall. Early yacht systems were quite large and required a permanent installation, but later compact hand-held receivers were developed and these low-cost units were often the primary position-fixing system on small craft that could not afford the high cost of renting a Decca Navigator receiver and did not have the space or adequate power supplies for installing it. The same applied to Loran where, although the service was free, the size of the receivers and the high power needed made them unsuitable for small craft.

There was a sort of reverse radio beacon where a shore station could take bearings of the transmissions from a ship and then radio this bearing back to the ship. It was through this ability to take bearings from the shore that our location was pinpointed when we hit the rocks in that first shipwreck of mine.

Aircraft were big users of radio beacons and these were generally located at aerodromes so that aircraft could home in on their landing-point. They were also established at significant points on aircraft routes and the aircraft beacons were operated on a more sophisticated system with a greater degree of auto-mation in the taking of the bearing and the way they were used for homing in on a destination. Aircraft beacons usually operated on VHF radio frequencies because these had a longer line-of-sight range from the transmitter when the aircraft was high. Marine beacons operated on medium wave frequencies that

The display of an aircraft radio compass showing simple left and right directions to home in on the transmitter.

would give an extended range compared with the short line-of-sight range of VHF at the surface of the sea. For aircraft the radio beacons became the primary means of navigating and more and more sophisticated versions were developed such as the VOR which became the standard short-range navigation system for aircraft worldwide, providing the pilot with an automated means of location with reference to ground stations that remained in use until it was superseded by GPS positioning.

These first steps into the use of radio for navigation were the start of a major change in navigation, moving on from visual navigation into the realms of navigating with a 'black box' that was to change the face of navigation. The

An advertisement for a very early direction-finder for small craft.

An aircraft Bendix loop antenna for direction-finding.

change can be compared with the change that took place a couple of thousand years ago when mathematicians managed to solve the riddle of how the sun and planets moved in relation to the Earth and to find ways to obtain the latitude from observations of the sun and stars. The nature and behaviour of radio waves was beginning to be explored in a way that meant they could be used to establish a position in relation to the transmitter. When you think about it, navigators were now being offered a means to fix their position that was independent of the visibility and the cloud cover and which was available for most of the time. It was not 100 per cent accurate and it was not 100 per cent reliable, but it was a vast improvement on what was available previously from visual observations. From these early ventures into radio position-fixing, radio links of one sort or another were to form the basis of a new type of navigation that would transform it for ever.

The principles of a hyperbolic navigation system using radio transmissions had been proposed in the early 1930s. These new systems were mainly based on measuring the time difference between the reception of transmissions from two spaced transmitters. A master transmitter would send a triggering signal to the two outer transmitters to ensure that they both sent out their signal at the same time and the onboard receiver would then measure the time difference between the reception of each signal and this could be used to establish the position. It sounds simple but radio waves travel at a very high speed and so it was necessary to find a way of measuring the very small time differences with high accuracy. This was in the 1930s which was the time when radar was also being developed and radar depended on measuring the time between the sending and receiving of a radio signal as it was reflected from the target and so a similar system was used involving a trace on a cathode ray. So the basic idea of radio-based hyperbolic navigation was well-known in the 1930s.

In 1937, Robert Dippy proposed using two synchronized transmitters as the basis for a blind landing system. He envisaged two transmitting antennas positioned about 10 miles apart on either side of a runway. A transmitter midway between the two antennas would send a common signal over transmission lines to these two antennas, which ensured that both antennas would then broadcast a signal at the same instant. If the aircraft was properly lined up with the runway, both signals would be received at the same time, but if it was off-centre then one would be received before the other and indicate to the pilot the direction to turn to line up with the runway.

The system had a greater range than the 10 miles first envisaged and it was developed into a general navigation system in which the position could be plotted on special charts that had lines of time differences printed on them. The name of the system came from this printed grid, hence it was called Gee for grid. Instead of just using the original two transmitters triggered by the master, a development saw the master station also transmitting so that there were three hyperbolic lines on the chart that gave the ability to check a position when all three crossed in more or less the same point.

Experimental systems were already being set up in 1940, and it was found that the system was usable for at least 300 miles at higher altitudes. Eventually three Gee chains were established to give UK coverage, but it was not long before jamming by the enemy occurred. The concept of mobile Gee chains was developed to help counter jamming.

After the war further Gee chains were established for civil aviation use covering much of the North Sea, but more importantly the Gee concept using time difference measurements became the basis for the Loran A system that

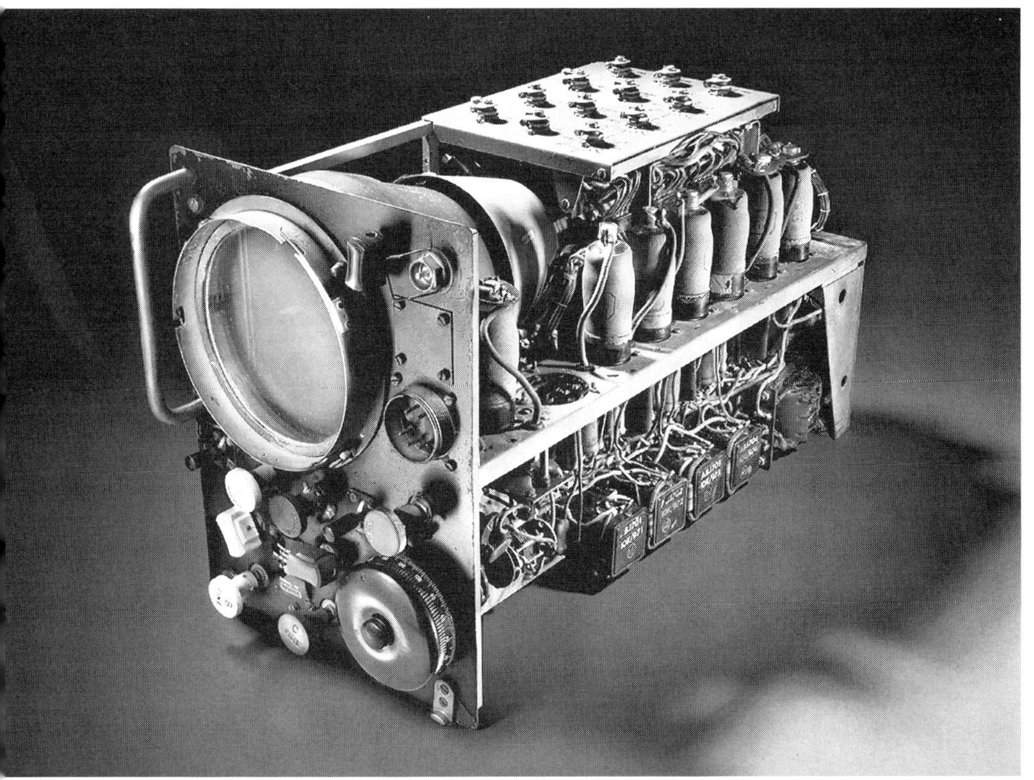

A Gee receiver, one of the early hyperbolic systems.

was developed in North America. Gee transmissions were taken off the air about a decade after the war ended and when it was largely replaced by the introduction of the Decca Navigator system.

Loran A, the extension of Gee, was developed to have a much longer range than Gee which was achieved by using long-wave transmitters. These frequencies allowed Loran to offer position fixes up to 1,000 miles from the shore and the system was widely used by shipping convoys during the war and by aircraft on transatlantic flights, but the main use of Loran was in the Pacific Basin where both ships and aircraft had to navigate to the many islands that dot Pacific waters which could be challenging to find after a long voyage. The effectiveness of Loran A to provide navigation information led to the establishment of transmitters across the northern parts of the Atlantic as well as in the Pacific so that there was full coverage across the northern oceans. After the war the operation and expansion of Loran was put in the hands of the US Coast Guard and a series of developments took place that initially led to Loran B and then to the familiar Loran C.

Loran C gave much improved accuracy even over long ranges and this was achieved by bringing in a type of phase comparison as well as the timing comparison of the pulses. It would be nice to think of a pulse being sent out that had a sharp start and finish so that it could be timed accurately, but in practice the pulse was a bit delayed in starting and stopping so that a clearly-defined timing was not possible. This is what led to the introduction of phase comparison into the system that gave the receiver warning that a pulse was coming and in turn allowed it to be timed much more accurately. This was entering the realms of much more complex electronics, but it came at a time when valves were being replaced by transistors, when electronics were becoming much more compact and the concept of the printed circuit board was emerging. Now complex electronic systems could be reduced in size so that Loran C could be condensed into practical packages for use in aircraft and at sea.

The receivers might have become more compact, but the transmitting masts supporting the antenna had to be very high and Loran C transmitters used masts over 600ft high. The use of Loran C still required navigators to use special charts with a lattice overprinted which enabled positions to be plotted directly onto the chart from the information presented on the receiver. Accuracy was adequate for most open sea navigation and demands for a higher level of accuracy for use in inshore waters were met largely by the higher level of accuracy of Loran close to the transmitters. Here accuracies could be measured in terms of a few metres, while even halfway across the Atlantic the accuracy might be half a mile which was still adequate for ocean navigation and certainly as good as and probably much better than could be achieved by using the traditional sextant sights.

Meanwhile in Europe, while Loran A and then Loran C were available, the range from the transmitters did not give the level of accuracy required for coastal navigation. During the Second World War the Decca Navigator system was developed as an alternative hyperbolic navigation system, but instead of using time comparisons of the incoming signals it used phase comparison between received signals. By using phase differences to establish positions it was claimed to be much easier to implement the receivers using 1940s electronics. Decca Navigator was invented in the US around 1936 by William O'Brian and it is one of those quirks of development that it was a US invention that led to the establishment of a European navigation system and a British invention Gee that was used as the basis for the North American system.

Decca Navigator was originally conceived as a system for aircraft, but development was carried out by the Decca Navigator Company in the UK and it became known simply as Decca. It was developed during the war with the first system established in 1942. It was deployed by the Royal Navy during the Second World War when the Allied forces needed a system that could be used for assault landings and it played a leading role in meeting the navigation requirements for the D-Day landings. After the war it was extensively developed with transmitting stations around the UK which were expanded to provide coverage over much of Northern Europe and later chains were established in many countries around the world. Because Decca operated on a higher frequency than Loran it had a shorter range that was limited to around 400 miles from the transmitters, which perhaps explains why it was used mainly by shipping rather than aircraft.

Decca's primary use was for ship navigation in coastal waters, offering position accuracies in the region of a few metres in good conditions and when the hyperbolic position lines offered a good cross such as when they crossed almost at a right angle. The fishing industry was quick to adopt Decca because of its good position repeatability, allowing fishermen to return to previously-fixed positions such as good fishing grounds or to spots where they had left gear. It was also extensively used in the North Sea oil arena. After the war Decca chains were established covering much of Northern Europe with other chains in Japan, South Africa, Canada, India, the Persian Gulf and Australia. When I worked on Trinity House Lighthouse tenders the accuracy of the Decca positions was good enough to be used for positioning buoys in many areas, particularly when buoys were required to be placed out of sight of land.

The Decca receivers were complex units with the 'black box' of the unit being fitted with seventy-two valves, but the display comprised a box with four dials, three of which could be read to give the red, green and purple grid numbers that were then plotted on the special charts that were overlaid with the grid of curved lines required to plot the positions. The whole Decca system was operated privately and the Decca Navigator Company relied on the income from these rental units to maintain the system and for profits. In 1980 the patents for the Decca system expired and shortly afterwards receivers began to be produced by other manufacturers who took advantage of the advanced electronics and computers becoming available to translate the Decca positions into latitude and longitude so that these could be displayed as a direct read-out, meaning that special charts were no longer required. A similar approach was being adopted for Loran and these compact Decca and Loran receivers revolutionized the use of electronic position-fixing in the 1980s and beyond, opening it up to vast numbers of small craft.

This change spelled the end of the Decca Navigator Company which had relied on rental income for the receivers and the UK Decca transmitters were taken over by the Ministry of Transport with the lighthouse authorities having responsibility for their operation. The system continued until 2000 when it was no longer viable with the advent of GPS satellite systems, and much the same happened in the US with Loran where compact receivers giving latitude and longitude read-outs came into widespread use but with the advent of GPS the transmitting stations were closed down. In Europe the last of the Loran transmitting stations has been shut down, but there are now calls to re-establish a version of Loran called E-Loran as a back-up for GPS.

While the Decca Navigator Company was focused on the marine side of hyperbolic navigation, they did propose an aircraft system that would cover much of the North Atlantic routes. Called Dectra, it was proposed to operate at lower frequencies than the normal Decca, thus giving a longer range, and a similar system Delrac was proposed to give worldwide coverage with an accuracy of 10 miles or less, but both were abandoned in favour of the range and distance system called VOR/DME that only required one transmitter rather than the four for the Dectra system and the emerging inertial navigation systems.

To enhance the accuracy of both Loran and Decca Navigator, differential systems were introduced. The accuracy of both systems was adequate in the most part for general navigation, but people like surveyors wanted a higher level of accuracy and were prepared to pay for it so differential systems were the answer. A differential system records the position given by say the Decca at a known position on the shore and this enables the error of the Decca position to be established with accuracy. Decca was prone to a number of fixed and variable errors and by measuring this error and then transmitting it out to

The author's first shipwreck, the *Tapti* cargo ship, lies on the rocks after a navigation error in 1951 before electronic systems were widely available.

the surveyors in their location at sea the measured error could be applied and a much higher level of accuracy was possible. This type of differential position-fixing was used a lot in the early days of oil and gas operations in the North Sea for the positioning of rigs and platforms and it could offer position accuracies of perhaps 1 to 2 metres. In some cases redundant transmitters of the old radio beacons were used to transmit the correcting signal and these corrections were usually viable up to a range of about 50 miles from the transmitter. Differential position-fixing is a viable navigation technique that is being used quite widely where high accuracy is required and it had considerable application in the early days of GPS, of which more is to follow.

You can't get anything more basic in concept for navigation than an inertial navigation system. From a fixed position you measure the distance a craft has travelled and in what direction to work out the craft's current location. It is just like a dead-reckoning position where you apply course and speed to establish a new position, but the difference with inertial navigation is the accuracy with which the measurements are made to arrive at the new position. An inertial navigation unit comprises a series of accelerometers that can measure the speed of the craft in two or three dimensions and highly-accurate compasses that will measure the heading. These very accurate measurements can take into account the speed and direction of leeway and tides and currents as well as drift in the air with the measurements being made with a high degree of accuracy. Accelerometers are used because they can measure changes in speed and if there is no change in speed then that indicates that the current speed has been maintained. The speed will be measured in three dimensions for aircraft and submarines which are the two main types of craft that use inertial navigation because of the lack of any alternative in many of their operations.

The accuracy of an inertial navigation system is highly dependent on the sensors and it is the cost of these very accurate sensors that makes the cost of inertial navigation systems very high and limits their application. The position accuracy of any system of this type will deteriorate with time and so they tend to be used when other systems are not available. They originally came in a package of considerable size, but like every other navigation system the package has become smaller with development and there are modern inertial systems that operate on an atomic scale, using the rotation of atoms as sensors. Like so many developments in navigation, just when a system offers compact and relatively cheap units, new technology appears that offers better and more reliable accuracy and in the case of inertial navigation it is the ubiquitous GPS that has taken over.

Mention must also be made of Omega which was a hyperbolic navigation system operating on an even lower frequency than Loran that was the first electronic system offering worldwide coverage but at reduced accuracy. Its very low-frequency transmissions meant that it could even be received by submarines underwater and its main reason for development was as a positioning system to be used as a back-up for the inertial navigation systems. The accuracy of an inertial navigation deteriorates with time so the Omega signals could be used to update the inertial navigation positions. The accuracy of Omega was at best about 1 mile and at worst probably 2 miles, but as a worldwide system it had attractions and it had adequate accuracy for ocean navigation. Aircraft were using inertial navigation and the Omega system was a good back-up for these aircraft systems. Its use at sea was limited, but it certainly challenged the traditional sextant and chronometer method of position-fixing by matching its accuracy while providing day and night availability. For aircraft, using a sextant for fixing the position had limited success, particularly as the speed of aircraft increased. By the time the position had been established the aircraft could be a long way from the position found. Aircraft tended to favour Decca Navigator and Loran for position-fixing and these were mainly available where the aircraft needed greater accuracy when approaching land and on the more popular oceanic routes.

As part of its aim to expand its portfolio of navigation offerings, the Decca Navigator Company developed the MNS 2000 which as far as is known was the only navigation receiver to offer the possibility of fixing the position from every system available at the time – around 1985. It could be switched to Decca Navigator, Loran C, Omega and the one satellite system available at that time, the Transit Satellite system. When we set out to make our attempt on the out-and-out Atlantic record in *Virgin Atlantic Challenger II*, a pair of these MNS 2000 receivers was fitted. We had two, partly as an insurance against failure and partly to enable position comparisons. In the event one failed anyway, so as the navigator I was left with just one but I realized that having two was not a good idea. If they show different readings, which one can you trust? We should have had three on board so you can have a voting system and go with the majority: two against one. Another problem with the MNS 2000 was that you had to switch off the system you were using in order to switch to another source of navigation information. So coming in from the Atlantic to make a landfall in the UK, I had to shut down the Loran C which was reaching the limits of its coverage and the accuracy was poor and try to establish contact with the Decca system which was also at the limit of its coverage.

This was when I discovered the Achilles' heel of the Decca Navigator system. In order to get it up and running you need a reasonably accurate position for the system to acquire and interpret the signals. In normal use this would be the position when the system was switched on in harbour and it would keep working until the next port of call. However, if the power supplies went down or the Decca failed, getting it up and running again could require considerable effort. It was much the same when coming in from seaward and trying to make contact with the Decca system so you could get its accurate position-fixing. Your position as you started to make landfall might only be accurate to perhaps 5 miles so it could take some time to get a good fix from the Decca. When you are travelling at 50 knots in rough seas it can become even harder and it took me more than half an hour to get accurate positions from the Decca as we were making the final run in to the Bishop Rock Lighthouse. Even then it went down again when we were just 20 miles out when a violent thunderstorm interfered with the signals. So Decca was a great and accurate navigation system, but as with most navigation you had to treat it with caution and not rely on it 100 per cent.

When radar started to enter into general use for shipping in the 1950s one of its important uses was to fix the position. Although the primary use of radar was collision avoidance, it could be used to fix the position either using radar ranges or radar bearings or a combination of both. To use radar in this way it was important to positively identify a feature that was showing on the radar display and reference it to the feature on the chart. You have to remember that radar was presenting a horizontal view of the land that was not always compatible with what the chart might show. With just one such feature identified such as a significant headland, then a range and bearing from the radar could be used to fix the position. Radar bearings tended to be less accurate because the ship's heading had to be applied if the radar was in relative mode and on smaller craft the heading might be swinging about considerably. Radar ranges could be taken accurately whatever the ship's heading and this was the preferred method of fixing the position by radar. Three such radar ranges could provide a position with considerable accuracy so that a pair of compasses started to replace the parallel rules as a means of plotting on charts.

One electronic aid to navigation that could help this radar-plotting was the introduction of Racon beacons. These beacons were mainly established on significant lighthouses and lightvessels and they produced a distinctive signal on the radar display when they were interrogated by the radar signal. This enabled the returns from these navigation aids to be clearly identified on the radar display so that you could use bearings and ranges from these targets to fix the position of the vessel. Racon beacons were particularly useful in crowded waters where there were many ship targets on the display.

So by the 1980s electronics were taking over much of the role of traditional navigation systems, but none of them were offering the 100 per cent accuracy and reliability that navigators crave. It was a transition period and for many navigators it was a big learning curve with many problems along the way. This was when space systems were starting to make an impact.

Chapter Eleven

Passage-Planning and Weather

Today it is a legal obligation for navigators to carry out passage-planning before the commencement of a voyage; probably the first time that any form of navigation has been made compulsory. The legislation demands that a whole passage is planned in detail before the commencement of the voyage and the level of detail demanded is from the berth of departure to when the ship is tied up alongside at the end of the voyage. Passage-planning is something that navigators have been doing probably right from the time that man first ventured out onto the water, although much of the passage-planning has been done mentally, working out in your head how you will get from A to B without actually writing anything down on paper.

Aircraft do their own form of passage-planning but here they are working in three dimensions and the planning now tends to be dictated from control centres rather than the pilot working out where he wants to go and finding the best route. Aircraft tend to follow a dictated path along the airways, although there is a degree of freedom in uncontrolled air space usually at lower levels and outside the main airways but whether controlled by the pilot or by the air traffic control centres there has to be passage-planning before departure.

Right from the early days when man first took to the water, probably using craft to cross a river, there would be passage-planning. The departure point would be on one riverbank and arrival would be on the other side which would be in sight, but the question about how to make the journey had to be considered. Were there currents in the river or perhaps the tide coming in or out? Was there a wind blowing that might be used to help make progress? This was all passage-planning and at this stage there was probably little consideration given to what action to take if things went wrong. Part of modern passage-planning is to have a back-up plan and to build in safety margins so that you have a plan if things do not work out as planned in the primary passage plan.

In those very early days of navigation there was every chance that things would go wrong with the initial plan. Unknown currents could take a craft downstream so that the planned landing-place was not possible. The weather would not have much effect on a short crossing, but it seems quite likely that the first craft to venture out to sea did so when they were swept out rather than as a planned manoeuvre. It is hard to picture what it must have been like when early man first ventured onto the water, but it seems likely that navigation was by instinct rather than by following a planned route. There seems little doubt that the route of many early voyages was determined by the prevailing weather rather than by design and throughout history weather has played a significant part in voyaging, both at sea and in the air. We will look at the role of weather on navigation later in this chapter, but in the early days of navigation it would be the wind that would have determined the direction of travel rather than the desire to reach a certain destination. It does appear that there was not the pressure of time to complete a voyage that we see today and so a voyage might be delayed for days or even weeks until the winds became favourable. However, to try to understand early navigation we must look at the motivation for travel and for taking to the waters.

Travel on land might be to forage for food and other supplies and as we have seen throughout history, to dominate other tribes and their possessions and much the same motive would dominate travel at sea. Trade was also an important factor and once seamen developed the means to travel relatively safely on the water, history suggests that it was trade and war that dominated the motives for travel and both of these required a degree of passage-planning to ensure arrival at the destination. It would also appear that fishing was an activity of early navigators, but for that the challenge might have been more in finding their way home with the catch rather than heading out to a destination. These activities were probably preceded by simple exploration, following man's natural inquisitiveness to explore into unknown territory. For exploration, passage-planning is not a lot of help because you don't know where you are going but it would have formed the basis for future voyages with the development of early charts which may have been simple memory charts or perhaps details written down in some form. If we look at the early Polynesian voyages around the Pacific that were studied and copied by that great navigator David Lewis, he cites simple curiosity as one of the motives for these voyages, although fishing and trade were other possibilities. It should be remembered that in the area in which these navigators operated the weather conditions were more consistent and predictable than in other regions.

So for early voyages a form of passage-planning was developed and after the early exploration there would have been a destination to head for. Factors such as the wind direction were vitally important for any passage on the water when the vessel was under sail and the wind direction would dictate the possible direction of travel that would be restricted to an arc of approximately 180° with the wind astern. This was a severe limitation on sailing craft, although as far as trading craft were concerned there was not the pressure of time. It is not surprising to find that when it came to more warlike ventures, craft were propelled by oars or paddles which within reason would have allowed them to proceed in any desired direction. Propulsion by oars or paddles required a considerable crew to man them, but on warlike ventures such a crew could also have provided the army when the destination was reached. Planning the passage to the destination would have been much more straightforward under oars, but without a compass it still left the question of direction a bit vague. The captain would have known where he wanted to go, but his arrival at a destination might have been a bit less reliable without the navigation tools we have today.

In these early days of navigation the weather was the big unknown. Even under oars making headway into a head sea could have been challenging and under sail it was impossible. With early navigation taking place largely in the Mediterranean, Red Sea and the Indian Ocean the winds are a lot more predictable and here you can find seasonal wind where the winds blow largely from the same direction either according to the seasons or even on a daily basis which helps to make the planning of a passage a lot easier and more predictable, but there was still a big element of uncertainty for a passage that might last more than twenty-four hours. As the early navigators started to venture into more northern waters this unpredictability would grow and the depressions that sweep in from the Atlantic would have made any attempt at weather forecasting beyond twenty-four hours very unreliable. Given the extensive availability of today's longer-term weather forecasts, it is hard to visualize making a passage at sea with such a high level of uncertainty.

As navigators ventured out onto the oceans they had to be prepared to meet a wide variety of weather conditions and without enough warning of changes in the weather to vary the course to any significant degree. Even as late as the 1950s, forecasting extreme conditions still had a large level of uncertainty which was why when I was on a ship approaching the Caribbean we encountered a hurricane with not enough warning to escape its clutches. Today hurricanes are tracked every inch of their way to give as much warning as possible and certainly enough for a ship to take avoiding action. Back in the 1950s passage-planning was also in its infancy and when we wanted to make a passage from port to port we simply drew a line on the chart and followed that to the best of our ability according to the prevailing conditions.

Wind the clock back 1,000 years and you can see how much uncertainty there was in planning any voyage. The charts in use would have a high degree of uncertainty and while they might depict a coastline, there was no guarantee that it was accurate. The compasses used to follow a course had a poor level of accuracy, if indeed they would work at all, and position-fixing was very inaccurate, perhaps at best fixing the position in the ocean with a latitude accuracy of 3° or 4° and a longitude accuracy that was largely determined by guesswork or dead reckoning which was far from accurate. It is not surprising then to find that the level of attrition was high and some figures suggest that no more than 50 per cent of ships setting out on an ocean voyage returned safe and sound. The risks were high with unpredicted storms being a major cause of shipwreck followed by grounding when making a landfall or on uncharted shoals or rocks. Without radio communications the cause of the loss of a ship would probably never be known, with few survivors living to tell the tale. Even across relatively well-travelled routes such as across the North Atlantic or to the Caribbean, the risks were still high.

Picture the situation of a ship about to leave port with a cargo and/or passengers on board. Apart from the risks that were inherent in the state of repair of the ship and its equipment, the captain would have very little information about what lay ahead. His immediate concern in choosing when to depart would be fair winds for leaving the harbour so that he could navigate through the harbour approach channels. The time required for this part of the passage could be quite short in a harbour such as Plymouth where the passage to the sea is compact, but it could be a major challenge in a port such as London where there are long and winding channels before the open sea is reached. This might entail anchoring if the wind changed or when the tide turned and this part of the passage plan would be subject to short-term change as the prevailing conditions altered. The tides might be predictable but any weather forecast would probably be developed by the captain from his personal experience of the weather and so might only be valid for perhaps twelve or at best twenty-four hours ahead. Beyond that time the course of action and the passage plan would depend almost entirely on the weather and in particular on the wind direction that would enable him to head down channel and out onto the open sea. When the wind was adverse there were anchorages that could be used until a favourable wind arrived, and it could easily take a week before the ship entered the Western Approaches and could go into ocean-sailing mode where the ship would sail in the optimum direction that was allowable by the wind direction. So for hundreds of years the passage-planning for ships tended to be made up as the ship went along and would rarely be planned for more than twenty-four hours ahead except in some sea areas where the winds were consistent such as in the trade wind zones. With hindsight it is easy to see why these areas were so-named and why they were much sought-after by navigators looking to make a good passage even if it meant sailing more miles, a significant factor in passage-planning.

The introduction of good compasses and logs helped navigators and an experienced captain would know the general wind and ocean current patterns of the seas. This would enable his general passage-planning to have some

Plotting the route is still an essential part of navigation, but these days it is done on electronic systems.

order so that maximum advantage could be taken of these. For a ship that was probably not capable of sailing at more than 5 knots a favourable ocean current of 1 or 2 knots was a major benefit, particularly as many of these ocean surface currents were generated by winds, so there would be the double benefit of winds and current to help the ship along. Columbus knew something about these wind and current patterns when he followed the trade winds out from Europe to cross the Atlantic and then headed north before heading back across the Atlantic to pick up the northerly favourable winds and currents for the eastbound journey.

By the eighteenth century the focus of trade had moved from the Caribbean to North America and major trade routes were established across the northern part of the Atlantic. This was a much more challenging route for navigators as there were no favourable winds and currents for the westbound voyage, but the Gulf Stream would give a good push for the journey back to Europe. By heading on a route further north it would be beneficial to follow a Great Circle route across the Atlantic, but this would take a vessel further north towards Newfoundland and up among the icebergs so compromise routes were developed with each captain following his own favoured courses. Even so, the North Atlantic was a challenging area for navigators with extensive shoals and low-lying land for making a landfall on the North American coastline in addition to the fog and icebergs along this coast. As you can imagine, casualties were high and as steamships started to replace sailing ships there was an increasing risk of collision to add to the navigators' woes.

Non-mandatory shipping lanes on the Atlantic were established in 1854 following the collision between the US passenger liner *Arctic* and the French liner *Vesta* that resulted in the loss of more than 300 lives. These shipping lanes were proposed by the shipping companies rather than by safety authorities, although a number of international conferences were held to discuss the idea of shipping lanes in various parts of the world. This voluntary system on the Atlantic was the first attempt to establish shipping lanes for vessels travelling in opposite directions and was the forerunner of the mandatory shipping lanes that now exist in many busy shipping channels around the world. The westbound lane was further north to avoid the Gulf Stream and the eastbound lane was designed to take maximum advantage of this major current. These eastbound lanes roughly followed the 42° line and when records were starting to be set by the liners for the fastest to cross the Atlantic, the liners were supposed to follow these recommended routes.

It was at about this time that an officer from the US navy published his book *Sailing Directions*. This followed extensive research into the log books and charts of thousands of both sailing and steamships which Lieutenant Maury found in the archives of the US navy when an accident at the age of 33 cut short his sea-going career. He started work analysing these log books and charts in 1842, extracting information, and after five years of collating the information from them he was able to develop a picture of the winds and currents in the Atlantic. This was published as the *Wind and Current Chart of the North Atlantic* and represents the first attempt at providing captains with a definitive study of the ocean that could help to significantly optimize ocean voyages. The book became a sort of bible for navigators operating in Atlantic waters and is credited with transforming the understanding of Atlantic winds and currents. The book also marked a turning-point in methods of passage-planning and set the pattern for future planning, although the term passage-planning had not yet been developed at that stage.

Maury pointed the way to a future in which navigators could plan their voyages to take maximum advantage of the prevailing winds and currents, but there was still one important element missing. While Maury's charts and book had shown the winds that might be expected, this was only an estimate of the prevailing winds and there was no actual real-time information about the winds and the weather. Maury's charts might work reasonably well in the areas of the trade winds where the winds were fairly consistent, but further north in the Atlantic and the Pacific the weather tended to be governed by the flow of the low-pressure areas that swept from west to east. The winds here were prone to short-term changes in both strength and direction which

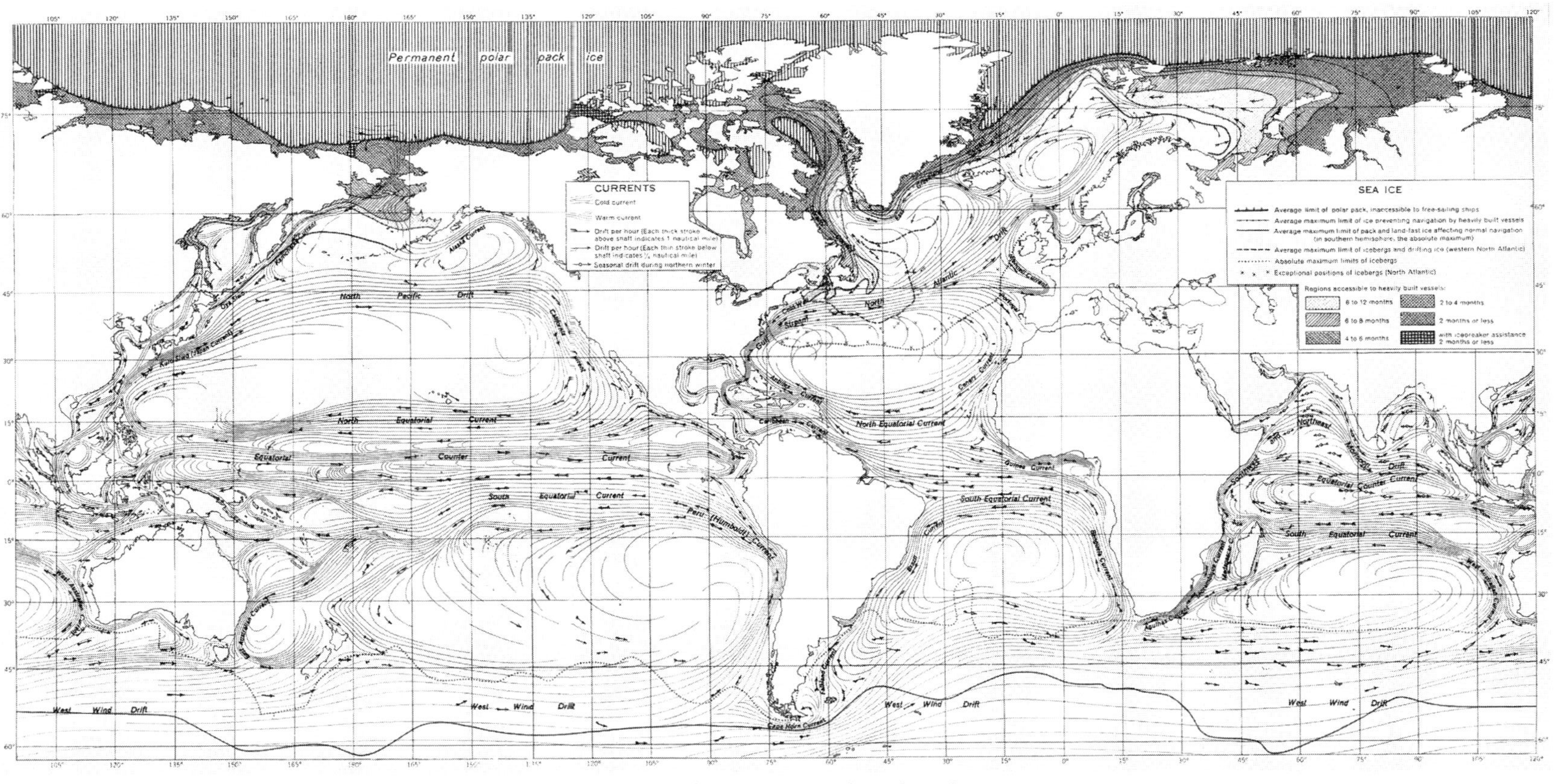

A chart of the circulation of ocean currents; a significant aid to progress in the sailing ship era.

made passage-planning in the longer term difficult and while in the short term an experienced navigator might be able to read the message from the clouds and anticipate short-term changes, progress was largely at the mercy of the changeable wind and weather and therefore difficult to anticipate.

With the advent of steamships progress was less at the mercy of the winds, but for sailing ships everything depended on the strength and direction of the wind. The development of the barometer had provided navigators with a possible way of anticipating changes in wind direction and strength, but in the eighteenth century the understanding of the weather and what caused changes was still fairly basic. In areas where the weather was largely governed by low-pressure areas the barometer readings would show whether a ship was moving into the depression or out of it and there was the understanding that a rising barometer reading tended to show that the weather might be improving and that the wind would probably be veering in a clockwise direction. It was the changes in barometer readings that were more important than the actual readings themselves and if the change was rapid then the wind strength was likely to be higher, but any interpretation of the barometer readings was only reliable for a maximum of twenty-four hours ahead so any long-term planning was not possible other than by using experience.

It was the barometer that started the understanding of the weather and allowed navigators to be able to predict conditions at least for some time ahead rather than relying just on looking at the clouds and relating what you saw there to what might lie ahead. One of the main uses of the barometer was found in giving captains and navigators some sort of warning when it wasn't a good idea to head to sea. A rapidly-falling barometer was a fairly sure indicator that there were strong winds ahead so staying in harbour was probably the best idea. The traditional mercury barometer was quite an expensive piece of equipment that was mainly beyond the means of most captains and owners, and it was not the easiest piece of equipment to accommodate on board a moving ship where it had to be mounted in gimbals to keep it upright. However, they were often found in ports and harbours on public view so that anyone preparing to head out to sea could see the behaviour of the barometer before deciding to do so, so the barometer was probably the first instrument that was used, at least for short-term passage-planning.

The development of the aneroid barometer changed that and here was an instrument that was both compact and relatively cheap that could be carried on board ships and even vessels such as fishing boats. It was Admiral Fitzroy in Britain who was responsible for developing the use of barometers as a means of informing seamen of what the weather might be doing for perhaps twenty-four hours ahead, which was a significant development when you think that it would give time for coastal shipping to head for shelter and thus

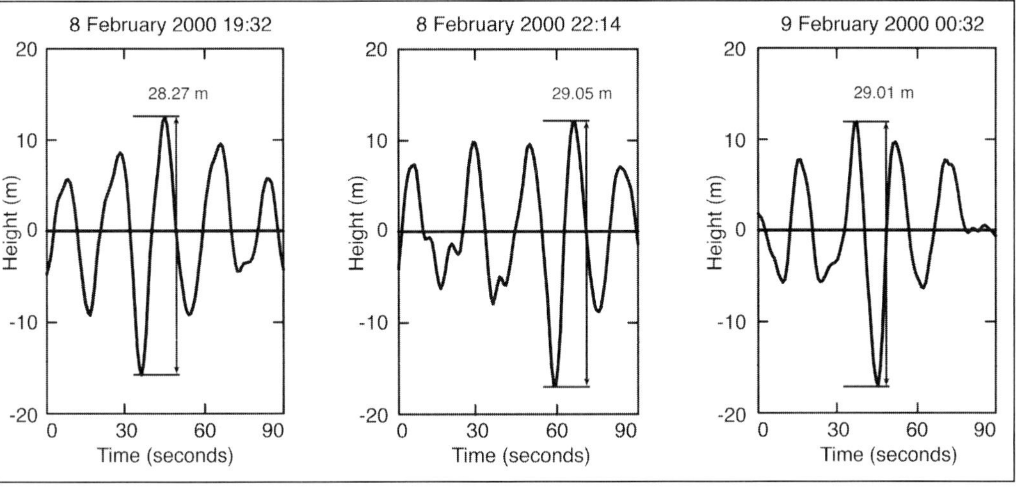

Wave-recorder trace of the largest wave ever recorded at more than 29 metres high; a real hazard to shipping.

reduce the risks. It was in the nineteenth century that a deeper understanding of the weather was being developed, and how the barometric pressure and the air flowing from areas of high pressure to areas of low pressure were being understood and used for early forecasting. Combined with a greater understanding of how distinctive cloud patterns could also give indications of the weather that was to come, this enabled navigators to navigate with a degree of forward planning. What was still lacking with weather forecasting was a way to generate a more global picture of the weather over an area of land or sea. For this a means of communication was needed so that barometric pressures and current weather could be transmitted for correlation at a central location so that a broader picture of the developing weather could be generated.

The first attempts to do this were around the turn of the twentieth century when the telegraph was invented. This allowed signals to be transmitted over land lines and was the first means of being able to transmit messages over distances. If readings such as the barometer, temperature, wind direction and strength taken at one time could be correlated into one 'weather map' then it might be easier to predict what lay ahead in terms of weather conditions. These early attempts at synoptic forecasting were only for land areas because that was where the readings were taken and they had communication links, but they could provide warnings for shipping along a coastline. It was a step in the right direction, but the ideal was for ships out at sea to be able to receive weather warnings and that had to wait until the development of radio links that would allow shipping to communicate, which took place around 1910. The most high-profile use of this radio telegraphy was the warning about icebergs sent out to the RMS *Titanic* before she hit one. Icebergs are a danger to navigation and so have to be taken into account when passage-planning.

A Force 12 storm in the North Atlantic. (*Author*)

While it now became possible to send messages to ships at sea, it was still a long way from developing reliable weather forecasts for shipping. Obtaining the weather readings from ships at sea was still in its infancy and only a few passenger ships had the luxury of radio communications. So getting enough readings to develop a synoptic chart of the sea areas was still a vague science and like the forecasts on land the science was still developing with forecasts mainly only extending to twenty-four hours ahead. It would be many years before ships could receive reliable weather forecasts that could be used as the basis of passage-planning and most of these early forecasts were rather weather warnings rather than actual forecasts. Once the concept of developing synoptic charts for the weather had been developed there was a desperate need to get weather readings from ships at sea. Otherwise there were big blanks in the charts that an imaginative meteorologist might be able to fill but left the quality of weather forecasts for ships at sea sadly lacking and so trying to plan a passage to take advantage of fine weather or to avoid bad areas was still a challenge.

The pressures of war helped to develop not only communications but also the quality of weather information and naval ships at sea were encouraged to send back weather information so that the quality of forecasting could be improved. Following the Second World War when these naval weather submissions were greatly reduced there was international agreement to station weather ships in the Atlantic with the main purpose of obtaining good-quality weather information from mid-Atlantic. With the main weather patterns flowing from west to east on the Atlantic, these mid-Atlantic weather reports led to a considerable improvement in the weather forecasting over the land masses of Europe. However, the forecasts for shipping were still the poor relation and so passage-planning still tended to be limited to following the recommended routes rather than trying to take advantage of possible good weather conditions.

By this time steam and motor had taken over from sail and so there was a reduced requirement to try to follow the favourable winds across the oceans. The passenger liners were in decline with competition from aircraft and so the requirement for trying to optimize the passage was not high, although being able to avoid storms was always a requirement. Such avoidance could probably be achieved with twenty-four-hour forecasts which were the norm at this time and a ship might make short-term deviations in order to avoid the worst of a storm. It was in the 1960s that small sailing boats started to sail the Atlantic and the famous single-handed transatlantic race was introduced. The disparity of possible routes for this race is shown by one entrant taking a route well north to follow the Great Circle as far as possible to take the shortest distance. Another took a southerly route in the hope of getting more favourable winds and to avoid the mainly easterly flow of winds and currents, while the third took the middle route as a compromise. This does demonstrate the conflicting views about passage-planning in respect of the weather and currents and even on ships it was left largely to the navigator's preference and instinct rather than to any careful planning.

Aircraft were increasingly crossing the Atlantic and it was probably demand for accurate forecasts for these aircraft that led to a significant improvement in the quality of weather forecasts. The need to know where the jet stream was located and its height was vital to an aircraft crossing the oceans and this demanded improved forecasts that could extend for two or three days ahead. For shipping this opened up the possibility of optimizing the route that could be taken and the science of passage-planning was born. Storms could be forecast and tracked ahead and shipping could be routed to avoid them. This was the safety aspect of passage-planning, but it was realized that there could be significant savings in costs if the route could be optimized to shorten the time at sea with savings in both time and fuel. Ship-owners were prepared to pay for information to make these savings and initially some meteorological offices offered a routing service to shipping and then later private companies were set up to offer this commercial service. Much the same was offered to aircraft, but here the routes taken tended to be dictated by air traffic control as well as expediency.

Even with modern electronic navigation systems, fog can still create a hazard for shipping.

The passage-planning undertaken by specialist private companies might be used by ships that were carrying sensitive cargoes where the rolling and pitching of the ships had to be minimized. This was a new type of passage-planning in which information about the way the ship behaved in waves had to be taken into account in the calculations. This meant that the science of wave forecasting had to be developed to a much more refined degree. There are many factors that can affect both wave size and wave direction and in most seas there can be a combination of wave trains to be taken into account as well as the prevailing wind strength and direction and any legacy swells. It is a complex area of forecasting that demands both accurate forecasts for several days ahead as well as knowledge of both waves and currents. Also coming into this equation is the phenomena of rogue waves that ships want to avoid because of their potentially destructive power.

This type of active passage-planning changed the face of navigation. For the first time navigators were being routed from the shore rather than making their own decisions on board. Of course, the final decision about the route to be taken was always with the captain of the ship, but the quality of the advice coming from the shore was hard to ignore. Initially this routing advice was used to avoid areas of adverse weather that could slow ships down and it might be the case that a longer route might be quicker because of the higher

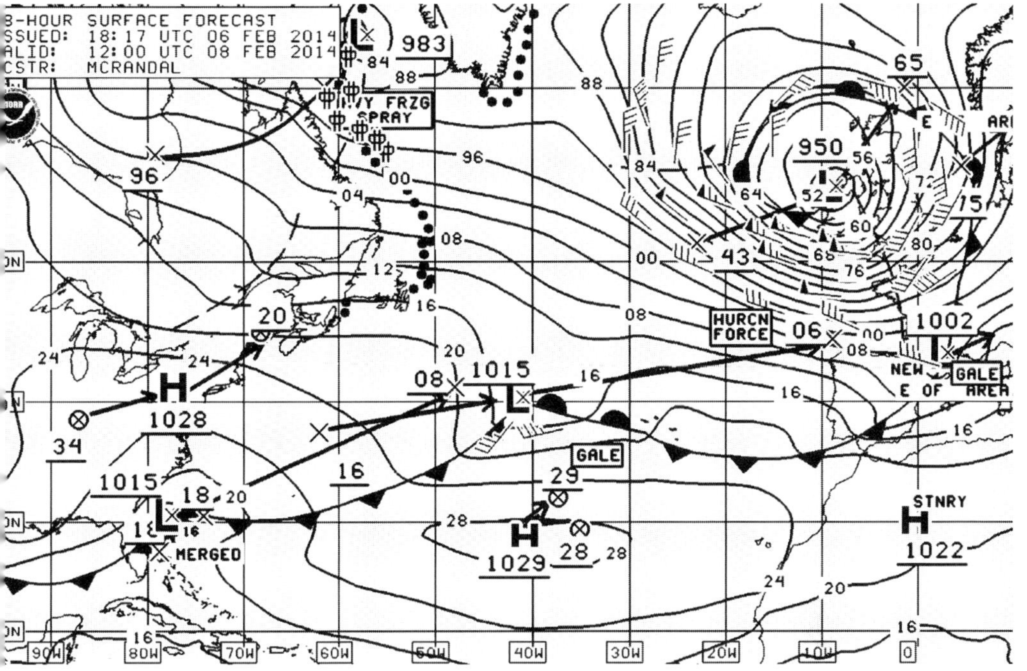

Weather forecasts are an essential part of navigation and these are now readily available to ships and aircraft en route.

speeds that could be maintained. Later it was realized that ships could also be guided to follow the most economic route, taking the one that would use the minimum of fuel. Another alternative, perhaps combined with fuel-saving, was to take a route and to maintain a speed that would ensure arrival at the vessel's berth at a specific time. As shipping became more and more cost-conscious and delays involving large and expensive ships could have a high cost, this type of time-sensitive routing was used extensively, both to ensure a punctual arrival and also to avoid arriving early and having to wait. It was also used by cruise ships where the need to maintain a tight schedule was paramount to their operation. This type of passage-planning required the planners to have a detailed knowledge of the ship's operating parameters such as the speed that could be maintained in different sea conditions and the fuel consumption in these differing conditions.

Avoidance of storms was also a requirement for this type of passage-planning, particularly as many modern ships are no longer fully equipped to survive a major storm. They could probably fight their way through but at the risk of incurring damage. The loss of containers overboard from container ships is one of the risks of encountering a storm. The large cruise liner *Anthem of the Seas* sailed from New York bound for Bermuda when she encountered the remnants of a hurricane and suffered some damage, demonstrating that weather routing is not infallible, or perhaps it was the pressure to maintain schedules that prompted the captain to make the decision to sail into the oncoming storm. The pressures on the decision-makers can be very high in situations like this when delays can be very costly and the design of the ship suggests that it is not designed to cope with extreme weather.

Hurricanes and typhoons tend to be well tracked these days allowing shipping to avoid them, but this is quite recent. We had a radio warning about that hurricane we encountered in the 1950s in the Caribbean, but these storms were not being accurately tracked and we thought we were clear of its path. For centuries seamen had been aware of the dangers of hurricanes and cyclones and the warning signs in the sky of an approaching storm were drilled into the minds of navigators, as were the tactics to avoid the worst of the storm if the ship tangled with it. A hurricane is a severe test of the ship and its crew and we came out unscathed from our encounter apart from some damage to the ship, but only recently the large cargo ship *El Faro* heading from Florida to Puerto Rico was lost when it encountered a hurricane with the investigation suggesting that the captain was largely responsible for not taking adequate avoiding action.

Perhaps more concerning for shipping is the existence of rogue waves. Such waves, which can be several times larger than the normal waves surrounding them, are almost always associated with storm conditions so by avoiding the storm you avoid the rogue waves. However, in areas like the North Atlantic and North Pacific and in the Southern Ocean the storms can be so extensive

Icebergs are a navigation hazard in both northern and southern waters, but today their positions are well-tracked.

A rogue wave photographed by the author north of Iceland.

that it is not always possible to avoid them completely by diverting. There are various theories about how rogue waves are formed, but the main reasons are two or more wave trains emanating from a storm that are crossing each other and the combined crests of the wave trains produce a wave that can be considerably higher than the others. Another possibility is that waves of different height travel at different speeds so a larger wave is faster than a lower wave. As storms increase in ferocity they will generate bigger waves and these bigger waves are overtaking the waves generated earlier because they are faster. When wave crests combine, the resulting wave is the combined height of the two or more waves, creating a monster. We are starting to understand rogue waves and being able to predict where they might occur and satellite images are helping to detect them, but they are a transient event. Understanding and predicting rogue waves is far from being an exact science and so they can present a considerable challenge for navigators even with the resources of the modern weather routers and many modern ships are not designed to cope with such an encounter.

An early example of weather routing came when long-distance sailing races started. As we have seen, a vessel under sail can be limited in the direction it can travel and over a long distance such as trans-ocean trying to find the optimum route can be challenging when a sailing boat is trying to take the shortest time. The passage-planning is a case of trying to optimize the route, the speed of sailing and to be in the right position along the route to take maximum advantage of wind and weather conditions in the days ahead. The skipper might have access to only limited information on board and the concept of having experts on shore with access to the latest weather information for perhaps days ahead and with full information about the sailing qualities of the yacht made a lot of sense. They could advise the optimum course to steer and then hopefully also try to position the yacht so that it could take maximum advantage of the changing conditions that might lie three days or more down the route.

It sounds like a case for a computer to solve and optimize the many parameters that might be involved and indeed computer programmes were developed just for this. These programmes would have access to the sailing potential of the yacht showing the expected performance in different wind strengths and different headings and this would be combined with wind forecasts for several days ahead. The computer would then work out the optimum route to follow in order to maximize the performance. The route would be constantly evolving as the weather forecasts were updated and the conditions changed, but whether the computer was better at making this assessment than the human was an open question. The human was in a better position to make more subtle allowances for factors such as the way in which the sea conditions might affect the performance and the speed difference between day and night sailing. This is a challenging area of passage-planning but the requirements are similar in many ways to those of shipping where the quest might not be for the fastest speed but for the optimum fuel savings.

We were faced with a different problem more than thirty years ago when trying to set a new fastest time across the Atlantic in *Virgin Atlantic Challenger*. My job as navigator was to find the optimum time to leave New York in order to carry the best sea conditions across 3,000 miles of the Atlantic. Our 75ft boat was very sensitive to the sea conditions and high speeds of around 50 knots could only be maintained when the seas were slight. Trying to find slight sea conditions over the whole of the Atlantic was challenging, but in reality we only needed these conditions where we estimated the boat would be at any one time. It could be rougher ahead or astern of our predicted position as along as it was calmer where we were going to be. This was a new challenge for weather forecasting and an extra challenge was found in trying to translate wind strengths into sea conditions because that was what really mattered to us. To demonstrate how narrow the weather margins could be, it was after we were delayed for ten hours when refuelling on the Grand Banks of Newfoundland. With that delay the record looked to be out of sight and the logical thing was for us to give up and turn back to land, but the forecast suggested that there was a major storm coming up behind us that would have endangered our survival. The only solution was to head out into the Atlantic and outrun the storm which we did and luck was on our side as by keeping going we then broke the record by just two hours. This was a case of the navigator negotiating with the weather, which is a whole new approach.

When I was doing the weather routing for *Destriero*, the 67-metre vessel built in Italy to break the Atlantic record, the challenge was slightly different. The designer stipulated that this 65-knot vessel could only run at full speed in waves less than 6ft high. Now a 6ft wave might be considered to be close to a calm out in the wilds of the Atlantic and to try to find those conditions over the 3,000-mile route looked impossible. Wave heights are notoriously difficult to forecast, but then I hit on an idea that meant I did not have to actually forecast the wave height in the ocean; that judgement could be left to those on board who could see in real time what the conditions were and adjust the route accordingly. My plan was to find a weather pattern where there was a fairly mild low-pressure area covering much of the North Atlantic. By setting a course around the bottom of this low-pressure area, the vessel could keep heading as far north as was comfortable until the wave height started to be close to the 6ft limit. Then she could adjust the course in a more easterly direction that would take her away from the centre of the low pressure and into better conditions. So by feeling her way across the Atlantic in a series of 'steps' she could follow the optimum course as close to the short Great Circle route as possible, while at the same time keeping the wave height within the

The returns from wave targets cause clutter on this radar display.

6ft limit. The plan worked well until the forecast showed a secondary depression forming over Spain and heading rapidly north to join its big brother in the north. The door for *Destriero* was closing rapidly and she would have to slow down if she could not get through the gap between the two low-pressure areas. In the event she just made it through the gap before the wave height started to increase and she went on to set a new record across the Atlantic, averaging 53 knots for the 3,000-mile route, a record that will be hard to beat.

When these events were taking place we did not have the luxury of computers and detailed weather forecasts for several days ahead so the human input into passage-planning and experience was still vitally important. Over the years since the inception of navigation at sea it has been experience that has largely dictated the actions of the navigator in trying to optimize the route. This optimization might only be based on what might happen just hours ahead but gradually, as knowledge and experience have improved, as charts have become more accurate and it has been possible to fix the position with accuracy, the ability of the navigator to plan a route to a destination has increased dramatically. However, there are still unknowns out there and although weather forecasting has moved on from being 'intelligent guess-work' to much more detailed accuracy, there are still unknowns out there such as tropical revolving storms and rogue waves. The weather is still the one thing that cannot be relied on by the navigator and this reflects why it is still important to include margins for safety.

Chapter Twelve

Collision Avoidance

We have seen how over the years there has been an improvement in plotting positions and knowing where ships are and this has allowed navigation to become a lot more precise. By contrast the risk of ships colliding with each other has risen from virtually nil in the early days of navigation up to a considerable risk in the present environment. Collision avoidance is now a major factor in modern navigation, despite the introduction of new technology largely aimed at preventing this.

In the days of sails there were very few recorded collisions at sea, although quite a few in harbours. At sea ships were generally few and far between and so the risk of collision was small. There were no radio communications and if a ship was in trouble the chances of anyone coming to the rescue were dependent purely on chance. Communication was by line of sight only so a ship coming over the horizon when you were sinking was purely a matter of chance. Indeed, that ship might well have been the enemy more intent on sinking or capturing you rather than coming to the rescue. The risk of collision in these circumstances was therefore small and even if two ships did collide, the speed involved in any encounter was likely to be limited and so the damage involved would be minimal. There did not seem to be any need to have any formal rules of engagement, should two ships come close to each other, about who should alter course and when and how. It does seem that some ships carried a form of lighting at night to give warning of their presence, but this was probably only in crowded waters and a reluctance to display lights at night might have been to avoid disclosing the presence of the ship to the enemy or to pirates.

Collisions in harbour were probably much more frequent because the sailing ships of most eras did not have auxiliary engines to help them manoeuvre in harbour and so they were not very controllable. Smaller ships had the option of using oars to help make headway in the desired direction in harbour but manoeuvring would largely be by using sails when possible combined with ropes and anchors so there would have been quite a high risk of ships bumping into one another, but again it would all happen at low speeds so that damage would be minimal and the risk was accepted as one of the perils of harbour manoeuvring. These collisions come within the realms of pilotage which tended to be a specialized branch of navigation with pilots skilled in both local knowledge and ship-handling skills.

We start to see records of collisions at sea not long after sails were being replaced by steam engines for propulsion. This not only increased the potential speed of any such encounter but it was combined with ships having poor manoeuvrability so that in poor visibility by the time a ship sighted another one bearing down on it there would be little time for any avoidance tactics. During the sailing ship era various nations had introduced 'conventions' for the actions that ships should take in the event of a possible collision situation such as ships running downwind giving way to ships that were close-hauled, i.e. sailing close to the wind, because those heading downwind had more freedom of action about the courses they could adopt. These 'conventions' were established mainly on a national basis and even then they were not compulsory but based on what might be termed good seamanship practice. It was recognized that there had to be some form of cohesive collision avoidance actions in a situation where each ship should have some idea of what the other might do. Two pedestrians meeting head-on on the pavement might not know which way to go to avoid bumping into one another, but there the consequences of a collision would not normally be serious and would cause more irritation rather than harm. Ships do not collide with the same sort of impunity and both shipowners and insurance companies were keen to see some sort of code that would bring order and predictability into a potential collision situation.

Prior to the development of a single set of international rules and practices, there existed separate practices and various conventions and informal procedures in different parts of the world, as advanced by various maritime nations. As a result, there were inconsistencies and even contradictions that gave rise to unintended collisions. Vessel navigation lights for operating in darkness as well as the navigation marks in channels were also not standardized, giving rise to dangerous confusion and ambiguity between vessels at risk of colliding.

With the advent of steam-powered ships in the mid-nineteenth century, conventions for sailing vessel navigation had to be supplemented with conventions for power-driven vessel navigation. Sailing vessels are limited as to their manoeuvrability in that they cannot sail directly to windward or into the eye of the wind and cannot be readily navigated in the absence of wind. On the other hand, steamships can manoeuvre in all 360 degrees of direction and can be manoeuvred irrespective of the presence or absence of wind.

In 1840 in London, Trinity House, the lighthouse authority in the UK, drew up a set of regulations that were enacted by Parliament in 1846. These Trinity House rules were included in the Steam Navigation Act and the

Admiralty regulations regarding lights for steamships were included in this statute in 1848. Note that these laws were aimed at steamships which were coming more and more into use at that time. In the US, Congress included lights for sailing vessels in their requirements for ships in US waters. Ten years later an Act of Parliament in Britain required coloured sidelights for sailing vessels and fog signals were required to be given by steam vessels on the ship's whistle and by sailing vessels on the foghorn or bell, while a separate but similar action was also taken in the United States, although British maritime law was also adopted in the United States which was probably the first attempt to get international agreement on maritime practice.

In 1863 a new set of rules that had been drawn up by the British Board of Trade in consultation with the French was initially aimed at bringing some sort of order to traffic in the English Channel. A year later these regulations had been adopted by more than thirty maritime countries in a major attempt at getting international agreement. In the US they were called 'Rules to Prevent Collisions at Sea'; the first time we see this phrase being used. In the UK they became known as 'The Rule of the Road'.

Individual countries introduced their own minor modifications to the rules so for navigators it was still a complicated situation to comply, but in 1889 the United States convened the first international maritime conference to consider standardization. The resulting rules were set out in 1890 but it took almost another ten years for them to be adopted, indicating at this early stage the slow laborious process of getting international agreement that we still see today. A series of International Conferences on Safety of Life at Sea (SOLAS)

A close encounter with a ship in fog.

followed, first in 1929 and then in 1948. This last conference was the first to consider the need for rules that covered the use of radar, but as usual it was another six years before these became effective.

The formation of the International Maritime Organization (IMO) in 1948 was a considerable step forward in preventing collisions at sea. Although it was several years before the IMO became effective, it was formed under the auspices of the United Nations and its brief covered not only rules to prevent collisions, but also safety at sea and oil pollution. Its first major work was the introduction of the International Rules for the Prevention of Collision at Sea which were adopted in 1972 but only entered into force in 1977. Prior to this there had been the Collision Regulations which I remember having to learn off by heart as a young apprentice when I went to sea in 1950. These 1977 rules also introduced the concept of Traffic Separation Schemes (TSS) to provide shipping with one-way systems in busy shipping areas and in port approaches. Although the IMO ratified these in 1977, the first one had already been introduced unilaterally by Britain and France in the Dover Straits following a series of major collisions in the shipping free-for-all that existed prior to that.

These rules, which became known as the Colregs, are a masterpiece of rule-writing that are constantly being interpreted by the courts as to the exact meaning when a collision occurs. Apart from prescribing the lights, shapes and fog signals that a ship or boat must exhibit or sound, they also prescribe the actions that ships and boats must take in order to avoid collision. In many respects they are common sense and based on long experience, but the clever writing of these rules comes in the way that they do not leave any loopholes. While they indicate which vessel might be the 'give way ship' and which might be the 'stand-on ship' in a variety of circumstances such as meeting end on, overtaking and ships crossing, they do not relieve the stand-on ship from taking action if the situation demands it. So a stand-on ship could still be held to blame if there was a collision that initially might have been set up by the give way ship not taking action or not taking enough action. Then the stand-on ship must also take action. Then there are the catch-all phrases such as requiring the exercise of good seamanship and sound navigation practices: 'Nothing in these Rules shall exonerate any vessel or the owner, master or crew thereof of the consequences of any neglect of any precaution which may be required by the ordinary practice of seamen or by the special circumstances of the case.'

That does not leave much room for negotiation when it comes to pointing the finger of blame following a collision. Many books have been written about the rules and how to conform to them and there have been many court cases that have resulted. I have been involved in some as an expert witness and it

A close encounter with a ferry; the sort of situation that is now a common part of modern navigation.

is fascinating to hear the legal arguments that can be presented in some of these cases.

I had my first collision at sea in the Dover Straits on my first voyage when I went to sea in 1950, heading out to sea from London Docks. Twenty-four hours out from London we had dropped the pilot off at Dungeness and were heading out into the Channel in thick fog when we hit this ship coming the other way. It was a bow-to-bow collision, just a glancing blow so no real damage done but it did demonstrate the vulnerability of ships operating in thick fog without radar. Radar was just starting to be introduced in those days after its development during the Second World War, but it was to be another four years before I went to sea with radar and even then it was a fairly basic display compared with what you see these days. The radar was so large that the works of the system had their own 'cabin' and you had to walk in to switch it on. Within ten years radar had transformed navigation and collision avoidance with radar ranges providing accurate position-fixing once they were transferred to the paper chart and ships showing up on radar even in the thickest of fogs to give some warning of what lay out ahead.

Most collisions between ships took place in the more crowded coastal waters and there was no doubt that the pinch points in the shipping lanes such as the Straits of Dover and the North Channel heading out from the Irish Sea became the focus of the authorities when it came to introducing the traffic separation schemes. Collisions out on ocean water were of course less frequent, but there were probably quite a lot that were not recorded either because ships sank without trace before the advent of radio or the damage to each ship was minimal. The introduction of the eastbound and westbound shipping lanes across the Atlantic already mentioned highlights the potential collision risk even in these open waters and this separation was probably responsible for a significant reduction in collisions in pre-radar days. On the Atlantic the collision risk increased significantly at both ends of the Atlantic route, around the Nantucket lightship/buoy on the American side and at the entrance to the English Channel on the European side. These were areas where ship numbers tend to be more concentrated heading in both directions and the prevalent fog that was a regular feature of the weather along the East Coast of North America added significantly to the collision risk.

Heading out of the Saint Lawrence River to cross the Atlantic in 1914 there was a major disaster almost rivalling the *Titanic* collision when the Canadian Pacific liner *Empress of Ireland* was in collision with a collier when fog came down. Like the *Titanic* the liner sank quickly, apparently due to portholes being left open and watertight doors not shut and around 1,000 of her passengers and crew drowned in the icy waters out of a total complement of 1,500. The collier was mainly held to blame for the collision.

The Nantucket lightship moored some 45 miles south of Nantucket Point was the focal point for ships heading in and out of New York and in 1933 was herself hit and sunk by an Atlantic liner, the *Olympic*, a sister ship of the *Titanic*. Three of the lightship's crew died in the collision which took place in thick fog. Lightships were being fitted with the new radio beacons that allowed ships to fix their position even in zero visibility and ships coming in from the Atlantic would home in on the beacon fitted to the lightship. The crews reported that they were constantly the victims of near-misses in fog as ships homed in on their beacon until that fateful night when the collision occurred.

Wartime brought its own problems when ships were running without lights at night. It was reminiscent of the past when ships did not want to be detected by the enemy. A cargo ship, the *Oregon*, running without lights, was a few miles south of the Nantucket lightship when it was struck by the US battleship *New Mexico*, also running without lights. Seventeen crew members of the *Oregon* were either killed or drowned and the remainder were rescued by a trawler fishing in the area.

The liner *Queen Mary* was another wartime collision victim when she collided with her cruiser escort north of Ireland. Shortly before the end of the war she was carrying around 10,000 US troops at close to 30 knots to outrun any U-boats and zigzagging to make her course unpredictable. Her escort the cruiser *Curacao* was running at 25 knots in a straight line and confusion on both vessels about who should give way made a collision inevitable with the *Queen Mary* slicing the elderly cruiser in half. Some 337 lives were lost on the *Curacao*, and the *Queen Mary* with a damaged bow maintained speed as ordered, to dock in the UK.

It was close to the Nantucket lightship that one of the major collisions in the Atlantic took place in 1956, this one between two Atlantic liners that were both equipped with probably the best radar equipment of the time and this led to the phrase 'radar-assisted collision'. The ability of radar as a collision-avoidance device had been questioned by some experts when it was introduced after the war. The year 1956 was still early days in the use of radar by

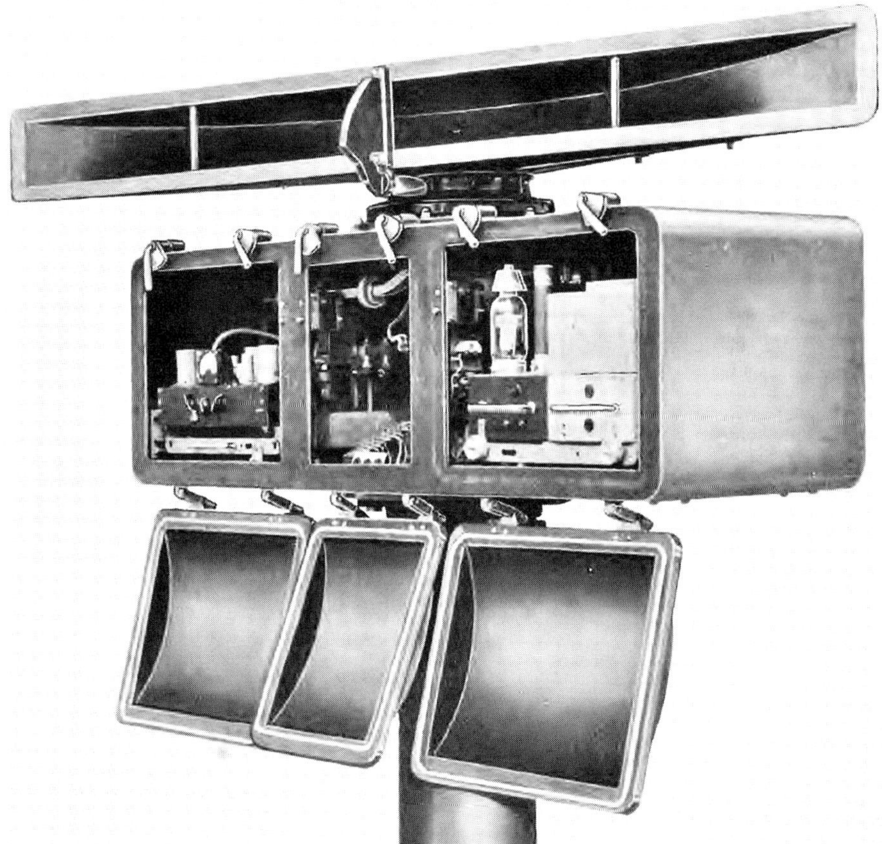

The antenna units of an early radar. (*Kelvin Hughes*)

A very early marine radar display. (*Kelvin Hughes*)

ships and the techniques for collision avoidance were still being developed. The problems stemmed from the fact that the radar display showed other ships in what is known as a relative display, i.e. showing them in relation to the ship rather than the true type of display which would show other ships as they would appear if plotted on a chart. When using a relative display navigators were encouraged to plot such a chart of other ships so that a proper assessment could be made of the collision risk, but these were early days with radar and the outward-bound Swedish liner *Stockholm* steered into the side of the inward-bound Italian liner *Andrea Doria* close to the position of the Nantucket lightship which was a turning-point in both of their courses.

Fifty-one passengers and crew on board the *Andrea Doria* were killed in the collision, which ripped a great hole in the side of the Italian vessel. Both ships were equipped with sophisticated radar systems, and authorities were puzzled as to the cause of the accident. Both were modern ships and only slowed down slightly in the fog in order to maintain their schedules, confident in their ability to see and avoid other ships on the radar. Both ships picked up the other on radar when still miles apart but it was when taking incorrect avoiding

A very early plan-position indicator from Western Electric which was a very early type of radar.

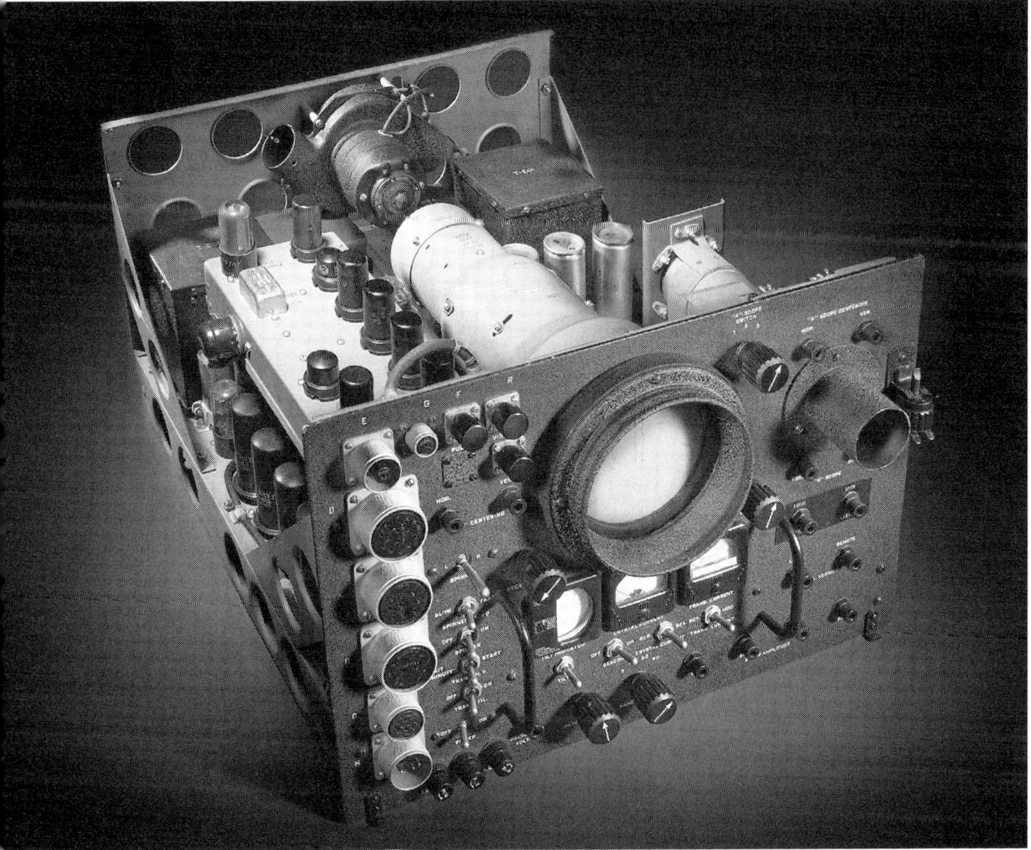

action that the collision occurred, both thinking that they were taking suitable avoiding action when in fact the *Stockholm* T-boned the *Andrea Doria* almost at a right angle.

This was a wake-up call for ships with radar thinking that they could see and take avoiding action in good time to avoid a collision. Radar gave a misplaced confidence to navigators in fog and there was a general feeling that with radar operating it was not necessary to reduce speed in poor visibility. There were also concerns about whether small craft could be detected on radar, partly because of their size but also because of the materials from which they were constructed that could be wood or fibreglass which were not strong radar signal reflectors. From those early days with radar it became obvious that there was a lot of work to do to make radar reliable for navigation in poor visibility and the accidents continued.

The Norwegian tanker *Stolt Dagali* was sliced in two by the Israeli liner *Shalom* in 1964 off the coast of New Jersey, in an area that has been called Wreck Valley because of the number of shipping accidents that have occurred there. Nineteen crew members on the tanker were killed when their stern was sliced off. The remaining twenty-four stayed afloat on the bow section which comprised watertight tanks. Fortunately the oil cargo on board was not highly flammable which prevented a fire starting. Again this was an accident in thick fog and was blamed partly on the poor use of radar and lookouts.

Icebergs presented their own collision risk and this was particularly the case before the advent of radar. The *Titanic*'s collision with an iceberg highlighted the risk and led to the formation of the International Ice Patrol that would track the paths of icebergs and send out radio bulletins to shipping. It was said that icebergs would not show up on radar because the ice was a poor reflector of the radar signal, but from my experience when setting records across the Atlantic the bergs showed up well. We were travelling at high speed at night in poor visibility in the vicinity of Cape Race, the southeasterly tip of Newfoundland, and we could see the icebergs clearly on radar in plenty of time to take avoiding action. Our risk of ice collision was with the 'growlers' (small bergs/ice floes) and bergy bits that tended to collect around the waterline of the icebergs and as they were just awash they were not detected by the radar. However, they do tend to lie upwind of the iceberg as the berg is being driven downwind faster than these small bits of ice that are hardly affected by the wind.

Collision avoidance is a significant part of navigation these days and just when it seems that technology can come to the rescue and make finding good solutions to collision avoidance relatively easy, the challenge can become significantly more difficult. In the past it was always keeping a good lookout that was the key to collision avoidance. This was followed by an assessment of the situation and the risks of a collision backed up by taking regular compass bearings of an approaching ship. If the bearing does not appreciably change then it has to be assumed that there is a risk of collision and the necessary action is taken to avoid it. In fog or other poor visibility such as heavy rain or snow then sound signals were the key to detecting other vessels around you and, as the rules dictate, you were required to slow your speed or stop until the danger was past.

The rules worked reasonably well, but that requirement to stop or slow down was so often ignored and many modern ships cannot stop quickly enough or turn quickly enough in an emergency situation. Picture a large oil tanker that could take several minutes for an alteration of course to take effect or perhaps ten minutes and 5 miles to come to a stop. Here it could be a challenging situation to meet the requirements of the rules and yet such ships were allowed to be built and to navigate the high seas. The Traffic Separation Schemes went some way to providing a solution for these large and unwieldy ships because they would mainly only be involved in being overtaken or over-taking themselves but even in one-way systems there can be crossing ships so the problems have tended to arise not so much from non-observance of the rules but from having ships that are not very manoeuvrable. There is such a diversity of shipping out there on the high seas that trying to write rules to fit every situation can be impossible.

Today we are seeing a move towards electronic solutions for collision avoidance. Electronic solutions have virtually taken over position-fixing and navigation and now the same is happening with collision avoidance. Radar is now well-established and has become much more sophisticated in its capabil-ities so that finding a solution to first establishing that a collision risk exists and then enabling a suitable avoiding action is much easier. For this the radar does many of the calculations for you and it does this first by establishing the course and speed of an approaching target and then translating this into a vector line ahead of the target on the radar display so that the project track of the target in relation to that of your own ship can be seen and the risk of collision established. Numerical information on the display will also indicate the closed point of approach and when this will occur, so that the risk of collision can be established. For the computer it is a simple calculation and should go a long way towards collision avoidance. The navigator still has to establish his own safe parameters as to what is a safe distance to pass but if his is the 'give way ship' he can carry out trial manoeuvres on the radar to help establish what will be the best manoeuvring solution to avoid collision.

The technology on a modern ship's bridge is a bit like a large-scale com-puter game and it is the younger navigators who can cope with this better than the older ones who have been brought up using traditional techniques. With

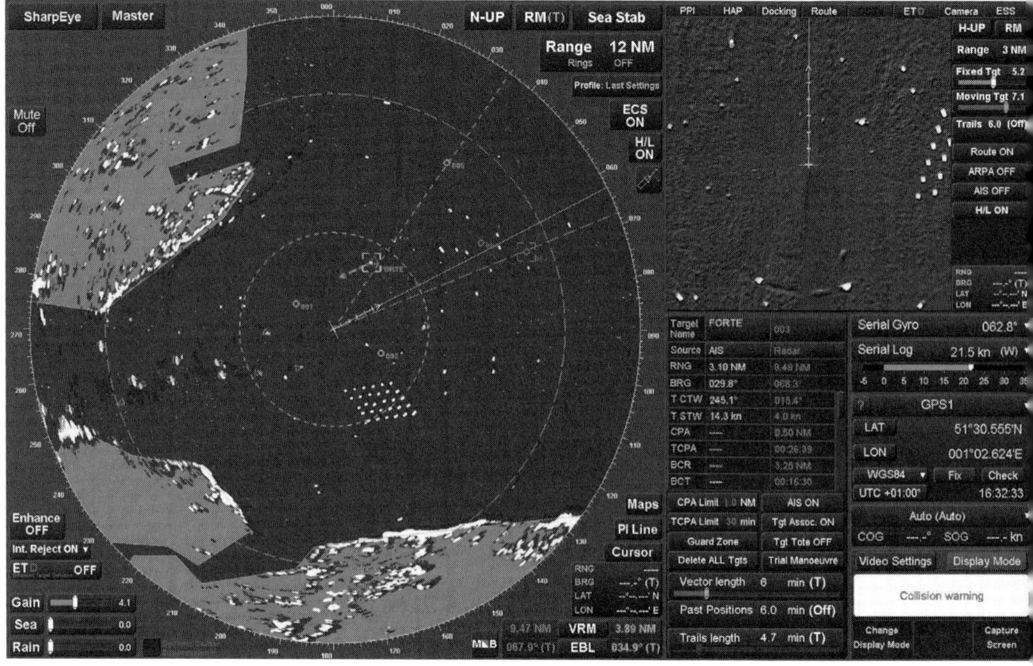

A modern ship's radar display of the Thames Estuary showing wind farms and ship targets and a host of numeric information. (*Kelvin Hughes*)

single-ship encounters where one ship has to take action to avoid another it is relatively easy to find the right solution and action to be taken but the situation can become much more complex when there are several vessels in the vicinity and where action taken to avoid one vessel might take you into the path of another. There also still exists the reluctance to use slowing down or stopping as a collision avoidance manoeuvre and most navigators tend to rely on helm manoeuvres when taking avoiding action. The reluctance to use the engines for collision avoidance probably stems from the past when the engine-room would require notice before slowing or stopping the engine and when it would immediately bring the captain rushing up onto the bridge. A change in the engine speed or noise can also alarm passengers because it can be felt throughout the ship whereas helm changes can pass unnoticed. Size also comes into the equation and it is not easy to slow or manoeuvre a 100,000-ton ship and persuade it to stop quickly.

This technology is advancing in a world where the speed of ships is also increasing. Where a cargo ship in the past might have travelled at 10 knots, a modern version will be doing 15 knots. Very large passenger ships and container ships are now often capable of speeds in the mid-20 knots and there is a new generation of fast ferries that can travel at up to 40 knots. This means that the time available to take action to avoid collisions is decreasing and navigators have to be able to respond much more quickly. So much of their focus on the bridge of a ship these days will be on the technology on the display screens on the bridge rather than on keeping a visual lookout and making their own visual assessment of a developing situation. This was brought home to one captain who arrived on the bridge of his ship and the watch-keeper commented that there was a vessel 2 miles ahead that he was monitoring. The captain commented: 'Yes, there is a yacht 2 miles ahead.' 'How do you know it is a yacht, Sir?' 'Because I can see it out of the window!!'

A new development that was originally aimed at security for ports and harbours is now widely used for collision avoidance. The Automatic Identification System (AIS) provided a means for those on shore to identify a ship at sea because it would automatically send out signals over a VHF radio connection that would not only provide the ship's name but also its position, speed and course and other information in a coded signal. This AIS information has now been incorporated into the electronic systems on board other ships and it can be displayed on the electronic chart and radar. This means that other ships in the vicinity have access to this information and the target on the radar can be shown with a vector that can help show its interaction with other shipping. Perhaps more importantly, by clicking on the target it can show the closest point of approach (CPA) so that you immediately have an indication of whether collision avoidance action is necessary. The advent of AIS is one more step in providing information to the navigator on the display screens on the bridge and it has been argued is one more step in

Radar displays can now be picked up by phones and tablets, but quality may be questionable.

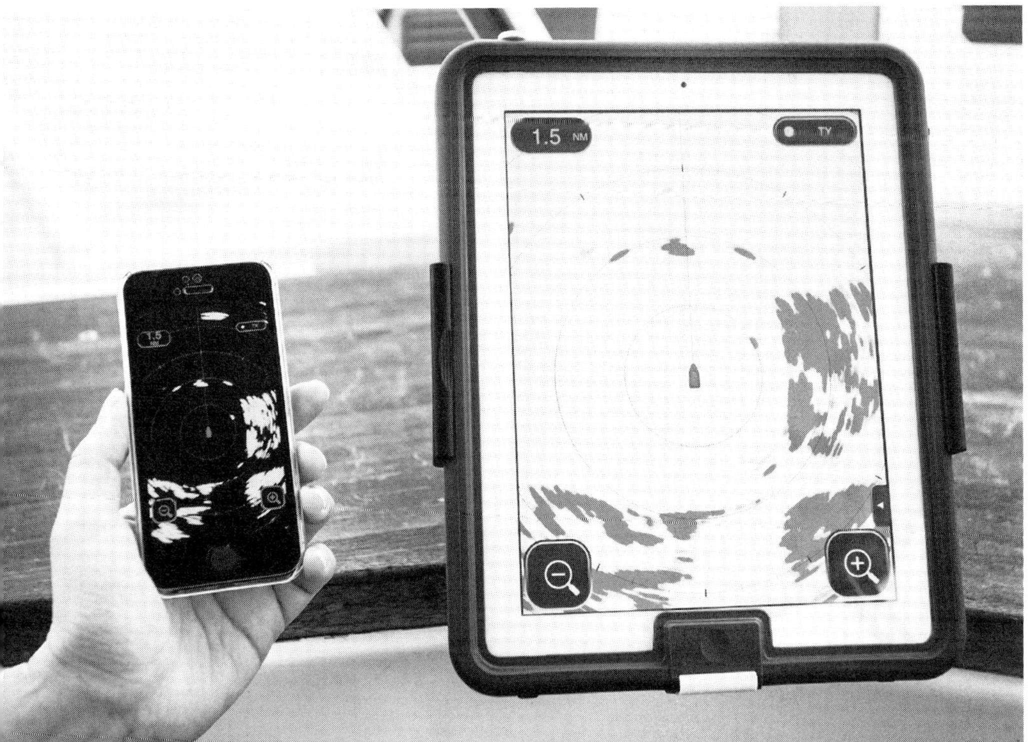

reducing the need for navigators to look out of the window to see what is going on in the real world.

The downside of AIS and using it for collision avoidance is that it is easy to make the assumption that all the AIS targets shown on the display are the only vessels around and they are the only ones that need to be considered in collision avoidance. While ships of over 300 tons are obliged to have AIS, there is no guarantee that it will be working, no guarantee that the information displayed is accurate and has been updated and, of course, no guarantee that there are not a lot of smaller vessels out there without AIS. The use of AIS for collision avoidance is rather like the situation with radar in the early days when 'radar-assisted' collisions occurred as navigators took time to appreciate the way in which radar had to be used as a collision avoidance tool. AIS is changing the face of navigation in a similar way because now not only does the navigator on board know exactly where he is through GPS positioning, but everybody else at sea and on shore also has access to the position. This, of course, is a stepping-stone towards the automation of ships which we will look at in a later chapter.

One of the dangers of AIS has become apparent with recent collisions between US navy ships and commercial ships. Navy ships often turn off their AIS because they wish to appear anonymous to other shipping and to shore

AIS targets in the busy Dover Straits shown on the radar display which can make collision-avoidance challenging.

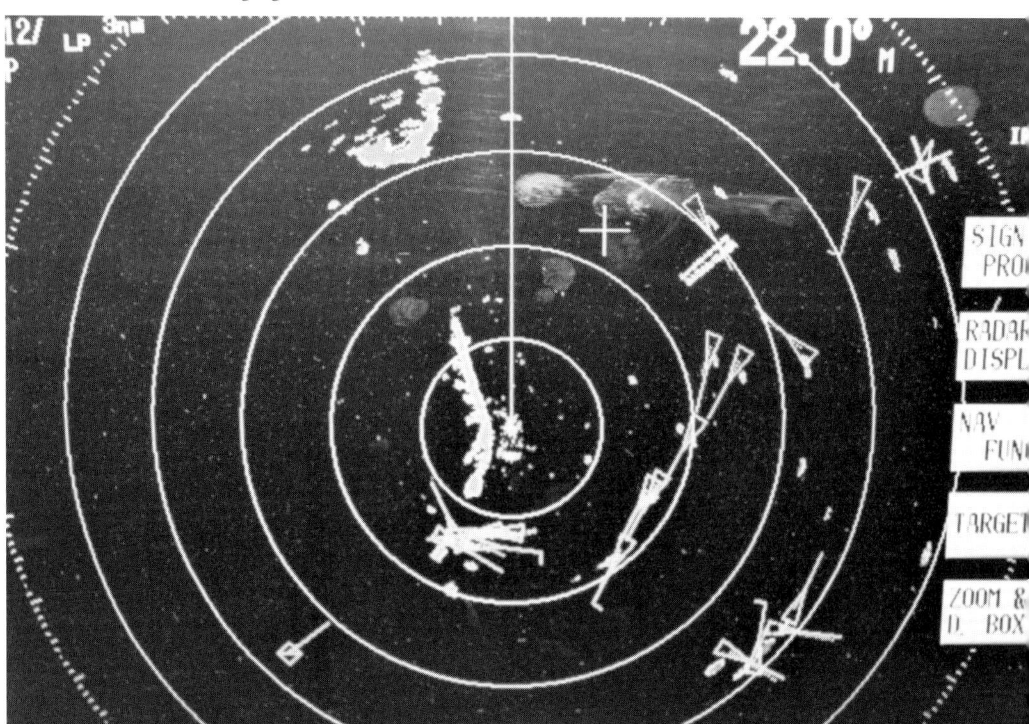

authorities, but it appears that they failed to realize that if they do this they tend to disappear from the knowledge of commercial shipping navigators who are relying entirely on their electronic displays to detect other shipping and to undertake anti-collision manoeuvres. The same may account for the rise in collisions between fishing boats and commercial ships when it seems likely that the fishing boats do not have AIS and so become second-class citizens out at sea and remain undetected. Navigation is moving into dangerous waters in the way that electronic information is being used for collision avoidance and in many instances small craft are virtually disappearing from the displays of larger ships.

One of the problems with radar is that the radar pulse will be reflected by anything that is in its path and this includes waves on the surface of the sea. This appears on the display as what is known as 'sea clutter' which can extend possibly a mile or two out from the centre of the display. These sea clutter returns can be just as strong as the signal that might be returned from a small craft which can then get lost among the clutter. Today's radars are using sophisticated software that analyses the returned radar pulse in order to try to separate out small craft radar returns from the sea clutter and it does this by looking for consistent returns from the same point suggesting a small craft as opposed to the more random returns from the waves. It is not a 100 per cent guarantee that small craft will be detected, but it helps.

The situation is made worse by the fact that many small craft do not make a strong radar target, particularly those made from composites or wood which do not reflect the radar pulse strongly. These small craft may also have navigation lights that are weak or not well displayed so the risk of collision is heightened at night. In poor visibility the chances of a ship seeing a small craft in its vicinity either visually or by radar can be minimal and we are seeing small craft adopting defensive tactics such as keeping in shallower water where the big ships cannot go. The past ten years have seen quite dramatic changes in the way that both large and small craft cope with the danger of collision avoidance which is now probably the top navigation risk. Statistics suggest that a collision occurs every five days on average somewhere in the world, but those are only the reported ones. It does seem likely that a big ship colliding with a small vessel would not even be aware of the collision and the disappearance of the small vessel might only be considered when it did not arrive at its destination.

One solution here is alternative detection systems. There are two that are currently available, but at this stage they tend to be used just for specialized application. Both were originally developed for military applications and it is only in the last few years that ruggedized versions capable of standing up to installation on small fast craft have found application at sea. Video cameras are quite widely used on ships and boats to give a view of what otherwise might be hidden areas. This might be mainly for security purposes to detect unlawful activities, but there is a growing use for navigation and in particular to provide a view astern when the design of the bridge or wheelhouse does not give a clear view astern to detect overtaking vessels. It is not known whether video cameras used in these roles constitutes 'keeping a proper lookout by sight and hearing' as required by the Collision Regulations but it is certainly becoming common practice.

Apart from saving the navigator having to go out onto the wing of the bridge to get a view astern, these video cameras do not add a lot to the detection of small craft. However, there is a form of video camera that can help here and this is the low-light camera. This is for use at night when there is little or no natural light and the camera can pick up barely visible light from objects floating in the water and this is magnified to produce a useable picture of otherwise hidden floating objects. At present the cameras for these systems need to be pointed in the right direction and they can be moved manually or programmed to scan an arc ahead, but the display is not integrated with the radar. They do offer a means of detecting items like boats without light or unlit buoys or even floating debris in the water. The range is normally about 2 miles ahead which should be enough for practical purposes and these low-light cameras can be a boon when vessels are navigating in inshore waters where unlit hazards might be expected. Because they are not integrated into any automatic detection system, they have to be interpreted manually once something is sighted on the display.

The other type of camera is the infrared camera that picks up heat differences in objects. This could detect boats and possibly buoys because the heat from the engine would show up or even the heat from a human on board. A buoy or floating debris might be a bit more of a challenge because the heat difference could be minimal but it is surprising how sensitive these cameras can be. At least an infrared camera is another weapon in the anti-collision armoury, but again it is a self-contained system and at present is not integrated into other systems. One big advantage of the infrared camera is that it can see through fog as can radar so it is complementary to the low-light camera rather than an option to replace it.

With each of these alternatives being stand-alone systems it means that the navigator has to monitor three displays if he wants to be sure that there is nothing around that might be a collision risk. It would be good if these three detection systems – radar, low-light cameras and infrared cameras – could be fully integrated so that an object seen by any one system could be displayed on a central screen such as the radar. Not only would this show all the possible targets around a vessel, but it could also help confirmation if two or more of these systems were to detect a single target. Then you could be pretty sure that it was a definite target and not just wave clutter. We are still some way off with this type of detection integration, but it does seem to be a worthwhile route for further research.

The history of collision avoidance has seen a dramatic change over the years. From the days when avoiding a collision was a very minor part of navigation, it has grown into a significant factor and is probably now the main challenge to safe navigation. History has shown that when there has been an increased risk of collision then steps have been taken to reduce this risk. The establishment of separate routes across the Atlantic for eastbound and westbound traffic was one of the first attempts at separation to avoid collision and the modern Traffic Separation Zones are another example of how separating traffic heading in opposite directions reduces collisions. This is quite logical and the results have been mainly good. However, such separation zones do not take into account the crossing traffic such as ferries that are a feature of most narrow channels and which can be a major part of the collision risk in these areas. This crossing traffic can present a serious collision risk through several factors. The ferries tend to operate at high speeds, often between the 20 and 30-knot bracket, but perhaps the major factor is that shipping in the main channels through the strait or channel often thinks that it has priority because of the large arrows on the chart showing the direction of the flow in the main channel. Then the crossing ferry traffic is two-way and so the ferries also have to avoid each other. In the Dover Straits this crossing traffic has adopted its own routing system to separate out the ferries travelling in each direction, a bit like the voluntary routes adopted on the North Atlantic in the past. The potential for a major disaster involving ferries carrying upwards of 2,000 people is considerable and there have been ferry collisions in the busy Strait of Messina between Italy and Sicily and also in Hong Kong waters.

So now we are seeing the collision risk increasing, largely because of the rise in the use of technology for collision avoidance. The consequences of a collision can also be more serious with large cruise ships carrying upwards of 6,000 passengers and container ships carrying cargoes valued in billions of pounds rather than millions. The increase in the size of ships can also reduce their scope for active manoeuvring to avoid collision so there is the potential for a major casualty in this high-risk navigation area. There is a disturbing increase in the number of collisions between ships, although at present these tend to involve a large ship colliding with a small vessel. History shows that for every step forward in collision avoidance such as the introduction of radar and AIS there is also one backwards as the technology seems to suggest that it gives navigators more warning and more freedom, whereas in reality the view out of the bridge window is still the best collision avoidance system ever developed.

Chapter Thirteen

The New Stars in the Sky

The development of the very accurate clock by Harrison that would eventually enable navigators to determine their longitude and thus solve the position-fixing problem is seen as a defining moment in navigation history, but an equally defining moment has taken place with the development of satellite navigation. The concept of putting satellites into space that could send signals to establish a position anywhere in the world seems to be from the realm of science fiction, but it has become a reality and today knowing precisely where you are is now taken for granted. It is a revolution in navigation that has changed not only the way we navigate in the remotest parts of the ocean, but also on land and in the air. For the first time we have highly accurate, three-dimensional navigation that now enables navigators to concentrate on where they are going rather than finding out where they are.

The first satellite, the Russian Sputnik 1, was launched in 1957 and I doubt whether anyone at that time could appreciate just what a change satellite technology would bring about in modern life. The information that can be provided by satellites has invaded every aspect of modern life, but as far as navigation is concerned it has made a dramatic change, not only in the way we navigate but also in the quality of weather forecasting, the tracking of ships and aircraft and in understanding the oceans and their behaviour. Instead of having a two-dimensional view of the oceans as we do from the bridge of a ship, we can now get a three-dimensional view with observations from above.

That first satellite did little more than transmit radio signals that allowed it to be tracked. Just days after the launch of Sputnik 1 in 1957, two physicists at the Advanced Propulsion Laboratories (APL), William Guier and George Weiffenbach, were able to work out the orbit of the satellite by analysing the Doppler shift of its radio signals during a single pass of the satellite. The Doppler shift is the change in frequency of the radio signal as it approaches or retreats from the observer and it was suggested then that if the satellite's position could be worked out in this way it might be possible to turn this around and locate the position of a receiver on the ground from signals from a satellite. For this to work the position of the satellite would have to be known with some accuracy. A year later the chairman of the APL's Research Center, Frank McClure, suggested that if the satellite's position was known and predictable, the Doppler shift could be used to locate a receiver on Earth and he proposed a satellite system to implement this principle. This idea was taken up by the US navy who wanted a worldwide position-fixing system as a reference for their Polaris submarines and so the Transit satellite system was born.

Development of the Transit system began the same year and a prototype satellite, Transit 1A, was launched in 1959. That satellite failed to reach orbit but a second satellite, Transit 1B, was successfully launched in 1960. Successful tests of the system were made in 1960, but it was four years later before the system entered service.

The delays were caused mainly by the weight restrictions imposed by the launch rocket and by excessive vibrations during the launch process. Several satellites malfunctioned but you have to appreciate that electronic systems in those days did not have the sophistication, ruggedness and compactness of modern electronics. However, sub-metre accuracy could be achieved by averaging a large number of Transit fixes to prove that the system was basically sound. The position accuracy achieved with just one fix was more in the region of 200 metres at best and usually much worse in the initial stages of development. This was still adequate for most navigation purposes and represented a significant development, although the main downside of the Transit system was that a position fix might only be possible once an hour. We used Transit when we were doing our Atlantic record attempts in 1985 and 1986 but this hourly fix proved to be a considerable handicap as we could be 50 miles away from the position indicated given the high speeds at which we were travelling.

The satellites used in the Transit system were placed in low polar orbits, at an altitude of about 600 nautical miles and they took around 106 minutes to complete a full circuit of the globe. A constellation of five satellites was required to provide reasonable global coverage for position-fixing, but while the system was operational there were at least ten satellites in orbit with one spare for each satellite in the basic constellation. These spares were considered necessary in order to ensure that the position-fixing could be maintained to adequate security levels.

The orbits of the Transit satellites were chosen to cover the entire Earth, crossing over the poles and spread out at the equator. Since only one satellite was usually visible at any given time, fixes could be made only when one of the satellites was above the horizon. At the Equator this delay between fixes might be several hours, while at mid-latitudes of say 45° the delay between fixes was of the order of an hour or two. At the poles the position-fixing was continuous because there was always a satellite in sight. As we have said, the primary purpose of the Transit satellite system was for Polaris submarines for updating their positions for which they needed only periodic fixes. Once the updating of the position was complete, the submarines could use their inertial navigation systems for position-fixing as required for missile-launching.

With later improvements, the system provided single-pass accuracy of approximately 200 metres and also provided time synchronization to roughly 50 microseconds. Transit satellites were also used to broadcast encrypted messages, although this was a secondary function. From 1967 onwards the Transit navigation system was in the public domain and with the cost of suitable receivers reducing considerably it was widely used by commercial vessels and smaller private craft such as yachts. Its use was mainly restricted to position-fixing in open waters as the interval between fixes made it unsuitable for coastal navigation.

For the user the Transit system was relatively simple, but its operation was complex. First it was necessary to determine the actual track of the satellites and this was checked at least twice a day in order for the position accuracy given by the receivers to reflect this accuracy. Checking the position of the satellites was done from ground stations in a reverse of the system used for establishing the position of a mobile receiver and this upgraded position information formed part of the signal that was received by the mobile user. From there it was necessary for the mobile receiver to measure the change in the Doppler frequency of the signal which would give an indication of the mobile position compared with the satellite's position. Two carrier frequencies were used to help reduce the effects of the signal passing through the ionosphere. It sounds complex and it was only the advances in computing power and technology that allowed the system to work. For the submarines for which the position-fixing system was originally intended there was an upgraded accuracy for the satellite position that allowed the position of the submarine to be measured with an accuracy of around 20 metres. If this had been generally available then it would have marked a significant development in navigation accuracy.

With the establishment of the Transit satellite navigation system, the concept of navigating by satellite was established. Transit worked but it also highlighted the challenges and difficulties that could be encountered by trying to navigate with satellite information. The measurements required had to be very accurate, particularly with regard to both timing and establishing the position and orbit of a satellite that was travelling around the globe in under two hours. It was only advances in computer technology that made this possible, but equally important were the advances in reducing the size and power requirements of the computer components. Weight and size can be a critical factor in putting satellites into orbit and reliability was a vital aspect of any satellite operation because it was expensive to get the satellite into orbit and once there it was virtually impossible to fix any faults.

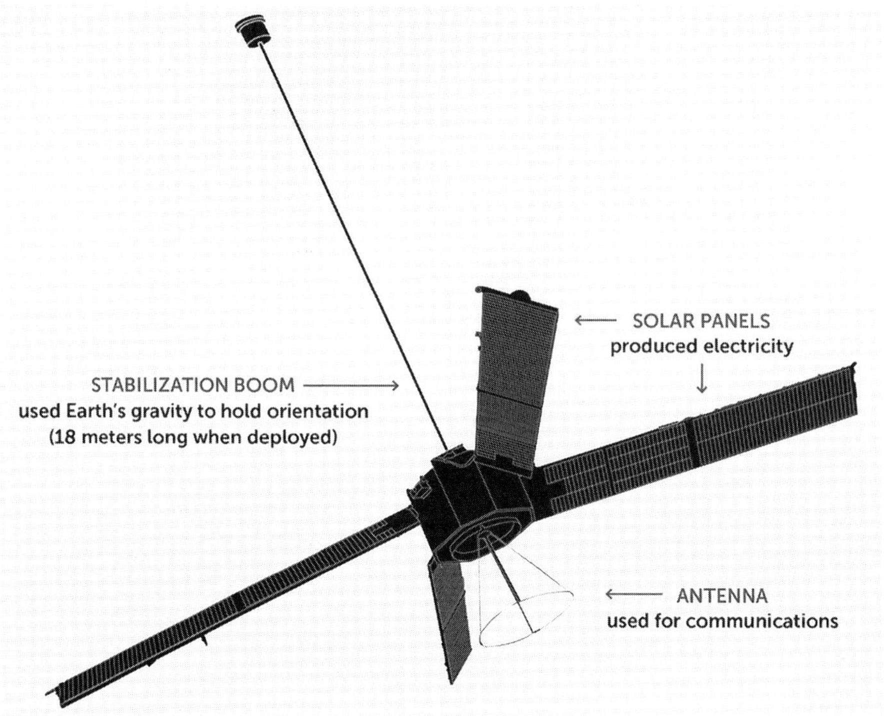

A Transit satellite that formed part of the first viable satellite navigation system.

By the time Transit was fully operational, thoughts were already turning to an improved system of satellite navigation that would overcome some of the inherent problems of the Transit system such as the intervals between fixes. Transit had shown the way and given a taste of what could be achieved with satellite position-fixing but the time interval between fixes was a source of frustration, meaning that Transit had severe limitations as far as general position-fixing was concerned. As early as the 1970s thoughts were turning to a new satellite system that could provide continuous position-fixing. In the meantime satellite data was also starting to provide other information that would be of benefit to navigation.

Most of this new information from satellites was in the form of weather information. Weather forecasters had always been frustrated by the lack of detailed information about what was taking place out at sea. Weather reports were coming in from ships, largely on a voluntary basis and some of it of dubious quality, but the detailed information needed to make accurate forecasts was lacking and the forecasters had to 'guess' what was happening in many areas. This meant that the quality of the forecasts for shipping and aircraft was not reliable, but satellite information changed all this. With its view from on high a satellite could look down on the oceans and not only give a picture of the cloud formations over the oceans but as the quality of satellite data improved also read the pressures and temperatures over wide areas of oceans and thus in effect give the forecasters a much higher quality of information that in turn led to improved weather routing.

The other factor that led to improvements in both weather forecasting and in navigation was the rapid development of computer technology. Weather forecast maps were largely developed as hand-drawn diagrams using the experience of the forecasters to fine-tune the data and develop forecasts. This human intervention tended to take the easy route and rely on historical data and in this way it could miss out the possibility of extremes of weather. It was a slow process to make the change from the human forecaster developing weather maps to a situation where the computer took charge and drew the maps from the raw weather data that was presented to it. Obviously the data from satellites went a long way to providing this raw data, but the increase in computer power was probably the most significant factor. In the 1970s what was considered to be a powerful computer would probably have the same power as is found in a mobile phone these days, whereas today the meteorological offices around the world are equipped with some of the most powerful computers available and it is this that has led to the ability to extend the timescale of forecasts out from perhaps a day or two ahead to around a week. For many professional forecasters it was a painful process having to admit that the computer could do a better job of forecasting than they could, but that was the price of progress. Today forecasting has a wealth of information largely obtained from satellites that can be fed into the computer which then uses advanced computational fluid dynamics to anticipate the movements of the air in a three-dimensional picture for some time ahead, much of this based on historical experience.

These same powerful computers were also what allowed the next stage in satellite navigation to be developed. The basis of the system was simple and relied on what were the basic tried-and-tested solutions to fix the position. For years navigators had used three bearings or ranges to fix their position and these bearings and ranges might be compass bearings from the land or measurements taken from the stars or, latterly, radar ranges from identifiable targets on the land. Both Loran and Decca Navigator used a similar concept when these first electronic systems were developed. Where the three ranges or bearings intersected was the location of the ship. So the next stage of satellite navigation took this principle and it was proposed that positions could be fixed by taking the range or distance from three satellites in space and where the ranges crossed would be the position. It sounds simple but the technology involved was very complex if any worthwhile level of accuracy was to be achieved. At this distance from its early development I still find it amazing that anybody could think that they could measure ranges from orbiting satellites possibly hundreds or thousands of miles away with any worthwhile degree of accuracy to fix the position. However, experience with fixing positions with 20-metre accuracy using the Transit system had shown what might be possible and gave confidence in the new concept.

The Global Positioning System (GPS) project was launched in the United States in 1973 with the aim of overcoming the limitations of Transit. There had been a number of design studies carried out in the 1960s on systems that might produce the Holy Grail of navigation: a system that could give high-accuracy position-fixing on a worldwide and continuous basis. Much of this development was classified because this was a military requirement and at this stage in the development there were no plans to make this a public service. Three people – Roger Easton, Ivan Getting and Bradford Parkinson – have been given the credit for inventing the GPS concept which was done under the umbrella of the US Department of Defense.

The system would depend on very accurate time measurements and for that they were relying on the atomic clock. When exposed to certain frequencies of radiation such as radio waves, the subatomic particles called electrons that orbit an atom's nucleus will 'jump' back and forth between energy states. Clocks based on this 'jumping' within atoms can be used to provide an extremely precise way to count seconds.

In a caesium atomic clock, atoms are funnelled down a tube and at a specific frequency these caesium atoms 'resonate' and change their energy state when subjected to radio waves. These radio waves have to be at a frequency of 9,192,631,770 cycles per second. When this frequency is achieved, it is measured by the system and this corresponds to one second. It is complex but the accuracy of an atomic clock is so precise that its accuracy is in the order of a maximum change of 0.03 nanoseconds per day, which is equivalent to a change of one second in 100 million years. The US navy began development of the Timation satellite which proved the feasibility of placing accurate clocks in space in 1964, which was one of the basic requirements for developing GPS.

The basic requirements for GPS were agreed in 1973 and at that time the project was named Navstar which then became Navstar GPS. The first ten satellites of the system were launched between 1978 and 1985 and the full constellation of satellites was finally established in 1993.

As we have said, the concept of GPS is simple but the execution is complex. There is a constellation of twenty-four satellites in orbit around the Earth and these orbits are arranged so at any point on Earth there would be at least six satellites in 'sight', although in practice there are more. This layout of the satellites allows a receiver to choose the best satellites from those available to give an accurate fix and this choice would be based on both the bearing and the elevation of the satellite. The orbits of the satellites are tracked with very great accuracy by dedicated ground stations because it is this accuracy that forms the accuracy basis of the whole system. When you consider that these satellites are travelling at 14,000km per hour relative to the Earth, tracking their positions to the required level of accuracy is quite an achievement on its own, but if you are measuring the distance from the satellite to your position to establish your position with a high level of accuracy, then satellite position accuracy is vital. The satellites are in orbit 11,500 miles above the Earth and each one goes around the Earth twice in twenty-four hours.

Knowing the position of the satellite at the instant of fixing the position is one thing, but then you need to measure your distance from it with the same high level of accuracy. This is done by measuring the time it takes for the signal from the satellite to travel to your position and when you consider that that signal is travelling at close to 300,000 kilometres per second the actual time that has to be measured is very, very small. Now you can begin to understand why you need an atomic clock with its very high level of accuracy. The receiver will measure the time and hence the distance from at least three satellites and from that it is possible to establish your position. It all sounds very logical when you say it like this but I find it amazing that anybody could even contemplate setting up such a system in the hope that everything would work as planned and that the extreme levels of timing accuracy that are required could be achieved. Add into this mix what would now be considered to be the very basic computing power that was available when GPS was being considered as a development and you can see that those involved in the early development were pioneers in every sense of the word

They had to pinpoint the positions of the fast-moving satellites to within metres at the time when they transmitted their signal, then they had to measure the time interval that that signal took to travel around perhaps 12,000km at a speed of 300,000km per second. This had to be done with at least three satellites at the same time and then the calculations had to translate those three time intervals into a useable latitude and longitude position. The time had to be measured in nanoseconds, one of which is 1/1,000,000,000th of a second which was only feasible using a very accurate atomic clock. Trying to pinpoint the position of a satellite to within a metre or less when it is at least 11,500km away is challenging and even more challenging when it is travelling at perhaps 20,000 miles an hour. It sounds like mission impossible, but that is what the pioneers set out to do and they achieved this with quite dramatic results so that a position can now be measured by a simple watch-sized computer unit!

The cost of GPS would never have been tenable on a commercial basis and it was only the requirements of the military for this level of accuracy to track their missiles and aircraft that made the cost justifiable. That first block of satellites went up by 1985 which made it possible to get two-dimensional position fixes and four years later the first of the Block II production satellites was sent up. A year later in 1990 GPS was declared operational and it was in 1995 that the full constellation of twenty-four satellites was fully operational. In 1983 a Korean Airline jet was shot down by the Russians because it had strayed into Russian airspace because of a navigation error and it was this that led the then US President Ronald Reagan to declare that GPS would be available to anyone on a free basis as a public service in aid of safety in the air and at sea. This free availability only gave limited accuracy of around 100 metres which was adequate for most general navigation requirements with the very high 1-metre accuracy only available to the US military and to trusted allies. Despite these restrictions, for the first time the world had what was then considered to be the ultimate in navigation systems: a system that provided high-accuracy position fixes on a continuous basis and with an adequate accuracy for many practical purposes. It was a milestone in navigation history.

For those wanting higher levels of accuracy from the GPS the concept of differential navigation was developed. Differential GPS (DGPS) means taking GPS position readings in a location where the position has been accurately established. This is usually land-based and this allows the error in the GPS position to be calculated and then the required correction is sent out as a radio signal to GPS receivers in the vicinity where it is applied to the position found there. DGPS allows the position accuracy to be upgraded considerably so that the possible 100-metre error in position found with normal GPS can be reduced to around 10 metres. It is a technique that was used earlier with both Loran and Decca Navigator and reference stations for DGPS were established in many areas, those in the US covering many of the important port areas and on the oil patch in the Gulf of Mexico, while in the North Sea DGPS was widely used for positioning rigs and platforms. Even higher accuracies could be established by taking position readings over a period of time and this could bring down the accuracy to centimetres which was a significant tool used by surveyors. I was on the tow-out of the largest concrete oil platform ever built at the time and the tugs were towing around 0.75 million tonnes which had to be positioned with a location accuracy of 1 metre and a heading accuracy of 5°. There was only one chance to get it right because once on the sea bed it was there permanently. It required position-fixing out in the open sea of the highest order. DGPS continued to be used for many

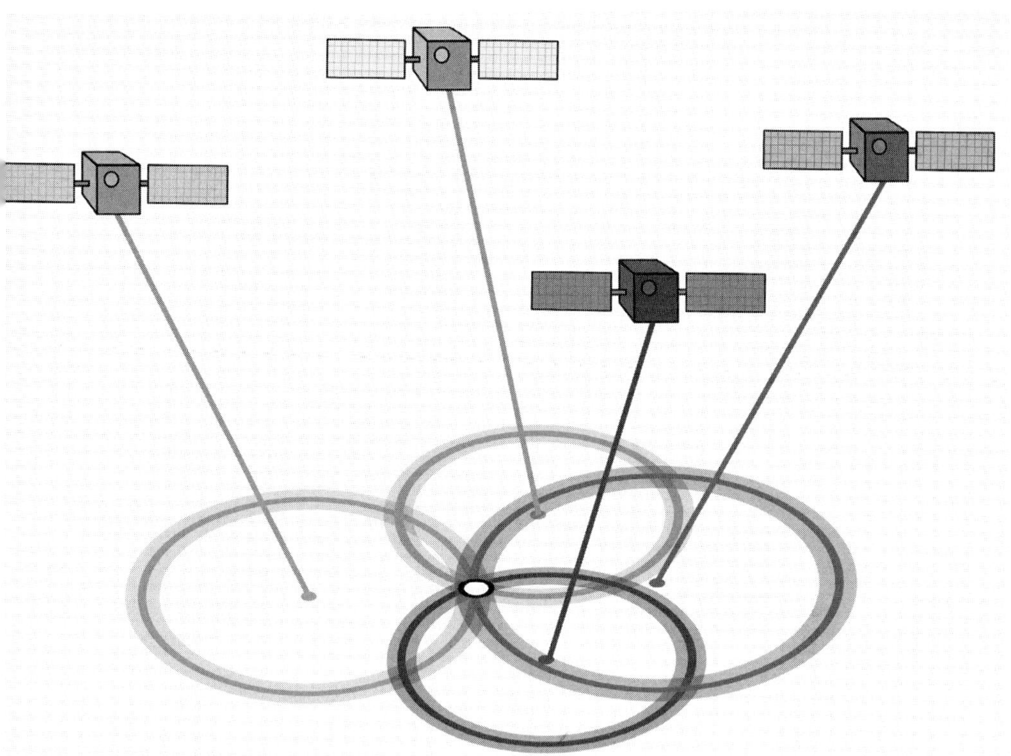

How the individual signals from GPS satellites interact to establish an accurate position.

years until the upgrading of the position accuracy of GPS and is still in use today where a very high order of position-fixing is required.

The concept of GPS did not come without problems. Because the positions developed by GPS were three-dimensional so that they could give height as well as latitude and longitude, they had to relate to a common datum and the one selected was WGS84. This datum took into account the fact that the Earth is not a true sphere; rather it is a spheroid and has some odd bits that are out of shape. Because it was adopted for GPS, WGS84 then became the international reference datum but around the world many of the maps and charts had been referenced to alternative datums, some international and some local. It became quite a task for map and chart-producers to make the change to the standard reference and for many year mariners were warned to apply corrections to the GPS positions before plotting them on older charts. Today the change has been completed and there can be a degree of confidence that the plotted positions from GPS will relate to adjacent land and other features. Another small change was that the GPS positions were displayed in degrees, minutes and decimals of minutes which was easier for the computer to deal with, but many of the charts still showed their latitude scales in the traditional degrees, minutes and seconds rather than the decimals which could lead to errors.

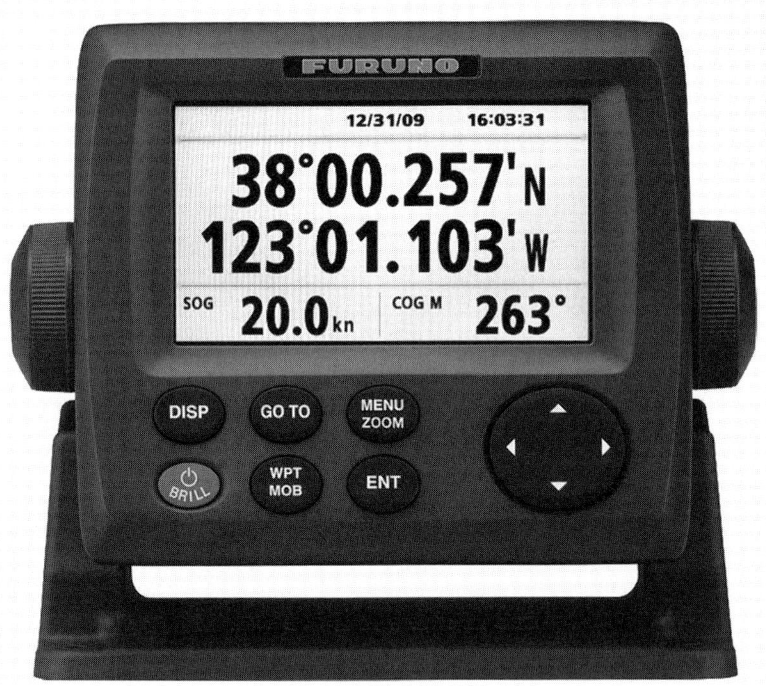

A modern GPS receiver that shows the position with an accuracy of just a few centimetres which is higher than normally feasible.

Another problem that developed and still exists today is that with GPS a navigator would plot the position given and take that as gospel and not relate where he was by any visual reference to the land or other navigation marks. It was the absolute positive display of the position on the GPS receiver that did not allow any room for negotiation, did not give any indication of possible errors and offered a sort of take-it-or-leave-it approach to navigation. This was reinforced by the display numbers where the latitude and longitude might be displayed to four decimal places of a minute which equates to something close to just a few centimetres of accuracy. This type of display seemed to infer that this was the level of accuracy on offer when in fact the position error could be many metres.

The initial 100-metre accuracy level that was on offer was fine for coastal and similar navigation requirements where high accuracy was not required. However, there quickly developed demands for a higher level of accuracy to be available as 100-metre accuracy was not adequate for harbour approach navigation and for aircraft landing, it did not meet the level of accuracy that was required for electronic charts to be viable and it was not accurate enough for land navigation use. By 1996 the selective availability that restricted accuracy was removed and civilian users were then offered accuracy of around 20 metres which was more than adequate for most practical purposes. Today the civilian accuracy available is around 5 metres which means that it can detect when you cross the road if you are GPS-enabled. These increased accuracy levels opened up a whole new navigation industry with electronic charting and road navigation systems becoming the norm rather than the exception. It was the ability for the position of virtually any vehicle including ships and boats to be plotted automatically on a moving map that has transformed navigation and almost made the navigator redundant in many peoples' eyes. All the hard work of establishing where you are is done for you and you don't even have to plot the position on the chart. In theory you can sit back and relax and let GPS do the work for you. In practice the prudent navigator will be constantly checking the position by other means if possible and particularly by reference to the land or navigation hazards but in reality you have to wonder just how much of this checking actually goes on.

While GPS was being established largely for the US military, the Russians were not idle and their GLONASS (Global Navigation Satellite System) satellite position-fixing system was established around the same time as GPS, but its use was restricted to the military and it is only in recent years that it has been made publicly available for general use but again with restricted accuracy. Work started on the system in 1976 and by 1996 there was full worldwide coverage with twenty-four satellites available. It was primarily aimed at providing position-fixing coverage over Russian territory, but offers full worldwide position-fixing. There have been one or two unexplained outages of the system which would be a worry for users, but today there are receivers available that can handle both GPS and GLONASS which makes a lot of satellites available and which should improve the availability of satellite navigation.

Waiting in the wings are several other satellite navigation systems all based on more or less the same technology that is used for GPS. Probably the most advanced is Galileo, the one being established by the European Union which is now available for position-fixing, although there are still a number of the satellites to be launched to make up the full constellation of thirty. Galileo will cost in the region of €5 billion to establish and the reason behind this deployment is to provide a service that is independent of the other national systems that could be shut down at any time. Galileo will have two levels of availability: one with a high level of accuracy that will be available on a paid

The latest version of the GPS satellite that is replacing earlier versions.

basis and another less accurate level that will have free access. Most satellite navigation satellites have several atomic clocks on board to provide back-up in the event of failure, but it has been reported that some of the Galileo satellites have suffered atomic clock failures. Included in Galileo is a search and rescue capability designed to pick up signals from distress beacons on a worldwide basis and to fix the position of the distress beacon within about 2km to aid rescue and this is likely to replace the ageing Cospas-Sarsat system. Galileo has suffered from lack of funding on occasions but is moving slowing forward and when fully operational it promises 1 metre position accuracy for all users and 1 cm accuracy for users who are prepared to pay for this level of accuracy. There is no military involvement so that unlike GPS the EU claims that the system should remain operational and effective and available to all, but in the event of hostilities the US has threatened to jam the Galileo satellites if they are being used by an enemy.

China has got in on the satellite navigation act with their BeiDou system. Initiated in 2010 with a small constellation of satellites, it is being expanded to have a total of thirty-five satellites when completed in 2020. There are claims that when fully operational the system will be able to offer position-fixing with an accuracy of around 1mm which sounds incredible and which will open up many new applications if this level of accuracy can be reliably maintained. Certainly general navigation does not require this level of accuracy so these new applications are likely to be for detailed movement monitoring and for the control of robots and similar applications. Japan and India are also reported to be developing their own satellite navigation systems, but these are likely to have limited coverage over their own and adjacent territories and sea areas.

The past ten years have seen dramatic changes in navigation and the availability of satellite position-fixing systems is becoming both widespread and commonplace. Finding out where you are is no longer the challenge so the navigator can now concentrate on where he is going. However, as history has shown there never seems to be quite the full promise in any new navigation technique or system and while satellite navigation seems to tick every box in terms of accuracy and availability, it is beginning to appear vulnerable. This vulnerability comes about because of the very weak signal that is sent out from the satellites. It has been compared with looking at a 100 watt electric light bulb from a distance of 50 miles. In other words it is barely discernible when it is picked up by the GPS antenna and this makes it very easy to jam. Just send out a signal from a transmitter on a frequency that is close to that used by the satellite system and you can prevent that very weak signal reaching the receiver so it stops working. This is already happening on a voluntary basis when people want to stop a GPS tracker from working so they cannot be tracked. This might be a very weak and local jamming problem, but it is possible to buy a jammer on the internet that could have a range of several miles and could cause serious interruption to many forms of transport. A more sinister problem comes in the form of spoofing where it is possible to send

The tiny size of a modern GPS chip such as those used in phones.

fake signals to a receiver so that it will show a false position. It has been demonstrated that spoofing could be used to direct a ship in the wrong direction or even into enemy hands with sophisticated spoofing. The fact that there are likely to be alternative satellite systems available for position-fixing is not a solution to this problem because they all work on adjacent frequencies and so any powerful jamming system is likely to interfere with all of the satellite systems at the same time.

Then there are the problems that come from the increasingly complex navigation systems found today and the lack of careful integration between systems. This can mainly relate to the alarm systems in use and there was the case where a container ship went aground because the alarms went off. The initial alarm was an indication that the GPS had failed, but GPS position information is now fed into several bits of equipment on the bridge and so there were alarms also emanating from the radar, the electronic chart, the AIS, the autopilot and of course the GPS receiver itself. These alarms were compounded as the effects of the GPS failure impacted on other equipment so that eventually there were eighteen alarms going off. In trying to track and eliminate the alarms, the navigator was so distracted that it was found the ship had been aground for ten minutes before he realized it. This may sound

An example of 1,000-watt GPS jammers that could cause serious disruption to GPS signals.

A Gincan unit that helps to reduce the possibility of GPS jamming when installed in the antenna system.

extreme, but it does demonstrate the need for a much more integrated and cohesive approach to navigation and the vulnerability of having just one source of position information.

The past twenty years have seen a revolution in navigation like no other in its history. Accurate positions are there for the taking and with navigation now being so easy you can sense a complacency setting in that has never been there before in navigation. It can perhaps be compared with the complacency that set in in the early days of radar when it seemed to offer the solution to navigating in fog. It is easy to take so much for granted when you have the apparent solution handed to you on a plate and we have got to this stage with satellite navigation. Maybe it will take a twenty-four-hour outage of GPS to bring us up with a round turn and appreciate just how vulnerable we are when using just this one system to the exclusion of everything else. That is not the way that navigation has ever been conducted in the past as we have seen in this history, so we will look at possible solutions in the next and final chapters.

Chapter Fourteen

The Human Element

In the earliest days of navigation when people first took to the water everything depended on the human. The eyes were used to detect features that could help to identify a location and also to help fix the direction of travel. Perhaps a sense of smell might be used to sniff out land smells and touch might have been used to check the depth of water, but essentially all navigation was conducted using human senses. Gradually over the years instruments have been developed to help navigation such as sounding poles and compasses and later quadrants and sextants. All of these required the human to handle and work the information given and the navigator was the focus of all the various elements of information that went together to find the way. In essence, everything was visual, so what we now term the view out of the bridge window was the basis of virtually all navigation.

It was the same with the weather which was always a significant part of navigation. It was the human who would look at the clouds and try to translate what he saw there into what sort of wind and weather might be expected. The human brain was the processor for all the information that was collected and from this information he could work out what the weather might bring in the hours ahead. Everything was visual, which had limitations in terms of the time scale for how long ahead the weather could be forecast. So much for both navigation and for weather forecasting which were based on personal experience with very little written down. The prime example of this was the Polynesians with their epic sailing adventures of which there is no written record. The log book that became an essential part of navigation in later years was one of the first attempts at bringing some form of written record to navigation and the experience gained in these records could be used to help plan future voyages.

Apart from early buoys and lighthouses and other sea marks such as significant headlands, the navigation relied on the navigator's experience. There was no guidance or help from the shore in these days, so that view out of the window was the navigator's primary source of information for both small boats and big ships. This practice existed right through to the beginning of the twentieth century when radio was being introduced as a means of communication to ships at sea. Radio could help in terms of advice on the location of icebergs and later with weather forecasts and it was these weather forecasts that were the first outside help that the navigator received. As we have seen through the latter parts of this book, there was a steady build-up of the position information that would emanate from the shore with systems such as Loran and Decca Navigator and it was these systems that relieved the navigator of much of the burden of fixing the position which was the basic key to navigation. With the advent of electronic navigation which in turn meant that position was fixed with information from the shore, the role of the navigator subtly changed. When the navigator fixed the position from the sun or stars or from bearings from the shore he would be aware of the possible errors and limitations of the fix. With the electronic position-fixing there was no such awareness and with position information presented in such a positive way it became more and more difficult to query its validity.

This is what leaves the navigator with a dilemma. Can you trust position information that is being presented in this way? I think the fault here lies with the people who design and produce the onboard receivers and they are working in a competitive market. It does not help a product if you suggest that it may not have full accuracy when the competitors are suggesting that theirs does. The navigator has to learn from experience or education just how much reliance can be placed on a position that is displayed when he has little or no influence on how the position was generated and what the possible errors are. Here we see a major switch in emphasis from the navigator who has worked hard to find a position through his own efforts and so has a good idea of the level of accuracy of his work to a navigator who is presented with a position generated by others where there is no indication of the accuracy or reliability. Human nature will almost certainly make the latter navigator take the given position as gospel because he does not have perhaps the experience or resources to query it. As we saw with that example of the navigator who was overwhelmed by alarms, electronic navigation is fine when everything is working properly but it can be a downhill slope to disaster when things start to go wrong.

There was a case a few years ago where there was a fault in the antenna cable of the GPS which led to the GPS not working. On that GPS receiver there was no audible alarm to indicate failure but there was a visual alarm that came up on the display which was missed by the navigator. The position information displayed then switched automatically to a dead-reckoning calculation using the previously registered course and speed. With the GPS failure passing unnoticed, the navigator then convinced himself that the buoys that he could see were the buoys marking the channel that he intended to follow, with the result that the ship ran aground on nearby shoals. The vessel was a cruise liner, the *Royal Majesty,* which ran aground close to the Nantucket

Shoals and even though the vessel had both Loran and GPS position-fixing, the navigators on watch had convinced themselves that they were on track and seemed to make what they could see fit with what they expected to see. This can be quite a problem when making a landfall and it is human nature to convince yourself in this way when you put your faith in what the electronics are saying rather than what your outside view is telling you. In the case of the *Royal Majesty* the lookouts were reporting features that should have indicated a deviation from the course but these were ignored.

The modern navigator is now put in the invidious position of being presented with perhaps too much information without having too much control about its quality. Modern electronic chart systems are a case in point and those fitted on the bridges of many modern ships are overly complex and can require considerable experience to operate them with each manufacturer having their own system. Consider the case of a navigator joining a ship in Rotterdam within perhaps just a few hours of sailing out into the busiest shipping lanes in the world. He has to become familiar with what to him is a new type of equipment and then operate it effectively. There is a strong case for some form of standardization of the systems and many authorities are calling for an 'S' mode to be incorporated into systems that would allow them to revert to a standard operating system common to all equipment.

The bridge and electronic displays of a modern ship.

This is the pilothouse of a modern lifeboat, which is beginning to look very much like that of a modern airliner.

There is a degree of standardization for ship equipment that has to meet laid-down standards, but for small craft equipment there is no limitation to what a manufacturer can include. In the early stages of development everything was kept simple because complication increased costs but today's equipment incorporates all the possible bells and whistles, probably 90 per cent of which the navigator will never use. Again complications like this can make it challenging to find just the basics of navigating information which in most cases is all you need. I can remember one electronic chart system where it required five key strokes just to change a daylight presentation to a night-time one when this should just be a simple one-key operation because you may have to do it in the dark. It seems to be part of a syndrome where manufacturers see complication as a sales benefit with little experience of what it can be like in the darkened wheelhouse of a boat at sea. Perhaps the inexperienced navigator is lured into buying such equipment in order to impress his friends when all it really indicates is a lack of experience.

While the electronic chart shows a very positive level of information where there is little room for negotiation by the operator, radar is different. With radar the operator's experience is the key to interpreting what the display is showing and I know from my experience that a quick glance at the radar display is never enough. You had to study the display in detail to discover all the small target returns that could indicate small craft or perhaps buoys and then translate these into what the targets could be. Even land targets can be difficult to identify sometimes because while the radar is presented to you as a plan view, perhaps suggesting that you are looking down from on high, it is in fact a horizontal view more or less showing what you might see out of the windows. Like the electronic chart, the modern radar display shows everything it can see in a very positive way that does not allow much room for negotiation. It is a great tool and the basis of what is used today for most collision avoidance manoeuvres, but what navigators need to realize is that what is important is not what the radar is showing but what the radar might not be showing.

This might sound like a very negative approach to navigation, but it highlights the modern navigator's dilemma. Should he just take everything that is shown on the screens as gospel and navigate accordingly or should he question the validity of everything? Human nature being what it is, the navigator will inevitably take the first course of action because it is often so hard to find any good reason to question the electronic information, even that offered by the radar which can never show 100 per cent of what is out there on the water. Back throughout the history of navigation we have seen how the navigator is always checking, checking, checking in order to try to validate what he thinks is his position and where he is heading. Soundings were used to back up position information and visual sightings were probably the most positive position information available. Today all the information required by the

The view out of the window is still a vital part of navigation, particularly on small craft.

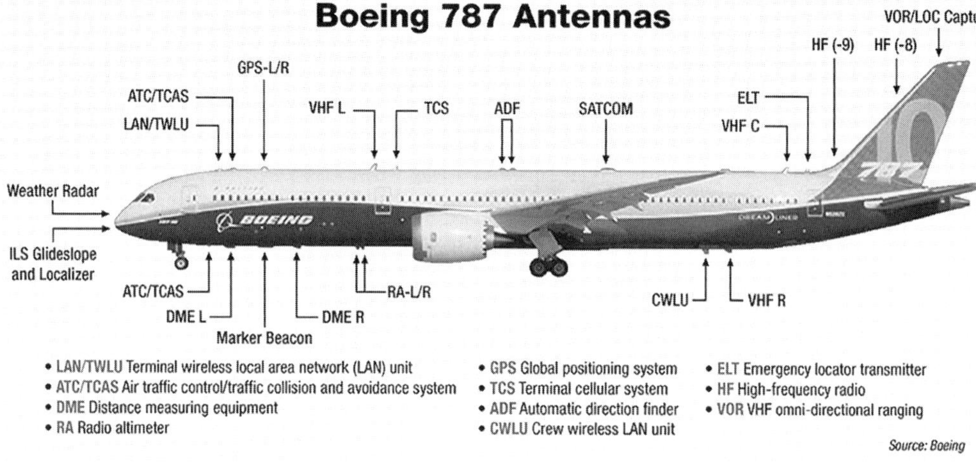

The wide range of antennas that have to be accommodated on a modern airliner, indicating the complex nature of modern systems for safe navigation.

navigator seems to be presented to him on a plate that does not leave much room for negotiation. We are hooked on GPS and what it says is taken as gospel by most navigators.

In the air the transition towards automation has gone a lot further and while the pilots have a window of sorts to look from they are reliant virtually 100 per cent on air traffic control offering them a clear route ahead in terms of collision avoidance. For navigation they will plan their route beforehand and the monitoring from the ground will be quick to inform them if they deviate from the planned route. Little is left to the imagination of the pilots of commercial operations, but for private flyers there might be a bit more flexibility and the need for navigation and collision avoidance can still occur but there the speeds are generally slower. Private flyers will soon be told if they stray into controlled airspace so they are pretty tightly governed as well.

On land you always have the luxury of stopping and working out where you are and where you are heading and there are signposts to help, but even here with the advent of GPS routing and positions plotted on maps the skill of navigating is disappearing and people get lost if their GPS stops working. The classic stories of trucks getting stuck down narrow lanes demonstrates that land navigation still has some way to go.

So navigating has moved on a long way from the days when a position fix was a luxury to one where a position fix is demanded and expected. From the days when a skilled navigator was an essential part of the successful completion of a voyage we have moved on to where the navigator, skilled or not, might be the handicap to the successful completion of a voyage. The days of automation are looming and with around 95 per cent of marine accidents, groundings and collisions and suchlike being claimed to be the result of human failures, perhaps the world of navigation might become a safer place with automation.

Chapter Fifteen

The Future

This story of the history of navigation has shown how navigation has developed over the centuries with the most rapid and changing development taking place in the last fifty years, mainly with the advent of electronics and the introduction of satellite systems. It would appear that we are on the verge of having the ultimate navigation systems that will largely prevent accidents at sea and in the air. We are almost there, but as always with electronic systems they do not quite achieve what they set out to do and there is always a question mark left that makes it necessary for human intervention and assessment. Navigation has taken massive steps forward in solving the problems of finding out where we are and where we are going, but there is still work to do so it seems appropriate to see what the future of navigation might hold and what solutions are in the offing.

We finished the last chapter looking at the human element and how it does appear that this is becoming the weak link in navigation these days. The way that the human interacts with modern electronic systems has become a considerable issue and in a world of increasing automation and electronic control there is becoming an increasing focus on many forms of transport taking out the human driver, navigator or pilot and operating under the control of the computer. It is easy to understand people's nervousness about this because if things go wrong there is always a human there to assess the situation and to sort out the problem and perhaps more importantly to take the blame. What such an argument fails to take into account is that it is the human part of the operation that is largely responsible for the mistakes in the first place, so take out the human and the operations, in theory, should be safer.

As far as road transport is concerned, there are already autonomous vehicles out there being tested and they seem to work. The navigation element of these vehicles is quite straightforward and very similar to the GPS navigation systems we use manually today. Close-quarter navigation such as the position of the vehicle on the road is more critical but certainly within the scope of modern technology, but it is collision avoidance that is the critical factor that makes people nervous. On the roads collisions can be with other vehicles, with fixed objects and perhaps most critically with pedestrians, so sophisticated collision avoidance systems are necessary. Experience with autonomous vehicles does suggest that they can operate relatively safely but the question will always be the public perception. You could have ten accidents involving a vehicle with a driver and these tend to be acceptable because we know that drivers are all fallible and can make mistakes. Have one accident with involving an autonomous vehicle and the whole concept is condemned. Is this because there is no one to blame when you have a driverless vehicle? Then of course there is the question of legislation which is currently all written around the concept of having a driver in the vehicle. It is a legal minefield and the worst-case scenarios will always be when there is a mix of autonomous and driver-controlled vehicles on the roads. From a navigation point of view, autonomous vehicles are viable and possible.

With aircraft, many modern aircraft are virtually autonomous already. They can fly themselves once the necessary instructions have been given and they can even land and take off without human intervention. Again it is current regulations which demand humans on board that is the main sticking-point in the implementation of autonomous aircraft, but drones are already in use by the military for many purposes which operate as a sort of halfway-house towards full autonomy. These are remotely-controlled aircraft on which the controller has access to the feedback from onboard sensors and is able to control the drone accordingly. It seems a small step from there to full autonomy, but these drones have no people on board and it would be a brave airline that advertised its flights as having no pilots on board. In many modern aircraft it can be argued that the pilots are on board to cope with emergencies, but this puts the pilots in an invidious position when they have to first recognize that it is an emergency situation and then take the necessary action. A pilot may only experience an emergency once or twice in a career and it is only intensive training that gives them the resources to cope. With standard

A view of what the future unmanned ship might look like. (*Rolls Royce*)

aircraft designs the planes are incredibly well-tested to extremes before being certified for public use and this testing gives the pilots a good resource to cope when things go wrong.

Compare this with shipping where currently it is very much a free-for-all on the high seas. Apart from vessel separation zones in some port approach areas and narrow channels, all vessels are free to roam the oceans with minimal control. Ships are required to have specific navigation equipment on board and trained and qualified navigators but the 'Freedom of the Seas' still exists, although now there is a growing trend towards monitoring shipping but that is a long way from controlling it. This will possibly make it easier to introduce autonomous ships where they can roam the high seas unmanned but take on a crew when entering and leaving harbours. The motive for doing this is largely economic but there are those who say it will be safer because it rules out human error.

The actual navigation on the high seas is quite straightforward and there will be the possibility of control from the shore in order to change plans to avoid adverse weather and other conditions. Electronic chart systems linked to an autopilot can control the navigation quite adequately using established technology; however, problems may arise with collision avoidance. Complex algorithms have been developed to control ships so that they conform to the collision regulations in the event of ships meeting at sea, but these are based largely on detection systems using radar and that could be the weak point. As we have seen, current radar cannot guarantee to detect everything that is floating at sea so are we prepared to accept a collision avoidance system that may have such a hidden flaw? I would argue that current collision avoidance tactics used by human navigators today are based almost entirely on radar detection anyway so the systems used on an autonomous ship would be no worse than what is happening today and indeed might be safer if we take the human out of the equation. After all, the statistics suggest that human navigators are responsible for most of the casualties at sea today.

There is the possibility of using supplementary detection systems to help the radar. As we have mentioned there is low-light TV and infrared cameras that offer the possibility of supplementing the detection of possible targets by radar. At present these both operate on separate displays and there has been no attempt to integrate them, but the possibilities are enormous. If all three detection systems could be integrated and displayed on one screen which in turn could be analysed to find collision risk and possible avoidance manoeuvres, then there could be a lot more confidence in automated collision avoidance and in turn the development of automated ships. In the air radar is mainly used for adverse weather avoidance with collision avoidance taken care of by ground control. The weather avoidance systems are becoming more and

An image of what the bridge of a future ship might look like, but it still contains the human element.

more sophisticated with the latest being a laser system to detect clear air turbulence which can be very disconcerting for passengers as it can arrive virtually unseen and unannounced. It is advanced detection systems like this that will make autonomous travel more reliable and at the time of writing there is serious research going on to find solutions.

As on land and in the air, it is current legislation that could be holding back development of autonomous ships at sea. The law, maybe by inference rather than actual words, requires people to be driving, flying or navigating ships at sea because that has always been the practice. It will take a brave politician who sets out to change that perception and so while there may be strong argu-ments in favour of autonomous vehicles of one sort or another we may be some way off implementation. What we will probably see is a step-by-step approach which is what seems to be happening in aircraft with the aircraft virtually flying itself but the pilots are there to set it up and to monitor pro-gress. At sea the start may be seen in having a manned ship at the head of a convoy of unmanned vessels with all the ships connected by an invisible electronic tow rope rather than the normal visible rope connection.

A much more immediate concern was that highlighted in Chapter 13 which is the vulnerability of satellite navigation systems to jamming and spoofing. This may happen accidentally, but in a world where there is a real possibility of terrorist attacks of one form or another jamming the GPS or other satellite system signals this could prove to be an effective way of causing mayhem on land, sea and in the air. We have become heavily reliant on satellite systems to provide position and timing information and if the system goes down there would not just be a risk to navigation but to a wide range of the infrastructure that keeps modern society running. The very accurate timing available from satellite navigation systems is widely used in the control of vital infrastructure and so could collapse in the absence of GPS signals. Navigation on land, sea and in the air is now almost wholly dependent on these satellite signals and the extreme weakness of the signal when it reaches Earth can make them very vulnerable to jamming and there is no back-up.

There are cries from many quarters to provide a back-up position and timing system and many would argue that this is provided by the competing satellite systems such as GLONASS and BeiDou, but as these have the same weak signals and operate on wavelengths close to those of GPS they are also likely to be affected by any jamming. The solution appears to lie in providing an alternative position-fixing system and it is claimed that an enhanced version of Loran, eLoran, would be the answer. As we have seen, Loran is a well-proven position-fixing system with a long range while eLoran would

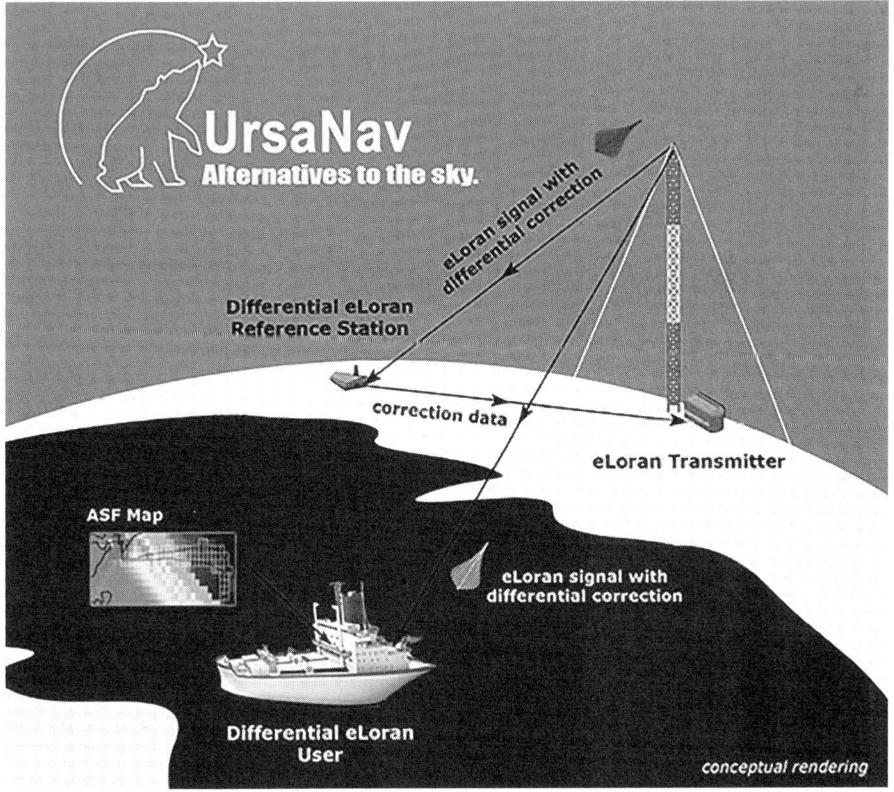

A diagram of how eLoran might work as a back-up to the vulnerable satellite systems.

keep much the same range and coverage as in the past but provide a much more accurate position fix that would be comparable with that of normal GPS by using differential enhancement. The big advantage of using Loran is that it operates with a very powerful signal sent out on long-wave frequencies that would be very hard to jam. It would not offer worldwide coverage unless there was international cooperation to establish a large array of transmitters, but coverage could be established over most of the main land masses and shipping and aircraft routes to provide adequate coverage. Another advantage of using Loran is that the signal also includes similar very accurate timing to that offered by satellites.

The provision of eLoran as a back-up is well-recognized in most navigation quarters, but the actual implementation remains in the hands of politicians who have to allocate the funding. This would be done on a national basis, but of course the benefits would be on an international basis because most transport is international. So the argument raised is 'Why should we pay for this when it is the international community that will benefit?' Then there is the question of when you have two independent position-fixing systems, if they show different readings, which one do you believe? With luck we may have a back-up system for satellite navigation in ten years' time or there may be a serious loss of satellite signals that leads to a major disaster. History has shown that it takes such a disaster before anything changes with the authorities becoming reactive rather than proactive, so we wait with bated breath for that disaster to happen.

Index